General Reinhard Gehlen:
The CIA Connection

By the same author

Breaking Cover
    (a collaboration with Bill Gulley, former director of the White
    House Military Office)

General Reinhard Gehlen: The CIA Connection

Mary Ellen Reese

The enemy of my enemy is my friend.
—Hebrew proverb

George Mason University Press
Fairfax, Virginia

327.12
Rees

Distributed by
National Book Network
4720 Boston Way
Lanham, MD 20706

Library of Congress Cataloging-in-Publication Data

Reese, Mary Ellen.
General Reinhard Gehlen : the CIA connection / Mary Ellen Reese.
p.   cm.
1. Gehlen, Reinhard, 1902- .   2. Intelligence officers—
Germany—Biography.   3. World War, 1939-1945—Secret
service—Germany.   4. United States.   Central Intelligence
Agency—History.   5. Intelligence officers—United States—
Biography.   I. Title.
DD247.G37R44   1990
327.12'092—dc20   90-13843 CIP

ISBN 0–913969–30–3 (alk. paper)

For Mitch

Contents

Introduction

General Reinhard Gehlen was a figure unique in the history of espionage. Chief of Eastern Front Intelligence for Adolf Hitler until the collapse of Germany in 1945, eleven years later he became head of the Federal Intelligence Service, Bundesnachrichtendienst (BND), for the democratic West German government of Konrad Adenauer. Among his senior staff in the BND were the same officers who had served with him under Hitler. And the instruments for this remarkable metamorphosis were agencies of Gehlen's former enemy, the United States: Army Intelligence—which acquired Gehlen and the core of his unit immediately after the war and nurtured them in deepest secrecy—and later the CIA.

How did this happen? Why was Gehlen whisked off to America and then returned to Germany to re-establish the unit he had run for Hitler, while others were tried at Nürnberg, convicted and hanged? That the United States Army, within weeks of liberating the concentration camps, would employ a section of the German General Staff is on the face of it startling. What did the Americans want from Gehlen? How much did they care whether he or his staff were Nazis? And what sort of control did they exercise over this group in which many of Germany's former military leaders found refuge? In short, what was the nature of the Gehlen Organization and what was the real relationship between it and American Intelligence?

Judgments about the Gehlen Organization and its relationship with

American Intelligence cannot be made without putting them in the context of the times. At first, immediately after the war, with revelations of Nazi atrocities pouring out of conquered Germany, the American people were in a vengeful mood. Nothing could have persuaded them that it was in the nation's interest to support a group of Hitler's officers, certainly not the argument that they could provide valuable information about the Soviet Union. Sympathy for America's Russian allies, the heroes of Stalingrad who had suffered such bitter losses, was widespread. Few seconded General George S. Patton when, at the end of the war, he proposed using captured German troops and leading them against the Soviet Union.

But before long the mood in the United States shifted. Clashes between Soviet and Allied occupation forces mounted, and as the Americans were withdrawing their troops from Germany as fast as they could, the Soviets appeared to be digging in in their zone of occupation. By June, anxious American military authorities believed themselves so overmatched by the Soviets that they seriously questioned whether, if a conflict arose, United States troops could retreat before being overrun. The operative word here is "believed."

The Americans did not *know* how many or what kind of troops the Soviets had, how they were armed, where they were, or what their leaders intended to do with them. Nor did they have the capability to find out. But they did have General Reinhard Gehlen, Hitler's expert on the Soviet military. In addition to his impressive store of knowledge, Gehlen claimed to have a network still in place in Eastern Europe which could provide the Americans with the information they desperately wanted. Under the circumstances, Army Intelligence did decide to do as Patton, in another context, had suggested: use captured Germans to fight the Soviet Union. Whether or not, as some at the time and more since have claimed, the Americans exaggerated the extent of the threat, this is the backdrop against which one can begin to evaluate the American action in taking on Gehlen.

A broader, more far-reaching issue is the United States' continued, ever-closer relationship with him. Once what was perceived as the desperate need for operational intelligence about the Soviet order of battle had receded, was the CIA justified in taking over responsibility for the Gehlen Organization from the Army? In so doing, the Organization was given a new stability and political legitimacy. No longer an appendage of Army Intelligence, dependent on decisions made in the Pentagon, adoption by the CIA meant that the existence and continuing support of the Gehlen Organization had the full approval of the highest political authorities in America.

The threat of immediate military confrontation between the Soviet Union and the United States developed into the long-term Cold War. By the summer of 1946 the Soviets, aware that Germany's great value lay in the populous, industrial West, not the Soviet-occupied East, supported the creation of a unified, neutral Germany to be controlled by a four-power commission. But the United States balked, believing the Soviets intended to exploit Germany's assets for their own advantage and block her economic resurgence. The Americans viewed a weak, unstable Europe, of which Germany was the heart, as fertile ground for communist expansion. Beyond that, they suspected the Germans might form some kind of alliance, open or clandestine, with the Soviet Union. They had done it before. In 1919, resentful of the terms imposed on it at the end of World War I by the Versailles Treaty, Germany entered into a secret agreement to rearm with Soviet help. The mighty German war machine which rolled across Europe at the cost of so many lives was the result.

The question of what to do about Germany continued to be discussed with the Soviets, but the Marshall Plan to rebuild Europe was America's answer. For political as well as humanitarian reasons, the United States would underwrite European economic recovery. Soon, only Berlin remained under actual rather than nominal joint Soviet and Allied control, and the line dividing West and East Germany became the frontier separating the combatants in the Cold War. This was a political battle in which espionage played a prominent role, and a full appreciation of the growing ties between American Intelligence and Reinhard Gehlen requires viewing it in the framework of America's history of anti-communism.

The military occupation of West Germany ended in 1949 to be replaced by an Allied High Commission whose duty was to oversee the new government of Konrad Adenauer. But the great shift in the relationship between Germany and the United States came in 1950 and was caused by events not in Europe, but in Asia: the Americans became embroiled in the Korean War. The Marshall Plan originally prohibited the use of any of its resources for military purposes, but suddenly the Americans needed to send the men and arms committed to the defense of Europe elsewhere. American aid would continue, but the European nations must rearm to help defend themselves, and that included Germany.

In assessing the continued American support of Gehlen's Organization it is important to note that as soon as he began to re-establish his unit under the auspices of U.S. Army Intelligence, Gehlen gathered in former military colleagues, senior General Staff officers who had had no connection with intelligence. Recognizing that Germany would be independent again one day, and that it would need an army, he gave them refuge. He used these men, respected by the German people, to forge alliances with the new figures on the political horizon. Thus, the rearming of Germany strengthened Gehlen's ties with the government of Chancellor Adenauer who remained Gehlen's staunch supporter until a final, dramatic rupture in 1962.

Historically, personal relationships have furthered political alliances, and in examining American ties to Gehlen it is worth noting some of these. Chancellor Adenauer and John Foster Dulles, Secretary of State under President Eisenhower, formed a bond so close it was said that on being asked who at the Department of State set the policy on Germany, a Foreign Service officer ruefully replied "Adenauer." John Foster Dulles' brother, Allen, was Director of the Central Intelligence Agency and strongly supported the Agency's connection with Gehlen. Finally, Gehlen's ties to Adenauer closed the circle which existed during the critical early and mid-1950s.

This background may help explain why the Americans had a continuing interest in Gehlen, but it does not address some fundamental questions about the relationship. Did the information he provided justify taking him on and allowing him to expand his organization? What compromises did the Americans make in dealing with him? Did American Intelligence find itself supporting a group of Nazis? Was American supervision of the Gehlen Organization adequate?

The answers are not to be found in published accounts. The sources for those works are virtually all German—heretofore there has been no reliable information from the Americans—and the Germans had a considerable axe to grind. Gehlen was the founder of their central intelligence agency and his influence continued to be felt, through his successors, long after his retirement in 1968. The BND had a heavy stake in maintaining Gehlen's reputation and in playing down the American connection, and this was what the Americans, for their own reasons, wanted as well. On the other hand, Gehlen's enemies and critics of the BND, of which there were many, were equally intent on disparaging the man and his Organization.

Thus, even the most serious attempts to discuss Gehlen were badly flawed, but in the absence of information from the Americans this distorted account was perpetuated. A senior CIA officer, a former member of the staff working with the Gehlen Organization who later did an extensive study of it for the Agency, explained the difficulties facing those writing about Gehlen. In an internal document later partially declassified and released by the CIA he wrote: "[They] suffer from a terrible disadvantage (whatever their scholarly integrity may be), in that they seldom if ever get hold of any basic source material . . . So I am afraid that the dissemination of nonsense will continue ad infinitum, as each successive writer draws on his predecessor."[1]

Despite this manifestation of sympathy for the plight of the serious writer on Gehlen, the CIA remained unmoved, refusing to release any information on the subject. Indeed, the Agency still refuses either to confirm or deny that any relationship between Gehlen and the CIA ever existed.[2] Since the CIA appeared to be the sole repository of the information, unless another source of documents was discovered or American Intelligence officers who had worked with Gehlen broke their decades-long silence, no more would be learned about the American role. Fortunately, both things happened. In response to Freedom of Information Act requests, hundreds of relevant documents from other agencies were released to me. And Americans in the Army and the CIA who had been closest to Gehlen and his Organization agreed for the first time to be interviewed. Much of the information in this work, therefore, has never before been available.

The most significant of these newly declassified documents came from Army Intelligence. Well over a thousand were released to me in batches of a hundred or so over a period of two years and in no coherent order. They ultimately fit together to form a picture which shed new light on Gehlen's relationship with United States Intelligence. While revealing dangerous defects in his organization, they also countered many of the more sensational charges leveled against it. And, as they provide insights into the American intelligence services' relationship with Gehlen, they also expose destructive tensions among the American intelligence services themselves.

It was not a full picture, however. To complete it would require the cooperation of Americans who had played a part in the evolution of United States involvement with Reinhard Gehlen. Fortunately, more than two dozen former American intelligence officers who worked with Gehlen over a span covering almost thirty years, and others connected with Army Intelligence, none of whom had previously revealed what they knew, agreed to be interviewed. Many, in many places, spent dozens of hours with me. Starting chronologically with the officers of Army Intelligence, they include John Boker, the former Army Captain who "discovered" Gehlen at a prisoner of war camp in 1945; General John Russell Deane, Jr., (Ret.), in 1946 the Colonel in charge of the Gehlen unit; Professor Eric Waldman, who as a young Captain worked closely with Gehlen as the group began its explosive growth; and every CIA case officer who handled Gehlen until the Organization was turned over to the German government in 1956, as well as senior liaison staff members during and after that time.

In view of the CIA position regarding information on Gehlen, I had been concerned that former officers of the Agency would be reluctant to be interviewed. And at first many of them were. There is a tight network among the top echelon of former CIA officers; they are constantly in touch with one another. When I first called on two of them they were polite but uncooperative. Later, perhaps influenced by the nature of the documents released to me by the Army, they decided the best course would be for me to talk not only to them, but to those who worked directly with Gehlen. A few telephone calls were made, and I was welcomed by several key people who previously had declined to see me. The door had been opened and one officer referred me to another. Among the many who helped me were James Critchfield, Gehlen's first CIA opposite number, who played a decisive role in shaping the Organization's relationship with the United States; Thomas Lucid, his successor; and Donald Huefner, the chief American representative at a particularly difficult time for that relationship.

It was clear from the documents as well as from my conversations with former members of Army Intelligence that American support of Gehlen was a highly controversial issue. It became apparent that the same held true among CIA officers. I found there was a sharp divergence of opinion on the most fundamental aspects of the relationship, ranging from the wisdom of the original undertaking to the effectiveness of his Organization and its value to the United States. I was struck by the degree of detachment some of those who had worked most closely with him brought to their evaluations of Gehlen and his Organization. As far as I can judge, everyone with whom I spoke was completely candid and forthcoming. In a single instance, when two former CIA officers gave me sharply conflicting accounts of an incident of considerable importance, I believe a lapse of memory on the part of one, who was seriously ill, was responsible.

Like those most closely associated with the operation, not everyone will agree on the answers to the questions posed by this account. But because I have been able to draw on wholly new information, what follows corrects a distorted picture and provides a basis on which the

American connection with Gehlen can be judged. It is the story, which has not been told before, of that relationship as it unfolded, of the pressures which drove it and, above all, of the individuals who shaped it.

Part One

The Birth of the Gehlen Organization

Chapter One

Officer of the German General Staff

Flight Into The Mountains

Hitler's Wolfslair was a five kilometer, twenty minute ride through lovely countryside from General Reinhard Gehlen's headquarters. It was a trip Gehlen's officers dreaded. Far from viewing it an honor to attend a Führer Conference, it was a painful, frustrating, and often threatening experience. So, as they climbed aboard the Schienenbus— a sort of shuttlebus on tracks—the senior officers of Fremde Heere Ost (FHO—East Front Intelligence) covered their apprehension with wry humor. They called themselves die Gruppe Bosemueller, after a fictional embattled band of ordinary soldiers whose lives were at the mercy of capricious, bungling superiors. With paranoia thick in the air, and any disloyalty to Hitler a capital offense, even this kind of talk was dangerous. But it eased the tension.

Gehlen found another way to deal with the Conferences: he rarely went to them. Instead, he turned his intelligence reports over to General Guderian, Chief of Staff of the Army, and let him face Hitler with the increasingly depressing assessments of the military situation in the East. It was a wise decision to stay out of Hitler's way because as the German position on the Eastern front deteriorated, so did Gehlen's standing with his Führer. By Christmas of 1944 Gehlen was in deep trouble with his increasingly irrational leader. Fed up with him

and his analyses, Hitler considered Gehlen wrong-headed and a defeatist.

At the Situation Conference that cheerless Christmas Eve, Hitler
angrily brushed aside Gehlen's latest report, telling Guderian it was
rubbish. Two weeks later, on January 9 1945, on being presented with
another, even gloomier evaluation that pointed to an imminent and
fierce Soviet offensive, Hitler erupted. Calling the analysis completely
idiotic, he ordered Guderian to have Gehlen put in a lunatic asylum.

"The man who made these," Guderian retorted as he gestured
toward the pile of maps and diagrams for FHO, "is General Gehlen.
One of my very best staff officers. I should not have shown them to
you were I in disagreement with them. If you want General Gehlen
sent to a lunatic asylum," Guderian added, "then you had better have
me certified as well."

The finale came on March 28 1945, at two in the afternoon. This time
when Guderian brought him Gehlen's report Hitler charged that both
Gehlen and Guderian himself had repeatedly misinformed him, over-
stating the Russians' strength. This was too much for Guderian, and a
major scene ensued. Hitler ordered all the other officers, except Field
Marshal Keitel, to leave the room; by the time they had gone Hitler
had to some degree recovered himself.

"General Guderian," he said quietly, "your physical health requires
that you immediately take six weeks convalescent leave." Guderian
had been relieved of his command. Twelve days later it was Gehlen's
turn. On April 9 1945, without fanfare, indeed without comment of any
kind, General Reinhard Gehlen was given official written notice that
by decree of the Führer, he had been dismissed.[1]

In the days that followed his dismissal, as Germany became a
wasteland, the net began to close around Gehlen. Seen as a defeatist
and therefore a traitor, his position was precarious. But Gehlen was
ready. For six months, coolly, methodically, and in deepest secrecy,
Gehlen had been planning for this moment, and for what lay beyond.
Confident, as always, that his staff would carry out his instructions to
the letter, on April 28 1945 he tossed a rucksack into an old car,
climbed in next to the driver and quietly left his headquarters at Bad
Reichenhall.

Small and slim, his fair hair combed back from his high forehead,
the slight, soft-spoken Gehlen did not on first glance fit the image of a
member of the German General Staff. It was his manner, straddling
the line between self-assurance and arrogance, that conveyed author-

ity. He showed no lack of determination, but as the driver, an old comrade, started down the twisting road to the west, Gehlen knew the odds were against him and against the plan he had so meticulously worked out.

Self-doubt, however, was not part of his makeup. In years past, the first stirrings of spring here brought more wonder and held a richer promise of hope than elsewhere. But not now, not for Germany and not for Gehlen. The roads were jammed, and the war was suddenly only a few short miles away. As they crawled toward the Austrian border they ran into a division of their forces in retreat as the Americans swept through the mountain passes. Blocked on one road, the driver maneuvered the old car through the retreating soldiers and tried another.

In flight now both from the Army he had served and from the Allied armies opposing it, there was no turning back. What concerned Gehlen was gaining the time he needed if he was to win his gamble. But the Americans were moving so fast, and his own progress was so slow it seemed inevitable that he and his driver would be swallowed up by the advancing troops. If he, one of Hitler's generals, was captured by a first wave of Allied foot soldiers, fighting men in the violence of battle, there was no telling what they might do. At best he would be lost among the hundreds of thousands of prisoners being taken. Throughout the interminable night they were held up again and again. Bridges were out, damaged vehicles blocked their way, battles raged on the road ahead. Yet despite the hazards they reached their landmark: the Zipfelwirts, an inn on the Austrian frontier.

Hundreds of meters above where they stopped, beyond the treeline, lay Gehlen's destination. A hidden valley which, with story book irony, bore the name Elendsalm—Misery Meadow. When he took up his rucksack and said farewell to his comrade, Gehlen's goal seemed tantalizingly near, but as he struck out alone on foot he was suddenly more vulnerable than ever before.

SS units were scattered throughout the forests and by now were no respecters of rank. Hitler had ordered the removal of Army headquarters to Flensburg in the north; none of the Führer's generals had any business being in the south. Roving bands of SS troopers ranged over the mountains, fanatics armed with a blanket order to shoot deserters—a judgment they were to make on their own, carrying out their mission with a will. Brave but not a fool, Gehlen surveyed the terrain and opted to cut his own way up through the trees and deep snow rather than risk following gentler but more exposed hikers' trails.

Almost at once, as the trees closed in around him and his boots sank into the snow, he recognized a new enemy: the mountain itself. It was steeper and rockier than he had imagined, and he was weak and tired. Other threats receded as he fought the altitude and his own exhaustion. The intervals of climbing grew shorter, the periods of rest longer, and his thoughts gloomier. Perhaps, despite everything, his luck had been used up in the close calls he had had. Certainly a good part of it had been spent in rescuing his wife and children, and the treasure with which he meant to insure all their futures.

In January 1945, as the Russian advance picked up speed, reports of Stalin's order that the German people were to be annihilated, "the beast stamped out in its kennel," had reached Gehlen. They came hand in hand with horrifying accounts of the savagery of the Soviet troops. Those living in the line of march, a population of old men, women, and children who had been ordered to fight to the death, began to stream south away from the Soviets. Gehlen's wife and four children, the youngest of whom was two years old, were in Liegnitz, in Silesia, directly on the Russian route.

In February, Gehlen dispatched one of his best officers, the enigmatic but effective Major Hermann Baun to rescue his family and find a safe haven for them, and for the cases which contained documents, more precious than jewels, which he planned to use as barter. Bearing forged transport papers Baun collected the Gehlens and headed for Naumburg in Thuringia. Their road took them through Baun's home, Dresden, where his wife was running their small hotel and where the party planned to stop and rest. But the city was desperately overcrowded and they pushed on—escaping the merciless Allied bombing which devastated the city and killed tens of thousands, including Baun's wife.

Soon after, a copy of Eclipse, the Allied plan for carving up the conquered Germany, fell into Gehlen's hands. Thuringia, the refuge where Baun had left Gehlen's family, was designated part of the Soviet zone of occupation—and the final Russian assault could begin any day. Communication was difficult and insecure. Gehlen was sure his own movements were being watched, but his family and his passport to the future must be rescued. He immediately ordered his two most trusted drivers, one of them Baun's son, to take two trucks, find his wife and children, retrieve the cases of documents from the wine cellars near Naumburg where they had been stored, and get safely south to Bavaria.

The two drivers managed to locate and load into the trucks the cases, and Gehlen's family. The small caravan moved safely along the road as far as Leuna, where they were caught in an Allied air raid. But their luck held, no one was injured, and they pressed on. It was later that night, near Hof, that they suddenly faced a new threat, as great as the one they had just escaped, and the odds were against them. They were stopped by an SS unit and forced to proceed to their barracks, where the party's identification and transit papers, and the load they carried, would be examined.

Young Baun and the other driver were alert to the danger they faced. For a start, Hitler had expressly forbidden officers to evacuate their families to the West, and the fanatics of the SS were enforcing their Führer's will with a vengeance. And there was the matter of the authorization papers Herta Gehlen carried: they were forged. Legitimate travel documents being impossible to obtain, Gehlen had ordered his technical staff to create a set and duplicate the signature of the Gauleiter of Silesia. But most damning was the cargo. Orders had been issued to destroy all material which could be of use to the enemy, and it would be hard to imagine any of greater value than that in the two trucks.

In a daring maneuver, as they made their way slowly through the SS compound, Gehlen's drivers spotted an open gate at the rear, suddenly speeded up, drove the two trucks through it and made their escape.

A week later Gehlen was reunited, for a brief moment, with his family. Insofar as any place was safe, they had found refuge at a country house deep in the Bavarian forest near the Czech border. It was a melancholy reunion; both Gehlen and his wife were aware that at best their world was finished, at worst they would not meet again. But for this short time they retreated into family life and took comfort from its rituals.[2]

Now, leaning into the hill, exhausted and alone, in flight from both the victors and the almost-vanquished, it looked to Gehlen as if his string had run out. Yet he had no choice but to drive himself further up, to Misery Meadow. He had brought the whole of his intellect and all his organizational skill to bear on creating and executing this plan.

It had begun in October 1944 with furtive meetings among close colleagues, stolen hours of intense discussion, and all through the bleak winter the clandestine planning sessions continued. Gehlen was looking for survival, but not as a hunted creature, travelling on false papers, taking on a new identity, hiding out somewhere in South

America, simple as it would have been to arrange all that with the resources available to him. His goal was far more ambitious and imaginative.

He had no illusions about the course of the war, he had known for months that the game was up. The only question was what could be salvaged from the inevitable wreckage of unconditional surrender, and how it could keep him afloat as Germany and its leaders went under. The answer lay in his conviction that very shortly the Western powers would recognize that their ultimate enemy was their present ally, the Soviet Union. Then they would find themselves in desperate need of something only defeated Germany, only he and his coconspirators in Fremde Heere Ost, in fact, could give them: expert knowledge of the extent and real nature of the Soviet threat to the West. What they carried in their heads and in their files, Gehlen knew, was the fullest, most up-to-date information in existence on the Soviet Union's military capability, resources, performance and leadership. It was an invaluable asset he could and would try to exploit.

What Gehlen proposed was a bold gamble: he and his fellow officers would go into the mountains of Bavaria. There, away from the path of the Russians, they would bury their priceless hoard of documents, go into hiding, and wait for the advancing Allies. The risks of the plan were enormous. Discovery of their discussions alone meant death at the hands of their own High Command. Other lower officers had been summarily executed for merely voicing doubts about a German victory; Gehlen, a General, was assuming defeat and plotting how to meet it. Dangerous as their situation was, what lay ahead would be worse. The moment they set the plan in motion they would be entirely isolated in a world of enemies: fugitives hiding from their own people to the north and south; from the Americans, British, and French to the west; and to the east, from the Soviets.

This would be the most critical operation of Gehlen's career and he set about laying the groundwork for it with typical thoroughness. The secret plotting which began in October of 1944 was done by a small group which relied unconditionally on one another. This grounding in mutual trust, together with a complacent confidence in his intuitions about people, was to play Gehlen false one day. But at that critical time the conspirators maintained their loyalty and their silence. Gehlen, Gerhard Wessel, his successor as head of FHO, and Hermann Baun met at Bad Elster where they agreed to offer their joint services to the Allies in what came to be known as the Pact of Bad Elster. Under cover of their normal routine, they appropriated top secret

Eastern Intelligence files and made seven sets of copies. Then, taking ever greater risks, they buried them all in different locations in the mountains.

Baun was given a vital task. As officer in charge of the Frontline Reconnaissance Detachments, the so-called Walli units of agents who operated behind Soviet lines, he had established a network of secret contacts. Through these special channels he made contact with the British, to whom Gehlen put his plan. Gehlen proposed that in exchange for asylum—rather than imprisonment and whatever might follow—he would deliver to them the core of his whole intelligence organization. His senior staff, their expertise and, above all, their priceless files on the Soviets. He would sell his past to buy his future.

The offer was not even acknowledged. This apparent rejection by the British, whom Gehlen admired, not only was a blow to his pride, it dramatically raised the risk that his plan would fail. It left him with no alternative but to approach the Americans. But the Americans were young, raw, recent arrivals in the world of international politics and inexperienced in intelligence, where the British considered them particularly clumsy bulls in what they viewed as their china closet. Furthermore, Gehlen had no clear channel to the Americans as he did to the British, and he did not know what to expect from them, brash and unsophisticated as they were. Still, he had no choice, and added this unknown quantity to his already hazardous plan; he would surrender to the Americans, if he could, and then take his chances on making a deal.

Reinhard Gehlen

"As a young officer," General Reinhard Gehlen said of himself, "I stubbornly refused to learn a foreign language beyond what I had picked up in school, so that there could be no risk of my being posted to military intelligence work within the General Staff, let alone to the secret service itself . . ."[3] For Gehlen, as for most military men in the Western countries, Intelligence was at best a detour, at worst a dead end on the upward road through the ranks. The men who directed wars, the strategists, the commanders in the field, they were not Intelligence officers; those who made the battlefield decisions used information about the enemy just as they used other weapons at their disposal. Intelligence officers provided a valuable service, nothing more. Clearly this was the wrong turning for a young officer in search of promotion.

That Gehlen should have aspired to the General Staff at all is revealing; it shows that his small, wiry frame was animated by ambition. "He was very quiet, almost an introvert," a classmate said of him, "but this caused many of us to underestimate him. He was a first rate opportunist as well as a fine student. While we were muddling along in our careers, hoping to strike it lucky, Gehlen was always planning ahead, never missing a chance to better himself."[4]

Had Gehlen been asked at the end of the Second World War, or at the end of his life, to name his greatest accomplishment, it surely would have been that he was an officer of the German General Staff. It defined him as a member of an elite without parallel in Western societies, exemplifying military excellence and embodying the highest standards of honor for the German people. To Gehlen the German General Staff represented the finest essence of what it was to be a German. It was his touchstone.[5]

The force and influence of the General Staff on the life of Germany and therefore of Europe cannot be questioned. In the words of the historian Walter Görlitz, "The traditions . . . of the highest level of individual competence and responsibility within the corporate leadership, of the strictest moral and intellectual and also caste standards maintained within the framework of selfless devotion to the sovereign and the state—these were the traditions and the principles developed by the German General Staff through the 19th century . . . that they were widely admired and imitated is indisputable." By the turn of the century the German people saw it as invincible. What can be and is disputed, especially in the light of the rise of Hitler, is the character of the General Staff's influence.[6,7]

The General Staff did make an effort to resist Hitler, culminating in the July 20, 1944, Generals' Plot to assassinate him. But the plot failed, and on July 29, 1944, in the bloody aftermath of the attempt on Hitler's life, their capitulation was complete.[8] Chief of the General Staff, General Guderian, sent a notice to all General Staff officers that each one "must be a National Socialist officer-leader not only . . . by his model attitude toward political questions but by actively cooperating in the political indoctrination of younger comrades in accordance with the tenets of the Führer . . . " or "apply for his removal from the General Staff." No one did.[9]

Whatever its true nature, its influence on the life of Germany, or its humiliation at the end of World War II, in Gehlen's youth the General

Staff was a powerful, venerated caste apart and above, led by aristocrats. Had it not been for Germany's defeat in the First World War and its aftermath, it is unlikely Reinhard Gehlen, of middle class origins, would have been one of its number.[10]

In a democratic age to raise the question of social position is considered bad form; it is supposed not to exist—and if it does, it is unimportant. But in the Germany of Gehlen's boyhood (he was born in 1902) no one would have argued about, or apologized for, either its existence or its importance. Gehlen himself did not discuss his personal life, and this insistence on privacy, as well as being a professional necessity, allowed a certain cloudiness to form around the specifics of his background.

For the first six years of his life Gehlen lived in Erfurt, Thuringia (now part of East Germany). His parents had a small apartment at 63-64 Löberstrasse in a modest neighborhood of Erfurt, near the railway station. His mother, Katherina Vairuewyck, was of Flemish descent, and his father, Walther Gehlen, was a Lieutenant in the 19th Field Artillery Regiment. By 1908 the senior Gehlen's health was frail and he left the army and moved his family to Breslau. There his brother Max, a partner in the Leipzig publishing house of Ferdinand Hirt, arranged for him to manage a branch of the firm. The Gehlen family circumstances improved considerably as a result of the change. They now were living at the highly respectable No. 1 Königsplatz, and moving in the conservative circles of middle class Breslau businessmen.

At König-Wilhelm High School, which he entered in 1911, Gehlen showed a particular bent for science and mathematics, consistently ranking at the top of his class. By nature shy and serious-minded, Gehlen gained more respect than popularity among his classmates, from whom he tended to stay aloof. By the time the war was over and he had finished school he knew he wanted to join the army and be a General Staff officer, despite the fact that the military was not at first blush an encouraging place to try to make one's mark. By the terms of the 1919 Versailles Treaty both a General Staff and officer training for it were outlawed.

But the Germans, bitterly resentful over the Versailles terms, had set out on a massive and brilliantly successful deception, secretly rearming and rebuilding their military strength with the wholehearted cooperation of the Soviet Union. Negotiations leading to an agreement allowing the Germans to manufacture heavy armament and aircraft, as well as to build specialized facilities to train officers in Russia, began in 1919. In April, 1922 the Treaty of Rapallo, restoring diplomatic relations and establishing most-favored nation status, was secretly signed by Germany and the Soviet Union. By January, 1923, a further secret pact, between the Soviets and the German High Command, was signed. The Allies, out of negligence and indifference, ignored reports of Germany's gross violations of the Versailles Treaty, and simply looked the other way.[11]

Soon a Troop Office, along the lines of a national guard, and a program of Commanders' Assistants Training Courses were formed in Germany itself. Covers, in reality, for the clandestine re-establishment of the General Staff and the Staff Training College. Under the noses of its conquerors, the German military machine was back to business as usual. Now, however, it was necessary to go outside the traditional groups to find qualified men while attempting to maintain its exacting standards.

Only days after his eighteenth birthday, in 1920, Gehlen took his first step toward his ambitious goal by joining the army, and on January 1, 1921 he was posted to the 6th Light Artillery Regiment in Schweidnitz in Silesia. This was a time of intense upheaval which was bound to have an impact on the young Gehlen. Within only a few years he witnessed the Russian Revolution; the defeat of Germany; the collapse of German military discipline with the mutiny of the High Sea Fleet; the Communist uprising in Germany itself; and the hatred generated by the Versailles Treaty. All this could only have reinforced Gehlen's commitment to rebuilding a strong and orderly Germany.[12]

After finishing officer training programs at Munich and Jüterbog, Gehlen returned to Schweidnitz and hit a dry spell. There were few opportunities for advancement in this shadowy army. It was not until 1926 that his hard work and planning began to pay off and he was appointed to the prestigious Hanover Cavalry School. Not only was this a significant step forward in a career which appeared stalled, it plucked Gehlen from the dreary routine of an isolated garrison and thrust him into a lively and, by comparison, dazzlingly sophisticated milieu where his capacity for hard work as well as his keen and accomplished horsemanship won him recognition at last. It had taken eight years, but in 1928 Gehlen was finally promoted to the rank of First Lieutenant.

With that happy turn of events, however, came a less welcome piece of news: he was ordered to return to his former regiment in Silesia, where even his new duties as Adjutant of the First Battalion could not compensate for the brighter, more challenging world he had discovered in Hanover. He had seen and tasted better things; his ambition was further stirred.

Reinhard Gehlen married well when Herta Charlotte Agnes Helena von Seydlitz-Kurzbach became his wife in 1931. For an ambitious young soldier of middle class background it was a coup to win a von Seydlitz, even a hyphenated one. Indeed, the legendary hero to whom he was now related by marriage would be an ornament on any family tree, particularly one grown in Germany's martial soil.[13,14]

Allied to an old and prominent Prussian family with a distinguished military history, Gehlen was now measurably closer to his goal of winning a place on the General Staff. When Hitler came to power, declared the Versailles Treaty dead, and began his massive, overt rearming of his country, the outlook for Gehlen was brighter still. In June of 1935 he sat the demanding Staff College examinations, did well and was promoted to Captain. In 1936 he finally won the right to don the coveted Red Stripe of the General Staff officer.

When war broke out Gehlen was Senior General Staff officer of a reserve division of Army Group South, the 213th Infantry Division. His unit marched on Poland on the Army Group's left flank, but Poland collapsed before he and his men saw action. Despite this failure to achieve his baptism by fire, Gehlen was still credited with having had battle experience, all-important in a military career. But what tipped the balance for Gehlen, by now a Major, was that he had attracted the notice of the Chief of Staff of the Army, General Franz Halder. Within six months he had made himself indispensable to Hadler, who in June 1940 appointed him his Senior Aide; only four months after that Halder assigned him to be Chief of the Eastern Group in the Operations Section. His commander there was Colonel Adolf Heusinger, a man whose fate would be entwined with Gehlen's in a vastly different world five years later.

In Heusinger's section Gehlen concentrated on the problems Hitler's armies would face when the inevitable march on Russia began; it was the start of his lifelong preoccupation with the Soviet Union. Hitler invaded in June, 1941, easily cutting a huge swath eastward. But by end of the year the German army's apparently unstoppable machine began to falter in the face of Russia's ultimate defensive weapons: her weather and her size. Army Chief of Staff Halder belatedly and angrily recognized "lapses in the intelligence service" regarding the Soviet Union, and interest suddenly was focused on Fremde Heere Ost (FHO), the General Staff's Eastern Front Intelligence Service. It was clear its present chief, the gregarious Colonel Eberhard Kinzel, who lavished more attention on his blond, blue-eyed mistress than on Soviet intentions, would have to be replaced.

But who would that replacement be? Halder consulted Heusinger, who had just the man: his invaluable protégé, Reinhard Gehlen, on whose ability and "military dash" Halder himself had recently commented.[15] When nonetheless he pointed to Gehlen's lack of intelligence experience, Heusinger countered by pointing to his skill at organization, talent for planning and taste for hard work. Here, he argued, was a man equal to the task of stiffening a flaccid, undisciplined unit and making it productive. Halder was convinced and in April, 1942, Reinhard Gehlen was set on the convoluted path which one day would make him a unique figure in the history of espionage.

When Gehlen, reluctantly or not, took up his new post as chief of FHO, he had one consolation. He was in the same line of work as the enigmatic but respected Admiral Wilhelm Canaris, chief of the Abwehr, the Military Intelligence Service, whom he held in high regard. Canaris, like most of the military establishment, had no use for Hitler, and the Admiral's opposition was no secret. He was involved to a greater or lesser degree in a number of the plots against Hitler. The wonder is that he lasted as long as he did.[16]

Of all the schemes to depose Hitler, that of 1938 in which Canaris participated had the best chance of success, on paper at least. It was a serious attempt led by the former and current Army Chiefs of Staff, Generals Beck and Halder, and its purpose was not to kill, but to overthrow Hitler with the sanction of legal proceedings. Gehlen may have admired Canaris, but in this regard he did not emulate him. By his own account, the closest Gehlen came to acting against Hitler was knowingly to harbor in FHO several officers involved in the Generals' Plot of July 20, 1944.

Although he was unwilling at the outset, Gehlen embarked on intelligence work and soon surprised himself "for," as he was to say later, "It was precisely in this dreaded field of endeavor that I was fated to find my metier."[17]

Reinhard Gehlen (FHO) and Walter Schellenberg (SD)

The enmity between the officers of the General Staff and Hitler's Nazi Party ran deep and strong, but the Officers' Corps was no match for the Nazis. In a move long resisted by the military, the Nazi Party's instrument of terror, the SS, finally succeeded in gobbling up its Intelligence Services. On February 18 1944, Admiral Canaris, chief of the Abwehr, secret service of the High Command of the Armed Forces (OKW), was relieved of his post. By June, 1944, the dissolution of the Abwehr and of the Intelligence service of the Army (OKH), including FHO, and their absorption into the maw of the SS was complete. At last Himmler had control over all aspects of intelligence: internal and external, military as well as political. Integration of the services did not lessen the antipathy between the Nazis and the General Staff, however.

As head of the infamous Reichssicherheitshauptamt (RSHA), which oversaw the offices of State Security, General Ernst Kaltenbrunner answered only to the mild-mannered, bloodthirsty chief of the SS, Heinrich Himmler.[18] And Kaltenbrunner was delighted when he heard the news that on April 9, 1945, in a fit of rage over Gehlen's pessimistic assessment of the German position on the Eastern front, Hitler had dismissed him. "This little sausage of a von Gehlen [sic] now has to go West, too," he said with satisfaction, before continuing: "He probably relied too much on your poor intelligence service. Don't forget, I don't dream of courting one day reproaches by the Führer owing to your reports."[19] These pleasantries were addressed to Kaltenbrunner's subordinate, the smooth and wily General Walter Schellenberg.[20]

It is one of the phenomena of examining the Nazi state that, in comparison with someone like Himmler, other men of the Nazi regime, despicable by any normal standards, appear relatively benign. And so it is with the "university-educated intellectual gangster" and skillful political manipulator, Walter Schellenberg.[21] Schellenberg's understanding of the field, limited though it was, allowed him to appreciate the superior quality of Gehlen's work, but he himself was a sorry specimen of an intelligence officer and the cause of considerable grief and embarrassment to his subordinates.

Reinhard Gehlen's wartime reputation, and therefore that of the FHO, rested on his skill as an evaluator. But evaluation is only as reliable as the information on which it draws, and that was another matter altogether. Fresh intelligence about the Soviet position was constantly being recorded on the huge map table in Gehlen's office, much of it collected through the interrogation of Russian prisoners of war. By and large he did better getting information from the enemy than from his own side, since the level of professionalism in the other branches of German Intelligence was often low and occasionally laughable. In one of its gaudier and less distinguished efforts Walter Schellenberg was a featured player.

In April of 1944 two officers came to Schellenberg with a scheme to draw Winston Churchill into negotiations aimed at that favorite German goal, persuading Britain and the United States to stop fighting Germany and join with her in redirecting their energies against "the common enemy, Russia." This despite the fact that the Soviet Union was their ally, and President Roosevelt its wholehearted champion.

The instruments to be used to achieve this were "a French subject and proprietress of the noted perfumery factory . . . a certain Frau [Coco] Chanel" living in Paris, and "a certain Frau [Vera Bates] Lombardi, a former British subject of good family then married to an Italian," a woman who at the time was a political prisoner in Italy. Since 1941, Schellenberg was informed, Chanel had been having an affair with Hans Gunther "Spatz" von Dincklage, a dashing German who between the wars had earned a reputation as a playboy—and who since 1928 had been an undercover agent of German Intelligence. The officers convinced Schellenberg that Chanel, who believed the destinies of France and Germany were linked, was sufficiently well known to Churchill, and had suitable stature in Britain, to serve as a credible vehicle for proposing these delicate negotiations to the government of Great Britain.

Chanel confirmed that Lombardi was in fact an old friend and was very well connected indeed in British social circles—it was she who, twenty years before, had introduced Chanel to the Duke of Westminster, with whom the energetic Frenchwoman had embarked on a torrid and highly publicized affair. The nub of the scheme was that Chanel would write a letter addressed to Churchill, to be hand-carried by Lombardi to the British Ambassador in Madrid; he in turn would forward it to the Prime Minister. Lombardi could then proceed to England where she would see Churchill and make a personal appeal in support of the plan.

When the plan was explained and the letters delivered to her after she reached Madrid, Lombardi readily agreed to go to the British Embassy and see the Ambassador. Confident that their scheme was safely on track, the Germans sat back expecting to see their plan speed ahead; instead they watched as the whole thing went right off the rails. Vera Bates, it appeared, despite her marriage to Lombardi, was first and last an Englishwoman, a fact which apparently had not escaped the Italians who had interned her.

Loyal subject that she was, the minute she reached the British Embassy she revealed the whole cockamamy scheme and promptly denounced everyone involved, naming Chanel and von Dincklage as German agents. As soon as he realized what had happened, Schellenberg says succinctly, "contact was immediately dropped with Lombardi and Chanel." This sort of hare-brained scheme was not an everyday occurrence, but it is clear that the antagonists were unevenly matched and German Intelligence was systematically victimized by its enemies both to the West and the East.[22]

Given the unhappy state of German wartime intelligence as a whole, that Gehlen's FHO was able to amass the amount of reliable material it did on the Soviet Union is a considerable achievement, and Gehlen's professionalism, orderly mind and coolly objective evaluation of the facts were largely responsible for it. Under unrelenting pressure from Hitler for accurate predictions about Soviet intentions (information which Hitler then angrily rejected), Gehlen did engage in a practice widespread among Intelligence professionals of all nationalities, he did his best to appear to be specific but in fact often hedged his bets: an attack "might possibly" exceed local proportions, a counterattack was "not excluded," and so on.[23]

By fuzzing the outlines, by building an element of elasticity into his assessments, Gehlen was able to protect his reputation as something approaching a genius in his field, and historians of Intelligence agree he did have an outstanding record. By early 1945, when Hitler was past listening to anything but his own inner voice, it was a reputation worth preserving. By then Gehlen knew it was his ticket to the future.

On the face of it they were an oddly assorted pair, Schellenberg and Gehlen: the one glib, urbane, polished, adept in the many uses of charm; the other reserved, distant, aloof, disdaining small talk. But in practice their personalities complemented each other, and a shared grasp of the realities, a calculating turn of mind, and an instinct for self-preservation drew them together.

In March 1945, as cover for his real activities, Gehlen brought Schellenberg a scheme for the creation of an underground army to resist the occupation forces after the inevitable defeat of Germany. They met alone for three hours one evening, and Gehlen presented his proposal: the formation of a resistance movement patterned on that of the Poles, which had bedeviled and threatened the Germans until their putative allies the Russians extinguished it. Himmler, Gehlen proposed, would take command of the force, with Schellenberg and himself as the Reichsfürher's lieutenants.[24]

This was a more elaborate plan than that of propaganda minister Joseph Goebbels for the Werewolves, secret bands of patriots who would battle the Fatherland's invaders by stealth. The Werewolf plan in fact was an effort to inspire an exhausted people to fight on, and in the closing months of the war a miserable rabble of children and misfits would bring it into weak and ragged reality. But Gehlen's plan was serious, more than an idea, he told Schellenberg; he had already ordered the FHO staff to prepare a report on the subject. However, he added, to complete the plans he would need to take four weeks' leave so he could go to Army evacuation headquarters, code named "Frankenstrupp."[25][26]

As agreed, Schellenberg took Gehlen's study of the Polish resistance and its possible adaptation by the Germans to Himmler, whose reaction was swift and to the point. "This is complete nonsense. If I should discuss this plan with Wenk [Chief of Staff of the Army] I am [sic] the first defeatist of the Third Reich. This fact would be served boiling hot to the Führer. You need not tell your Gehlen. You need only explain to him that I strictly refuse to accept the plan. Besides—it is typical of the high class general staff officer to sit in Frankenstrupp nursing postwar plans instead of fighting." Himmler, wrong about so much else, was right on one thing at least: typical or not, Gehlen had indeed stopped fighting the hopeless war and was mapping a course for the future.

Now, six months after the start of his secret planning, Gehlen reached the first of his goals: a modest one, but profoundly welcome. When he finally broke through the trees into the meadow, there before him, solid, comfortable, inviting, was the haven he had been seeking. A large wooden hut with a sharply pitched roof, its eves stretching over the verandah, smoke curling from its brick chimney. Inside, nine members of his staff were waiting for him: six officers, two of them wounded, and three women assistants. The legend-makers have it that the first object Gehlen took from his rucksack was a small plaque bearing his family motto: *Laet vaeren nyt!* Never Give Up.[27]

Chapter Two

National Security and the Soviet Alliance

President Franklin Roosevelt's Commitment

Gehlen had charted his course. He would gamble on American appreciation of his expertise on the Soviet Union. This, of course, assumed the United States viewed its wartime alliance with the Russians as a temporary, necessary expedient, a marriage of convenience. But the American government, it turned out, did not. President Franklin Delano Roosevelt was still committed, as he had been all along, to the Soviet alliance. Winston Churchill called it "honeymoon madness," but Roosevelt's belief that he could win Stalin over left him unable or unwilling to recognize Soviet ambitions for what they were.[1] A letter sent by Roosevelt to every American war agency on March 7, 1942, demonstrates the lengths to which the President of the United States was prepared to go in his courtship of Stalin.

In his letter, Roosevelt ordered that any and all materiel the United States had agreed to send to the Soviet Union was to be given the highest priority regardless of the consequences to any other part of the American war effort. That meant the Soviet Union was given precedence over the British and all other American allies, and indeed over the needs of the United States armed forces themselves. General John Russell Deane, Chief of the American Military Mission in Moscow at the time, was to say later that this decision was, in his view, "the beginning of a policy of appeasement of Russia from which we have never fully recovered."[2]

The Germans, by contrast, accepted as fact that the future held a major, sustained and ultimately decisive confrontation between the Soviet Union and the West. To all Europeans, the fact that the United States—despite its having experienced a particularly ugly bout of virulent anti-communism in the Red Scare of 1919–1920—could so dangerously misunderstand and underestimate Soviet intentions reflected an astounding lack of political sophistication. Further, it demonstrated to them then what many Europeans believed to be the case: that the Americans, safe and half a world away, indulging in volatile policy swings from Brinksmanship to Detente, lacked the imagination and certainly the empathy necessary to appreciate what it was to live each day in the immediate shadow of the Soviet Union. Reinhard Gehlen, who planned to turn the Americans' ignorance to his advantage, spoke for many when he expressed his belief that the Americans suffered from the fact that they had insufficient knowledge and understanding of the East, its mentality or its positive and negative sides.[3]

The Americans were so committed to the maintenance of friendly relations with the Soviets that during the war there was a failure to take even the most elementary precautions to safeguard the nation's greatest secrets. After Hitler invaded the Soviet Union, and Russia swapped its role as enemy for that of ally, Roosevelt ordered a halt to censorship of mail to and from Russia, a move which led one outraged member of Army censorship to gesture at the stacks of unopened bags of Soviet-bound mail and say: "I only hope somebody around here had the sense to put a kettle in the back room and steam it all open."[4] In view of what was going on elsewhere in the government at the time, it is doubtful there were any kettles on the boil.

"We were convinced [the Soviets] had deep penetrations of the government," said Robert Collier, one of only three FBI agents assigned to the Soviet Espionage Division, "but nobody was paying attention to what was happening." Collier, William King Harvey and Lish Whitsun comprised the whole civil counterespionage effort against what was in fact a virtual army of Soviet agents operating in the United States.[5]

That nobody was paying attention was too bad, because a great deal was happening, much of it at Oak Ridge, Tennessee, and Los Alamos, New Mexico, where the atomic bomb was being conceived by the scientists and engineers of the Manhattan Project. Peer de Silva, who later, as a CIA officer, would work closely with Gehlen, was a security officer with the Manhattan Project. His assignment was to cooperate with the FBI in the surveillance of Soviet agents, but his role was to be strictly that of a spectator. "I was told not to take any action," he said later. "I was to watch them, to take note, but do nothing."[6]

As a result of this stunningly casual approach to the most sensitive military project in United States history, the stock of American secrets was systematically and persistently looted. Major George Racey Jordan, liaison officer between the United States Army and the Soviet Purchasing Commission at Great Falls, Montana, gave a Congressional committee a glimpse of the extent of that plunder when he recounted an incident that took place one night at the Montana airfield.

Great Falls was the first stop on the route between the United States and the Soviet Union. After leaving Montana, a plane would touch down again at Fairbanks, Alaska, and then go on to Siberia. One of the Major's tasks was to examine any luggage which was not protected by diplomatic immunity. The Major was a conscientious man who did his work so thoroughly that the Russians threatened to see to it he was relieved of his post. So it came as a considerable surprise to him when one night the previously hostile and notoriously tight-fisted Russians invited him out for a chicken dinner.

The dinner included a great deal of vodka, which the unexpectedly friendly hosts pressed on him, a gesture which raised the suspicions of the abstemious Major and led him to excuse himself to make a telephone call. He telephoned the airfield control tower to say that someone was to notify him at once if a plane headed for the Soviet Union came in. Shortly afterward the call came—and when it did the dinner party abruptly ended. The Major rushed to the airfield where he was confronted by two armed Russians who tried, with notable lack of success, to keep him from entering the plane. Once on board, he found a number of cheap black suitcases, each tied with cord and crudely sealed with wax. As the Russian guards bellowed that he was violating diplomatic immunity, the Major summoned his own guard; ordered him to stand with his rifle to his shoulder; informed the Russians that the cases were not immune from inspection; and proceeded to rip off the cord, break the unofficial seals and open them.

What Major Jordan found were documents from the Oak Ridge atomic testing site with words such as "Manhattan Engineering Department," "uranium 92," "neutrons," "protons," "energy produced by fission," and "cyclotron" appearing on them. There were also engineering documents with holes in them where the label "Secret" would have appeared, and maps on which the sites of industrial plants had been marked. Furthermore, he testified to the Congressmen, he found a memo from the White House. It read: "Had a hell of a time getting these away from Groves." The signature on the memo was "H. H." (This was not the only time Roosevelt's closest aide, Harry Hopkins, would come under a cloud of suspicion as a result of aggressively pro-Soviet positions.) But because Major Jordan was unable to find the word "Secret" on any of the papers, he did not have the authority to ground the plane, and it went on its way to Russia, cargo intact.[7]

Responsibility for the climate that spawned this flabby approach to national security must lie with Roosevelt. This unrealistic attitude was compounded by his physical condition which, by March, 1945, was rapidly deteriorating. Owing to the faltering leadership of the frail and ailing American president the Allies faced a crisis. What they needed was a definitive statement of the President's views on occupation policy.

All through 1944 an Anglo-American-Russian group, the European Advisory Commission, had been struggling with the daunting task of drawing up a mutually acceptable plan for the occupation of Germany, but by September there was still no official proposal from the United States. The American Departments of State, War, and Treasury all put forward their own plans but Roosevelt, although repeatedly pressed, had not expressed his views on the subject. "I dislike making detailed plans for a country which we do not yet occupy," he complained testily to his Secretary of State, Cordell Hull, on October 20 1944.[8] But when there was still no Occupation Directive, or indeed any political guidance five months later, in March 1945, with Germany all but defeated, Roosevelt's indecisiveness had become a major problem.

When Robert Murphy, the President's friend and personal representative to the Supreme Allied Command, returned to Washington for consultations in March of 1945, his highest priority was to have a private conversation with Roosevelt. So Murphy was relieved when the President invited him to dine at the White House. He set out confident that when he got back to Versailles he would finally have something substantial to report about the President's views on Germany. It was an intimate evening, with Roosevelt mixing the martinis before dinner and being, as always, the gracious and charming host. But from the moment the President appeared, Murphy's anxiety grew. For a start, Roosevelt looked terrible. Despite his light-hearted references to the amount of weight he had lost, Murphy was so dismayed by the President's condition that when Roosevelt observed that soon it would all be over, Murphy's first thought was not that the war was drawing to a close, but that Roosevelt meant he had not much longer to live.

When the two men left the dining room and settled down alone to talk, Murphy looked forward to the moment when Roosevelt would finally grapple with the basic issues and a course would be charted for the occupation of Germany. But Murphy's hopes were dashed and his concern about both his President and future American policy toward Germany reached their peak.

"The man who sat across from me that night," Murphy says, "was unable to discuss serious matters. He talked for an hour, but aimlessly . . . . Roosevelt was in no condition that night to offer balanced judgments upon the great questions of war and peace which had concerned him for so long. His conversation illumined for me why the Army during this period was making decisions which the civilian authority of our government normally would have made, such as the one relating to the capture of Berlin."[9]

To compound the problem created by lack of presidential leadership the United States suffered from a critical case of political naivete, which was reflected in its attitude toward intelligence in all its forms. Not only did the Americans not distrust the Soviets but, even had they wanted to spy on them, they did not have the capability.[10]

Herbert O. Yardley and William J. Donovan

Gehlen had offered his services to British Intelligence, an organization he respected. Rebuffed by them, he turned to the Americans, about whose intelligence services he was much less sanguine. Unlike generations of British royal courts and democratic governments which encouraged the development of professional intelligence services, American administrations had not given them a high priority until the outbreak of World War II.

"I think it can be said without successful challenge that before Pearl Harbor we did not have an intelligence service in this country comparable to that of Great Britain, or France, or Russia, or Germany, or Japan," said General Hoyt S. Vandenberg, an early director of central intelligence. "We did not have one because the people of the United States would not accept it. It was felt there was something un-American about espionage and even about intelligence generally.

There was a feeling that all that was necessary to win a war—if there was going to be another war—was an ability to shoot straight . . . All intelligence is not sinister, nor is it an invidious type of work."[11]

That the United States lagged behind Britain, France, Germany, Japan, and Russia in the business of clandestine foreign information-gathering is largely because it was not in the race in any serious way. Until 1940 foreign intelligence was handled by the military. In 1865 the Treasury Department established the Secret Service to combat counterfeiting and to give personal protection to the President. Many years later, in 1908, the Bureau of Investigation, forerunner of the FBI, was established, but it was not until 1939 that the President ordered the FBI to investigate espionage, sabotage, and subversion within the United States. The following year, 1940, the FBI was given closely circumscribed authorization to operate abroad, in South America. Its brief was limited to combating Axis espionage and sabotage; intelligence gathering was prohibited. And yet, almost in spite of itself, the United States did have some major intelligence capabilities, among them the balding, short, energetic Herbert Osborne Yardley.

Born in 1889 in Worthington, Indiana, Yardley learned telegraphy from his father, a railway agent, while at the same time learning poker at Monty's Place, the local saloon. Under the tutelage of such Worthington notables as Salty East and Monty Mull, Yardley became a master of the game which, along with the transformation of letters and numbers into other forms, became a lifelong passion. His talent for poker Yardley used for fun and profit; his gift for cryptography he put at the service of his country, which appreciated it only in fits and starts. A State Department telegrapher at the outbreak of World War I, Yardley, who had a messianic belief in the value and power of secret communications and who said "wars always afforded opportunities," seized on America's entry into hostilities to establish a Cipher Bureau, MI-8, for the War Department.

When the war ended, Yardley's bureau, which came to be known as the Black Chamber and which had performed brilliantly, was put under the joint control of the War and State Departments, with State responsible for the lion's share of its funding. But before long interest in and financial support for Yardley's bureau began to evaporate, and soon it was down to a skeleton staff. Hoping to pump new life into it after Herbert Hoover's election as President in 1928, Yardley decided to show off his department's prowess by sending a series of important overseas messages it had intercepted and decoded to the new Secretary of State, Henry L. Stimpson.

That turned out to be a mistake; Stimpson's response was literally shattering. Profoundly shocked and declaring that having within the government an organization which read the cables of foreign governments violated the principle of trust which ruled both his personal life and the professional affairs of State, Stimpson put an end to Yardley's work. He dissolved the Cipher Bureau by the simple expedient of ordering all State Department funds withheld from it and forbidding any further contact between MI-8 and the State Department. It was then that he made his famous observation that "Gentlemen do not read each other's mail."[12]

Yardley's small, brilliant cryptographic unit which performed prodigious feats of code-breaking, had run foul of the streak of puritanical high-mindedness that has a way of popping up among America's leaders. This noble revulsion at what was perceived as the unprincipled act of spying gave other nations, including the Soviet Union, a significant edge. While the United States was primly minding its own business, the Russians were carting home bushels of the most sensitive information about every aspect of American life: political, economic, scientific, military.

Their enterprise was greatly aided by the efforts of American communists and their active supporters. Whittaker Chambers was to say that some seventy-five government officials spied for the Soviets from 1936 to 1938, while another admitted Soviet agent, Elizabeth Bentley, said that Nathan George Silvermaster, a Department of Agriculture employee, not only ran a communist cell which gathered a "fabulous amount of confidential information" for the Soviets, but had such highly-placed sources in OSS that he knew the date of the American invasion of Europe four days before D-Day. So little understood or appreciated was espionage (spying out others' secrets), or counterespionage (protecting one's own), even by the military, that on being asked "How is the intelligence work in your force, Sir?" a naval flag officer answered: "We don't need any intelligence work. There are no Communists on our ship."[13]

While the Soviets had been busy at the work of espionage, the United States had done little either to protect itself from spies or do any spying of its own. But then, at 12:30 p.m. on June 18, 1941, Roosevelt issued an executive order that eventually would bring intelligence into the heart of American policymaking. He established the Office of the Coordinator of Intelligence (COI), an agency of the government which would have the "authority to collect and analyze all information and data, which may bear upon the national security," to "correlate such information and data," and make "such information and data available to the President and such departments and officials of the Government as the President may determine." Further, the COI was authorized to carry out "such supplementary activities as may facilitate the securing of information important for national security not now available to the Government," meaning that in addition to engaging in espionage, the Americans were in the covert operations business.

The Director of this new agency was Colonel William J. "Wild Bill" Donovan, and he immediately set about recruiting an extraordinary crew to carry out the presidential mandate. Writers, bankers, film producers, journalists, diplomats, professors—what has been de-scribed as "the most brilliant yet motley group of peacocks ever assembled in a Washington agency."[14]

Donovan was born on New Year's Day, 1883, in Buffalo, New York. His father, Timothy, like Yardley's father, worked for the railroad. He was a strong, feisty man of independent mind, and young Bill was certainly his father's son; in him ambition, energy, and intelligence combined with quantities of confidence and charm to forge his formi-dable personality. All his life Donovan would inspire intense loyalty or enmity, but never indifference. After working his way through Colum-bia University and its Law School, Donovan, a Roman Catholic of Irish stock, breached Buffalo's Anglo-Protestant social barriers when he established a successful law practice and married Ruth Rumsey, the daughter of one of the city's most prominent Protestant families. A man of action and a natural leader, Donovan went off to fight Pancho Villa's Mexican raiders, and then made an indelible mark as a hero of the First World War.

In that war—more medals would come in the next—Donovan was awarded the Congressional Medal of Honor, the Distinguished Service Cross, the Distinguished Service Medal, the French Legion d'Honneur and Croix de Guerre with Palm and Silver Star, the Italian Croci di Guerra, and the Purple Heart with two Oak Leaf Clusters. But for him the greatest honor was being Commander of that legendary regiment, The Fighting 69th, the corps of Fighting Irish whose feats of bravery cost them a staggering 3,501 casualties and won them an enduring place of honor in American military history. Donovan's extraordinary personal courage inspired his men and earned him the unbounded respect of his peers: after his death, General Dwight Eisenhower was to say of him: Bill Donovan was the last hero.[15, 16]

By naming Donovan his Intelligence Coordinator, Roosevelt put the new appointee in a visible and vulnerable position. If knowledge is power, then secret knowledge is power raised to a high degree, and in Washington, where power is the only game in town, the stakes were impressive. It was a challenge Donovan relished and he attacked it in a free-wheeling, free-spending fashion; by 1944 COI's predecessor, the Office of Strategic Services (OSS), had grown to the point where it employed some 15,000 men and women around the world. Among the remarkable throng he recruited to his new and some say haphazardly constructed organization were some who would play significant roles in American life in the future: such men as Directors of Central Intelligence Allen Dulles and Richard Helms, Ambassador David Bruce, historian Arthur Schlesinger, and Supreme Court Justice Arthur Goldberg.

Donovan, like Yardley, made an inestimable contribution to American Intelligence and, like him too, was curtly dismissed. Immediately after World War II, what Americans wanted most was to bring their boys home and be free of the international entanglements that in two generations had cost so many lives. They wanted to see the world in terms of black and white: Evil had lost, Good had won; that was enough. They did not want to examine the motives of the Soviets or anyone else. Furthermore, the new American President, Harry Truman, had a deep-seated aversion to the organization best equipped to provide such information, Roosevelt's OSS, and to its founder, Donovan. So deep was this antipathy that in October of 1945, when alarm bells were sounding, signaling danger from the East, he made an extraordinary move. Truman dissolved the OSS, which, despite its faults was the only broad-based, non-military foreign intelligence organization the country had ever had.

More damaging than other charges leveled against Donovan's edifice, and one which cast a shadow over the early days of its successor, the CIA, was that it had a leftward tilt politically. It is an accusation that has stuck as firmly to the OSS as the tired quip that OSS stood for Oh So Social. When that leftist characterization was repeated once again in a history of the OSS published in 1972, 27 years after its demise, it was still able to raise the hackles of OSS alumni. A heated reply appeared in a singularly literate journal whose book reviews, at any rate, deserve a wide audience but have a rigidly restricted readership: the CIA's in-house publication, "Studies in Intelligence."

The writer, an OSS veteran, reminds his readers, who, ironically, need it less than any others in the country, that: ". . . there were all kinds of people in OSS, ranging from Serge Obolensky (who wore his

Tsarist ribbons) at one end of the political spectrum, to some ideological Marxists and self-professing Communists at the other. . . . Just because a lot of OSS field officers were sympathetic to foreign leftist causes, and a lot more were unsympathetic with rightist ideologies related to that which we were trying to extirpate in general war, there was little reason to coalesce these individual (and in the circumstances quite normal) attitudes into a formal OSS party line. Those who knew General Donovan best knew that he had one overriding goal for his agency, and that was to do the enemy the greatest hurt in as many ways, in as many places, and as fast as possible. They also know that he was a stickler for observing broad lines of national policy where they had been clearly established, such as, for an obvious example, the maintenance of the solidarity of the alliance . . . It seems unnecessary to state that innate distrust of Soviet Communism was inevitably softened by the realization that the USSR was an ally, and an ally which was absorbing the overwhelming proportion of the Nazi war potential, and that, after all, the enemy was the Fascist Axis."[17]

Another reason the leftist label was pinned on the OSS was its exploitation of anti-Nazi sentiment among European workers. Hitler opposed the trade unions and the OSS saw an opportunity there. But others also saw Socialists, a species they found almost as threatening as Nazis. They were the ones who pointed anxious fingers at such figures as George Bowden, organizer of the radical Industrial Workers of the World and leader of the leftward National Lawyers Guild, who set up an OSS labor branch in Washington. The presence of this questionable political element, when it was combined with the fluent socialist rhetoric of some of the resident intellectuals, led a few within and a good many outside OSS to color that multi-hued organization a uniform shade of pink.[18]

While Donovan's own fate was being decided quietly at the White House, the War Crimes trials were getting under way at Nürnberg in a glare of publicity. At the same time, however, American Intelligence officers were quietly interviewing other high-ranking German figures with a view to using them in the difficult struggle to win the peace. As one observer says: "Stringing them up publicly in Nürnberg, while we were signing them up secretly in Frankfurt smacked, and still smacks, of hypocrisy. But it was a complicated time." Complicated and dangerous.

General John Russell Deane: American in Moscow

Just before Reinhard Gehlen hunkered down in Misery Meadow, William Donovan, choosing his words with care, had addressed a paper to his senior OSS staff. "The combat phase of the war in Europe is over," he wrote. Now they must work to win the peace. It was a struggle which, he added, "may prove more difficult than winning the war."[19]

For the Americans the effort to win the peace was hampered initially by a failure to get a firm grip on who the enemy really was. Threatened at first by phantom Nazism, slowly, one painful and occasionally false step at a time, they came to realize what some had been saying for years, that it was the Soviets who must be watched. Major General John Russell Deane, Chief of the American Military Mission in Moscow during the war, was one of the few with first-hand experience of dealing with the Russians.

By nature bouyant, energetic and optimistic, Major General Deane arrived in Moscow in 1943 "eager, hopeful, confident and happy." Two years later he left "with a deep affection for the Russian people but with high skepticism about the possibility of future American collaboration with her leaders."[20] Deane's long journey into disillusion follows a trail of Russian secrecy, suspicion and broken agreements. Trying to deal with the Russians then was, as it remained, infuriating. It may in fact have been more exasperating in 1943 because the Americans came in friendship and were startled by their reception. In their ignorance, the Americans dashed into Moscow with a well-defined short-term goal, victory over Germany and Japan, and relatively pure motives. They and the Russians, after all, were on the same side. The Americans soon discovered that not only were the Soviets not playing by the same rules, they often seemed not to be playing the same game.

Deane's task was to coordinate Russia's military requirements, to determine its most urgent needs and meet them. He soon discovered that there was no end to Stalin's demands despite the fact that the amount of material sent by the United States was gargantuan. Instead of thanks, the massive influx of American supplies was met with surly disdain, questions about America's sincerity in wanting to help the Soviet Union, and sharp demands for more. There was no quid pro quo of any kind. "We send the Soviets another 1,000 airplanes," Deane wrote General George C. Marshall, then Chief of Staff of the Army, "and they approve a visa that has been hanging fire for months. We then scratch our heads to see what other gifts we can send, and they scratch theirs to see what else they can ask for."

American largesse did not end with the hardware of making war, but extended to an extraordinary outpouring of secret intelligence infor-

mation, strategic and technical. Franklin Roosevelt, hellbent on culti-
vating Stalin and maintaining "friendly relations," discussed with
William Donovan the idea of establishing an OSS mission in Moscow,
and the two agreed it should be done. So in November 1943 the OSS
chief went to Russia where he had his first encounter with the NKVD
(predecessor of the KGB) on its own home ground, its dreaded
headquarters building, the Lubianka. Accompanying Donovan were
General Deane and Charles "Chip" Bohlen, who acted as interpreter.
As they entered, surrounded by armed guards, ghosts of the countless
Russians who had met their doom inside those walls seemed to close
in on them as well. It was a chilling start to an eagerly anticipated
meeting.

Their uneasiness grew as they were escorted through the unfamiliar
and strangely silent corridors to their rendezvous with two of the
NKVD's senior officials: Lieutenant General Pavel Fitin, head of the
Soviet External Intelligence Service, and Major General A. P. Ossipov,
chief of subversive activities in enemy countries. As the guards halted
and motioned them through the door into a large office, they were
greeted by the two generals, but despite their cordial tone, the atmosphere was highly charged. Although he was in civilian clothes while
his colleague Fitin was in uniform, it was Ossipov who was the more
formidable figure. "He was short, had brown eyes, brown wavy hair
and a sallow complexion," Deane recalled. "He spoke English perfectly and without a trace of accent. He was smooth and suave . . . and
one could easily picture him as the boon companion of Boris Karloff
. . . personally, after seeing him I was just as glad that Bill and Chip
were with me."

The seating arrangements for the meeting only added to the thin,
pervasive air of menace. There was no cozy corner with a couch and
comfortable armchairs clustered around a low round table, where men
with common interests could at least pretend to meet on equal terms.
The men and women summoned to this room sat across a long, serious
table from those who had business with them. Most striking, however,
was a chair which was placed so that a bright light shone directly into
the eyes of its occupant, an arrangement obviously intended for those
unfortunates who were required to Account For Their Activities.

As soon as the brief formalities had been attended to, Donovan
looked around, spotted this chair and went directly across the singularly inhospitable room to it. Once seated, he squinted against the
blinding light, faced the two Russians and solemnly announced that he
was ready for the third degree. It would be interesting to know just

how Bohlen translated Donovan's jibe, but apparently it succeeded in disconcerting the Russians and delighting the Americans.

The daunting Ossipov and his comparatively genial sidekick, Fitin, got down to cases with their American visitors. Donovan opened by telling the Russians he was there to let them know his agency was ready to cooperate with the NKVD and to inform them about OSS activities. As good as his word, Donovan then described for them the organization of the OSS, outlined the nature of the operations it was conducting, and listed the countries in which it was carrying them out. Clearly he got the Russians' attention; they immediately asked for details about OSS methods of infiltrating agents behind enemy lines, what kind of training the agents were given and where, and what equipment they carried.

Donovan answered all their questions, holding back nothing. He even volunteered descriptions of equipment the OSS had developed such as plastic explosives and suitcase radios. Then he moved in to close the deal he had come there to make: he proposed the two intelligence services exchange liaison officers. The Americans would send an officer and small staff to Moscow, and would welcome an equivalent Russian party to Washington.

In reply, Ossipov and Fitin, who at that point may have had trouble believing what they were hearing, angered Donovan by suggesting that perhaps he had not come to the Soviet Union only with suggestions for cooperation, but had some ulterior motive. Donovan indignantly denied the charge, and indeed it was stated United States policy, laid down by General Marshall, that American representatives were not to "seek information about Soviet equipment, weapons or tactical methods," for fear of offending the Russians. That cloudburst behind them, the Russians and Americans came to an agreement; as soon as the details could be worked out a small group headed by Colonel John H. F. Haskell would go to Moscow; Colonel A. G. Graver would take a similar team of Russians to Washington.

Deane reports that he and Donovan were astonished at the speed with which agreement on the exchange of OSS and NKVD officers was made. It usually took weeks or months to get a response to even the most innocuous suggestion, but in this instance the decision to accept Donovan's proposal was made on the spot. It was an event without precedent. The area of intelligence, Deane noted, was "marked by a degree of collaboration exceeding that attained in other fields." Considering how the balance sheet in that area actually read,

Ossipov and Fitin had good reason to smile as they bade farewell to the Chief of the American Secret Service.[21]

On Donovan's return to the United States arrangements for the OSS-NKVD exchange were well under way when, on March 16, 1944, Roosevelt sent a cable to the American Ambassador, Averell Harriman, informing him that the plan was to be "indefinitely postponed." The project had been killed at the insistence of J. Edgar Hoover. "The NKVD," the FBI Director tartly asserted, "has far too many representatives in this country already."[22] Harriman and Deane fired off a long cable asking the President to reconsider. For the first time, they argued, the United States had made contact with the Soviet Union's intelligence service, and that would lead to closer relationships with other departments of the government. Furthermore, the cable continued, canceling this project could jeopardize such cooperative efforts as did exist. But Hoover won the day. On March 30 1944, Roosevelt sent a cable reaffirming that the exchange was to be "postponed;" the reason he gave was the unfortunate impact word of such an arrangement could have on his Administration's chances for re-election that year.[23]

Deane, who admits at that time he "still had dreams of being chums with the Russians," was bitterly disappointed, and was not looking forward to Fitin and Ossipov's reaction to the President's decision. Nevertheless, the act of delivering the news to them provided one of the more exciting incidents of his stay in Russia.

When Deane first arrived in Moscow, every contact with an official had to be made through the Soviet Military Liaison Office (OVS). The chief of OVS was Major General V. N. Estigneev, a master at obstructionism, whom Deane describes as "the granddaddy of all stuffed shirts," and who combined more pomposity, condescension, and stupidity than he had encountered in any one man before. Deane soon discovered there was no way around dealing with OVS, since every official building was heavily guarded and seeing someone in it required getting through the door. In the absence of telephone directories, it was impossible to call anyone. He was understandably elated, therefore, when, at the meeting with Donovan, Fitin and Ossipov had given him a telephone number where they could be reached. Now he used that number to ask for an appointment, and was told by Fitin that someone from his office would pick Deane up that evening at six.

Deane already had discovered that for reasons of their own, whenever he had an appointment with Fitin and Ossipov they arranged to meet him in a different, obscure hideout. An NKVD officer would arrive to escort him there and back, and they would ride in Deane's American car. This time however, when his escort came he declined Deane's offer to use his car to travel to whatever out-of-the-way part of the city they were going. Instead he insisted they go in the waiting black limousine with shrouded windows, and Deane wondered why. The Russian's refusal of the ride was not without significance. In the virtually unrelieved deprivation and drabness of wartime Russian, here was a gleaming new, two-toned, cream-colored Buick, so clearly the most glamorous automobile in Moscow that Sir Archibald Clark-Kerr, the British Ambassador, referred to it as Greta Garbo. It was difficult to imagine a reason compelling enough to make the Russian spurn an invitation to taste its delights.

When it was clear the trip would be made in the Russian car or not at all, Deane instructed his driver to follow in the Buick. At that, the Russian issued some instructions of his own to *his* chauffeur, and there ensued a high-speed chase through the densely crowded streets of Moscow. For twenty minutes the Russian car sped at breakneck pace along an erratic course, tires screeching on the corners, sending up muddy waves of icy slush, soaking dozens of homewardbound comrades. Deane and his Russian host sat in the back seat, lurching from side to side, until finally the wild ride came to an end in front of a run-down tenement. As they got out of the limousine the two men looked back. There sat the Buick with the driver calm and still behind the wheel, an expression of bored indifference on his face.

When Deane told Fitin the story of the mad ride through the streets of Moscow and asked why it had been necessary to travel at such a clip, Fitin replied that his escort knew Fitin would be late for the meeting and wanted to spare Deane the embarrassment of being the first to arrive. Observing drily that they had travelled very fast indeed in order to be late, Deane then asked why the car's windows were covered with heavy curtains. Fitin answered: the curtains keep the passengers from getting sunburned. With that, Deane says, he gave up.

To Deane's relief, the NKVD men took the death of the exchange project in stride. Indeed, it is hard to imagine what more they could have gained by trying openly in Washington than they got by sitting still in Moscow. On March 31, the day after Roosevelt's second cable to Deane, Donovan sent Deane ''some intelligence items'' for him to pass on to Fitin. In his covering letter Donovan describes the materials he is providing:

"(1) *Raw and Unevaluated Intelligence:* This group is represented by a copy of a report turned over to us by Karl von
Kleczkowski, one of the German agents who recently came over
to us at Istanbul . . ."

"(2) *S.I. (secret intelligence) Reports of Intelligence Material
Received from the Field.* This group consists of brief Intelligence
Reports received from our agents in the field . . . May I call your
particular attention to Dissemination No. A-22449, a critique of
the Russian raid on Helsinki, 6th to 7th of February, 1944.

"(3) *Finished Intelligence Reports:* This category consists of
the reports prepared by the Research and Analysis Branch from
all available sources . . . The reports here transmitted represent
samples of the strategic, economic and topographic phases of the
work."[24]

Quantities of secret intelligence and special equipment began to
stream out of the OSS to NKVD headquarters. Not only were the
Russians being sent the most sensitive documents, but miniature
cameras, miniature microdot-manufacturing systems and microfilming
cameras were shipped over. A weak effort was made to get something
in return for all the instruction OSS was giving the Soviets about its
own organization, its sources and its methods, as well as the hardware
and agent-generated information it was passing on.

In his letter of March 31 1944, Donovan expresses his gratification
on receiving a "memorandum on Bulgaria, prepared by our Russian
friends;" and in his letter of April 11 1944, to Deane, John H. F.
Haskell says that together with the information he is sending for
transmittal to the Russians is a list of questions OSS would like them
to answer. There was small hope of reply. "As usual," Deane observes, "we gave the Russians, in the field of secret intelligence, much
more information than we received." Whatever the commodity, the
avenue which ran between Washington and Moscow was virtually a
one-way street.

Deane terms the failure of the Russians and the Americans to
understand one another a difference in temperament, but whatever it
was, it was reflected in the political behavior of the two nations. "We
will compromise the future to take care of the present," Deane says,
"while the Russians will compromise the present in order to shape a
pattern for the future." But it was in their personal dealings with
Russian officials that Americans found themselves at sea. They had
great difficulty dealing with Russian xenophobia, so alien to their own

experience. Distrust of the foreigner is deeply ingrained in the Soviet psyche and, as Deane discovered, there is no way to overcome the suspicions of the paranoid.

The Vodka Visitors, American officials on flying trips who were feted into near insensibility, failed to recognize the depth of this distrust and incomprehension. Even Deane may not have realized at the time just how profoundly suspicious and manipulative the Russians were. He would learn quickly.

The group in Washington which administered the Russian aid program, the President's Protocol Committee, was chaired by Harry Hopkins and its chief executive was James Burns. After Roosevelt issued his order of March 7, 1942, that materiel for the Soviet Union had precedence over that destined for the other allies and the United States forces themselves, this Committee, in Deane's words, "carried out [their mission] with a zeal which approached fanaticism." Supplies literally poured into the Soviet Union.

Maddening as the Soviet lack of appreciation may have been, more frustrating by far was the fact that much of the materiel was never even used. Of 126 diesel engines, only 3 had been installed, the rest were rusting where they arrived. These were engines which were in desperately short supply and were needed by United States forces for the invasion of Europe. But under the terms of the aid agreement, the Americans were not permitted to observe the use made of American equipment—and at the same time the Russians were asking for more.

An example which Deane calls "typical" is a complete tire plant which was dismantled and transplanted from the Ford Motor Company's River Rouge plant outside Detroit to Moscow. It was then a 10 million dollar undertaking which was expected to yield 1,000,000 tires every year for the Russians. It never produced one tire. When the Americans were finally allowed to send a team of engineers to help get the plant into production, the Russians refused to cooperate; they would not show the Americans their plans, refused to consult them and rejected their advice. The Americans left in disgust and the plant remained a shambles.

Finally Deane dug in his heels and sent a cable to the Chiefs of Staff advising a tougher policy and one which would require American assessment of the urgency of Soviet requests. Although General George Marshall replied approving Deane's recommendations, the White House overruled him. Instructions were issued that no strings of any kind were to be attached to American aid to Russia. When at last the war wound down the Soviet demands for materiel did not—

only now they were clearly directed at postwar use. With the possibility that the flow from the American cornucopia might slow, or even end, the Russians were stockpiling inventory for industrial machinery, port installations, oil refineries, pipe lines and the like. In the Soviet view, the United States could not do enough for them.[25]

This bitter experience of dealing directly with the Russians was limited to a relative handful of Americans, and in the climate of the times in Washington their reports more often than not were discounted as, at best, exaggerations. But their reactions were hardly new. Theodore Roosevelt, American President while William Donovan was still a student and Russia was still ruled by the Czars, summed up the frustration felt by others forty years later: ". . . it is so difficult to cooperate with the Russians because they are so corrupt, so treacherous and shifty, so incompetent."[26]

Nor were they alone in their alarm at Washington's apparent indifference to Soviet attitudes and actions. Winston Churchill warned that the Soviets were gobbling up Eastern Europe and were poised to seize more. "Meanwhile," he admonished, "the attention of our peoples will be occupied in inflicting severities upon Germany, which is ruined and prostrate, and it would be open to the Russians in a very short time to advance, if they chose, to the waters of the North Sea and the Atlantic."[27] Churchill later said that by May 1945 he himself had considered rearming the German troops "before the huge looming danger of the Russian mass."[28]

But in that victorious summer of 1945 the mass of people in the United States did not hear Churchill's words. A few intelligence professionals, however—some in OSS, most in the military—had arrived at the same conclusion as Churchill. This small but significant group began to empathize with General George S. Patton, who had conceived such a hatred for the Soviet Union that he proposed rearming the Germans and leading them against the Russians.[29] Quietly adapting Patton's principle, this group began to consider ways of using America's defeated enemy against her threatening ally.

Chapter Three

General Gehlen, Prisoner of War

In Hiding

Looking back, Gehlen is unremittingly defensive and high-minded about working for the Americans. He protests that he was concerned with what "my duties to Germany . . . should be," after the war, and determined that by offering his services to the West "we should be serving our fatherland as best we could."[1] It is true that his conviction that the Soviet Union posed an immediate and dire threat to the West, including his defeated fatherland, was deeply rooted. But other, more personal motives stirred this clever, secretive and ambitious man. While, hidden in the mountains, he waited for the moment to surrender, he had time not only to rehearse the offer he would make to the Americans, but to reflect.

Cool, analytical, pragmatic, a strategist by inclination as well as training, he was hardly a romantic. But from the moment he reached the silent beauty of Misery Meadow—hidden from view, untouched by the war which had consumed his days and nights—Gehlen was, if not moved, at least stirred. He long remembered "those truly enchanting days . . . rejoicing in the first signs of green shooting through the snows;" reliving a time when he had "grown accustomed to the peace." Possibly those days of suspended reality beyond the reach of the final bloody scenes of war were the most peaceful of his life.[2]

As Gehlen surveyed the beauty around him, his Führer made a last desperate attempt to cheat the victors. In a final crescendo of madness Hitler issued orders from his bunker that Germany be laid to waste, then invited his propaganda minister, Goebbels, and his wife to witness his marriage to Eva Braun. Outside the bunker there was an orgy of blood-letting. The battle for Berlin raged and its price in human life was an unknown number of soldiers and close to one hundred thousand civilians. There was fighting everywhere: in the Tiergarten; on the boulevards; in the Reichstag itself. The next day Hitler turned the destruction inward, to the heart of the bunker itself. He and Eva committed suicide. Shortly afterward Goebbels and his wife followed suit, after first giving poison to their six children.

It was a time of paradox. As Gehlen savored those unreal days, waiting, one man he hoped to meet—although he could not know it then—rode past on the road far below in a noisy, battered American Jeep, leading a column of tanks that had made the trip through France. It was James A. Critchfield, a 28 year old United States Army officer from North Dakota, and veteran of some of the war's bitterest fighting. Years later their paths would cross again, not far from this same place, and this time they would merge. But both would travel far before reaching that rendezvous.

For Gehlen it was a time of unexpected and unwarranted peace, far removed from the brutal world, but it was a fragile peace. He was still a hunted man and to avoid the possibility of being discovered, each morning at dawn Gehlen and four of his officers left Elendsalm Lodge. Every day they climbed higher into the mountains and set up a makeshift shelter, until they discovered a tiny, almost inaccessible hut at the edge of a sheer rock face, where they passed the long sunlit days.

But now trouble was brewing below. Elendsalm Lodge and the land on which it sat was cared for by Rudolf Kreidl, recently invalided out of the Army. A shrewd and suspicious country man, Kreidl had watched from a distance as Gehlen's men carried crates of food and supplies to the hut. His doubts about the group changed to alarm when he caught the flash of red on Gehlen's uniform, the coveted Red Stripe of the German General Staff, which Kreidl apparently mistook for the insignia of the dreaded and hated SS.[3]

Until then Kreidl had been uncertain about what to do, but as an old Bavarian of independent views, and no Nazi, he decided he did not want a pack of SS men on the run hiding out on land that was in his care. It could only spell trouble in the long run. So Kreidl went down into the valley. At the intersection of the road from Lake Spitzing he stopped an American solider and somehow conveyed the message that there were SS men on the Elendsalm and he should arrest them.[4]

The next day, while Gehlen was absent, a small detachment of Americans arrived, but even that episode had an uncanny unreality about it. Instead of being taken to a prisoner of war cage, or worse, the Germans still at the Lodge were subjected to the briefest of interrogations and then issued documents declaring they had been released by the American Army—without leaving their mountain hide-away.[5]

When Gehlen returned to the hut that evening he found the moment he had dreaded most, premature capture by the Americans, had left his comrades elated: the papers they had been issued by their captors meant they were now at liberty to go unmolested through their defeated land. What that signaled, Gehlen decided, was that the Americans had had time to organize, had their intelligence officers in place, and had an orderly procedure for dealing with prisoners of war. He was confident that as a General Officer he would be treated with respect, and as one with special knowledge of such value to the United States he also would be appreciated. Nonetheless, it was several more days before Gehlen was ready to leave peaceful Misery Meadow.

At last he took the next great step toward realizing his plan. Leaving the two injured officers in the hut, he and the other members of his staff started down the mountain and immediately ran into a small unit of French mountain troops. To be captured by the French would be a disaster; not only would it put an end to his plan, but the French were infamous for the ruthlessness of their interrogations. Having come so far it was unthinkable he should be stopped now by a chance encounter. Without breaking his robust stride, Gehlen called up his reserves of *sang-froid* and *bonhomie* and greeted one of the Frenchmen who eyed him curiously with a hearty *"Bonjour, Monsieur,"* and never looked back.[5]

His next move testifies to the full recovery of his shining self-assurance. Despite his run-in with the French, which demonstrated that by now enemy troops were everywhere, he knowingly exposed himself to capture in order to prolong for a few more golden days the enchantment he had found there in the Bavarian Alps. He led his party down from their mountain retreat and made his way through occupied country to the northern end of Lake Spitzing and the house of one of his officers. It was his intention to spend a peaceful Whitsun holiday there. And, as both the victors and the vanquished began to take the horrifying toll of this most savage of wars, that is exactly what he did.

Three days later the Alpine idyll came to an end. On May 22 1945, as he stood in the town hall of the tiny Bavarian town of Fischhausen, Gehlen faced the tired American boy to whom he must now surrender and saw bleak reality. He, a Brigadier General and proud member of the German General Staff, Chief of Eastern Intelligence, authority on Russia and the Soviet order of battle, grimly endured the humiliation of acknowledging defeat to a young American who neither spoke nor understood German. Gehlen's phony peace was over.

Prisoner of War

Three days before Gehlen's surrender, on May 19, 1945, another Allied prisoner of war, Major Borchers, was ordered to appear before a four-man Russian Commission at Flensburg. He wasted no time getting there. He and the other members of the German Demobilization Section had learned quickly to move with care. Their war was over, but a new, different and dangerous one had broken out around them and they were caught in the crossfire. Flensburg, on the Danish border, had been the German government's last military headquarters. It was also where some of the first shots were fired among the Allies themselves, while the Germans dodged the bullets and played for survival.

In a bureaucratic expression of their mutual distrust, the conquerors set up two separate Supervisory Commissions; that of the Western Allies under General Lowell W. Rooks, and that of the Russians led by Major General Trussov. A German Demobilization Section had been organized to aid both groups in disarming and disbanding the German military; it was an unenviable task. When Major Borchers presented himself before the Russians at 6:15 p.m. what they wanted from him was the man who could tell them about German intelligence operations against the Soviet Union. He explained that it was General Gehlen of Fremde Heere Ost they were after, and then added the unwelcome news that he was believed to be in the Southern, the Americans' Zone.[6,7]

This did not sit well with General Trussov's Commission. It appeared to Major Borchers that Gehlen's name and that of FHO were unfamiliar to the Russians, but they demanded that he produce a member of Gehlen's FHO for them by ten o'clock the following morning. News of Trussov's interest in Gehlen did not take long to reach the Americans—whatever else they may have been, most of the German military was fervently anti-Soviet, so the British and Americans were kept well informed about Russian activities—and they acted quickly. That same day, May 19, although no more familiar with the name of Gehlen than the Soviets, the Americans found his representative, Colonel Scheibe, who had been in charge of FHO's daily situation reports, and took him into custody.[8]

So the word went out, in Russian and in English: Find General Gehlen. Despite the fact he was thought to be in their zone, the Americans had their work cut out for them because the race would go to the swift, and the Soviets were better prepared for this kind of competition. The Soviets had been infiltrating agents into Germany throughout the war and now they were everywhere: among prisoners of war; posing as defectors from the Ukraine and Byelorussia; and moving westward with the swelling mass of displaced persons. Once the word sped through the network it would take fast footwork on the part of the Americans to beat them, and it would matter little if when he was found he was in American custody. In what was turning out to be a cram course in Soviet tactics, the Americans had already learned that if the Russians found the one they wanted and couldn't get him out, they would silence him.[9]

At about that same time, the man they were so urgently looking for was becoming increasingly annoyed. Gehlen was trying his best to explain who he was to yet another group of Americans who showed not the slightest interest. His patience was wearing thin. The Americans obviously did not appreciate him, starting with the officer to whom he and his four colleagues had surrendered. Now another American officer was being hopelessly obtuse, a fact which still rankled twenty-five years later. "We were unable to enlighten him as to just what a catch he had made,"[10] Gehlen complained; humility is another characteristic even his warmest supporters do not claim for him.

Resolutely unimpressed, the Americans ordered that the five be separated and Gehlen sent from Fischhausen for preliminary screening at Wörgl, near Kitzbühl. His reception there did nothing to improve the General's temper; his interrogation by a divisional intelligence officer he dismissed as "disappointing." The American was more concerned with the situation in Germany than he was with his captive's expert knowledge of Russia. Gehlen simply could not get the Americans to understand how important he was, and by his account the situation continued to deteriorate. He was ordered to be transferred from Wörgl to Counter Intelligence Corps headquarters in Salzburg, but he never arrived thanks to what he claimed was the bumbling inefficiency of the Military Police.

Instead of being taken, as he hoped, directly to a senior intelligence officer, the MPs escorting Gehlen drove around and around the streets of Salzburg, unable to find the headquarters building. After seeming to give up on the project, they deposited him in a deserted inn, posted two heavily armed G.I.s outside the door to prevent his escape, and then abandoned him. Three days later, Gehlen says, he was discovered by an officer who apparently gazed on him in astonishment and said: "We forgot all about you!"[11]

And the indignities did not end there. After being freed from lonely captivity in the inn, he was not questioned at Salzburg, but taken to Augsburg and yet another "disappointing" interrogation, this time at Army level. He was kept there and questioned for more than three weeks by a Lieutenant Drake who further irritated Gehlen not only because he showed no interest in the Soviet threat, but because he pressed instead for detailed information about the organization and staff of FHO. Information which, Gehlen confides with satisfaction, he was not inclined to give.

These frustrations soon paled into insignificance when Gehlen arrived at Wiesbaden. There the Americans finally took some notice of their captive. They looked at him; his biographical information; the skimpy reports of his interrogations; and promptly labelled him a Gestapo general. When he was thrown into Wiesbaden prison and treated with undisguised hostility, Gehlen's annoyance quickly changed into anxiety: so antagonistic were the Americans, in fact, that he "feared from their manner that there would be violence."[12]

Ironically, all this shoving and hauling through their zone by his unappreciative captors may have prevented violence and saved Gehlen's life. He had surrendered on May 22 1945, three days after the Soviets first questioned Borchers at Flensburg and realized that the chief of the organization which had more information about them than any other—and perhaps his files with him—might fall into American hands. It is quite possible that if Gehlen's progress from tiny Fischhausen to headquarters at Wiesbaden had been orderly and well-documented, agents of the Soviets might have kidnapped him along the way. Had they succeeded, Gehlen would not have complained of any lack of appreciation for his worth.[13]

After Wiesbaden was signaled to be on the alert for Gehlen, his representative Colonel Scheibe was interrogated by both the Americans and the British in Flensburg. They described Scheibe as "arrogant and believed to be a Nazi,"[14] but he provided a good deal of information about Gehlen and FHO which was considered to be accurate.[15] Army Counter Intelligence in Flensburg passed on what it had learned about Gehlen and FHO to General Edwin Sibert, Chief of Intelligence, G2, for the Twelfth Army Group. When he learned Gehlen had arrived there, Sibert ordered that special precautions be taken for his safety because, unlike the American intelligence officers Gehlen had encountered to date, Sibert was actively searching for former members of German Intelligence who could give him information about the Soviets. Among those of interest to Sibert were Gehlen's former superior officer, Walter Schellenberg, and the intrepid commando Otto Skorzeny, whose exploits were famous among the Allies.[16]

Skorzeny was being held by the Americans in the same camp as Gehlen, and was the object of considerable curiosity. Thanks to his daring rescue of Mussolini, and his leadership of a team assigned to assassinate General Eisenhower and the other Allied leaders, he had become a celebrity. It was a status that was gratifying to him, and Allied Intelligence would find ways to use him. But he was a different breed from the low-key, serious-minded political theorist, intelligence analyst and administrator Reinhard Gehlen, and one thing the Americans did not need was to have a celebrated Nazi hero working for them. The virtually unknown Gehlen was a better bet. His subsequent interrogation, and the relationship established between Gehlen and his interrogator would have far-reaching consequences.[17]

Plucked From Obscurity by Captain John Boker

Tall, handsome, slim and straight, John Boker "was smartly dressed and of cultivated manners . . . In his bearing and demeanor every inch an officer, as we understood the term in Germany," General Gehlen said.[18] Boker's family, with its roots in Westphalia, was studded with men prominent in their fields; judges, engineers, scientists, and pioneers in foreign trade. Even wearing civilian clothes he fit the popular conception of a distinguished member of the German General Staff.

John Boker, however, is a third-generation American, a graduate of Yale who was drafted into the United States Army in 1941, and at the time he discovered Gehlen, upon whom he made such a favorable impression, he held the less-than-exalted rank of Captain. But even as a young man Boker had presence, an air of cultivation and authority which he put to good use in his dealings with members of the German military.

Boker could point to generations of forebears who had made substantial contributions to German society, and in the best aristocratic tradition he could even lay claim to a brilliant but eccentric uncle. An astronomer and historian, the uncle devoted his life to the meticulous work of disproving, by scientific analysis of the actual condition of the heavens at the time, the astrological forecasts upon which such major figures as Napoleon and Hitler relied in mapping their military and political strategy.[19]

Had it been planned, and it had not, the Americans could not have found an interrogator better suited for Gehlen at the time. Boker, who had left a flourishing family business in New York when he was drafted, had no particular interest in intelligence, and had no reason to believe the Army would make use of his knowledge of German. Shortly after receiving his commission he was notified he was to be sent to Mexico, and began preparing himself for his posting by studying Spanish. But Boker never got to Mexico and spent the next three years studying and then teaching at the Intelligence schools at Camp Richie and Fort Hunt instead.

In the spring of 1944, just before D-Day, the June 6 Allied invasion of Europe, Boker was sent to England to join a British interrogation unit. It was the start of a period of intensive prisoner of war debriefings aimed at gleaning strategic and tactical information from the enemy quickly enough to be of use in the field. In October he followed the forward push to the border of Belgium, at Revin, and it was there that he encountered German officers with a profound knowledge of the Soviet Union.

Among these was Lieutenant Colonel Holters, chief of a Luftwaffe Intelligence Unit which specialized in Soviet information, and which had surrendered to General Patton with its aerial reconnaissance photographs, documents and files intact. In his efforts to hang on to the group and its material, and to keep them first from the grasping hands of the Russian Occupation Authorities, who were empowered to seize whomever and whatever related to Soviet interests, and then from the fiercely competitive British, Boker waged his first war against the military authorities. Further committed to the goal of keeping the documents and those who could interpret them together, Boker learned bureaucratic tactics which would prove useful in the bigger battles ahead.

In the course of his interrogation of Holters, a personal relationship developed. Among the confidences Holters shared with Boker was his description of how his home had been overrun by the Russians, his wife and daughter raped, and how in the aftermath his daughter had committed suicide. It was one in a series of horror stories Boker was to hear from those who had served on the Eastern Front, or whose homes lay on the Russians' westward line of march.

"The interrogations I made of several high ranking German officers who had commanded units on the Eastern Front, and interrogations which were made [earlier in the U.K.] had undoubtedly awakened what was an already strong antipathy toward the Soviets' brutally repressive system," Boker says. By the time he and Gehlen met, Boker was well prepared for the encounter. Not only was he knowledgeable about German military affairs, he had already done a detailed debriefing of Holters' Intelligence unit, and his already negative view of the Soviets and their intentions had been broadened and strengthened.[20]

The actual meeting between the tall young American Captain who looked like a German General and the slight, middle-aged German General who looked like a university professor was not precisely as the image-conscious Gehlen later wanted it remembered. To be caught fast asleep and half-undressed on a brass bed in the middle of the afternoon by an impeccably turned out young Conqueror was definitely not a dignified state of affairs. So Gehlen, who as Boker observes "was not built for frivolity," saw no humor in the situation and simply deleted the incident from his memoirs.

Gehlen had been released from Wiesbaden prison and transferred to a decidedly pleasanter location, the Twelfth Army Group's interrogation center, where he was quartered in The Generals' House. This was actually two fine Wiesbaden villas on the Bodenstedtstrasse, the von Bergen House which belonged to the former Ambassador to the Vatican, and the Villa Pagenstaecher owned by a prominent ophthalmologist. In them were billeted such luminaries as Hitler's former Chief of Staff, General Franz Halder, and the Reich's last leader, Admiral Dönitz.

Boker, by now considered an expert on German intelligence about the Soviets, set out to question Gehlen. The von Bergen House, where Gehlen was, was lightly guarded and on his first visit Boker was simply told the General "was someplace upstairs." After Boker found him in a bedroom, asleep, and asked one of his roommates to wake him, Boker introduced himself and suggested that when he was dressed Gehlen come down and meet him outside on the terrace. And it was there, at a secluded table on that terrace, that life first was breathed into the grandiose scheme whose viability Gehlen himself had begun to doubt on the long climb to Misery Meadow.

Rapport was established early. As Gehlen describes it, Boker was the first American officer he had met with extensive knowledge of Russian affairs and no illusions about Soviet intentions. For Boker, Gehlen confirmed his worst fears concerning the Soviets and held out the possibility of providing the United States with a source of expert knowledge about them. Above all the two men shared a sense of urgency in the need to recognize and counter what both believed was an imminent Soviet move to take advantage of the disorder in Europe.

Gehlen was convinced that Russia's true long-standing agenda was a Communist takeover of Europe, using whatever means presented themselves. Believing that the pact between Russia and Germany was a sham on both sides, Gehlen held that the Soviets had planned all along to invade Germany, then move on through Europe after the war had weakened both her and her enemies. In Gehlen's view Hitler had simply beaten Stalin to the punch with his invasion of Russia in June of 1941.[21] He saw no reason to think the Soviets had abandoned their long-range plans and stressed to Boker the point that the Germans had been keeping track of the Russians longer, better, and more thoroughly than anyone else. Not only did Boker see eye-to-eye with Gehlen about Soviet intentions, he respected what he considered to be the General's cool, objective analysis of the current precarious political situation.

Further, and of critical importance in deciding what action to recommend regarding Gehlen, Boker was convinced he was no Nazi and perceived a line which divided the Nazi Party and the Army, the Wehrmacht. The Army, which early on misjudged and underrated Hitler, did put up some resistance to him, although first too little and then too late. A military branch of the Nazi Party such as the SS, however, was heavily weighted with Hitler loyalists. To most Americans the distinction was a subtlety without meaning: they all fought Hitler's war and carried out his insane program, so they were equally culpable.[22]

Boker understood, as Gehlen did not, the depth and strength of Allied revulsion against the Germans, and he also recognized its political ramifications. Any attempt to get official sanction to engage the services of a German general not only would be rejected out of hand, it would result in drawing attention to Gehlen. Since the Administration in Washington was determined not to antagonize its Russian ally, an effort it had not yet recognized as futile, bringing to light the fact that the Americans were holding a man who probably knew more about the Soviet military than anyone else—and for whom the Russians were looking—would almost certainly have resulted in his immediate delivery into Soviet hands.

Surveying the situation, Boker recognized that if the idea of putting Gehlen's Soviet expertise to work for the United States was to get any kind of hearing he would need support in high places, and getting it would not be easy. The ground that would have to be crossed to reach someone with sufficient influence to force consideration of the plan was a political minefield, and so he set to work devising a strategy which would provide safe passage and minimize the risk for all concerned. Boker had reason to believe the Chief of Intelligence for the European Theater, General Edwin Sibert, would be sympathetic to the idea of using Gehlen, but at the same time he understood it would put Sibert in an impossible position, as well as jeopardize the scheme, to discuss it with him directly. So Boker turned his attention to wooing Sibert's second in command, Colonel Russell Philp, an artillery officer seconded to Intelligence, who had General Sibert's ear.

The reputation of German Intelligence left a good deal to be desired, but Gehlen set out to demonstrate both the caliber of the work produced by his unit and the potential value to the United States of their accumulated knowledge of the Soviet Union. Working closely together toward their common goal of acceptance by American military authorities, Gehlen and Boker drew up a list of reports Gehlen and his men would produce for Philp. Before he could do that, however, Gehlen would need his men and his files.

Immediately after the war the volume of work, the number of people, the rush of decisions, the sheer confusion with which the American Army was faced, encouraged taking shortcuts and invited manipulation of the system. And manipulate it Boker did. Having learned the British had taken an interest in Gehlen and requested that he be turned over to them, the first thing Boker did was have Gehlen's name removed from the list of prisoners in U.S. custody. (Elements of American Intelligence still had Gehlen's name on their wanted list several years later.)[23] Next, working with American Army Lieutenants Paul Comstock, Ulrich Landauer, John Zorek and Franz Brotzen, all but Comstock fluent German-speakers, Boker went to various other POW camps and rounded up key members of Gehlen's late unit, FHO.[24]

Finally, with the help of Gehlen's men, they recovered the precious files from their hiding places. Five of the eight caches of documents were rescued from under the floorboards of remote foresters' lodges and out of deep holes in the ground. Of the remaining three sets of papers, one had been burned, one was retrieved from the Twelfth Corps Documents Center before it could be forwarded to the Joint British and American Documents Center at Höchst, and one had been found by the British and already taken by them to the Hochst repository. Nothing could be done about the files which had been burned, but the ones taken by the British were another matter. Producing "facsimiles," forgery, is one of the basic tools of intelligence, and Boker had no difficulty creating documents authorizing him to commandeer the materials he required for transfer to Wiesbaden.

An imposing figure with a commanding presence, Boker allowed the officer in charge of the Repository a glimpse of his authorization papers while asking to be directed to the proper section of the warehouse. He made it clear he had no time to waste. Affecting the brisk, indifferent air of a man on a somewhat tiresome piece of routine business, Boker walked up and down the aisles, his eyes running over the great stacks of documents. Having been given a full description by Gehlen, Boker knew just what he was looking for, but there was always the chance that the documents had been moved, or even that they were already on their way to England.

Suddenly he spotted the containers, which took up some four feet of one shelf, but he continued past them, not breaking his stride. Finally, retracing his steps, Boker said he had found what he wanted: the material he indicated took up roughly a quarter of that section of the warehouse, included a Russian printing press, which had been used to forge documents, and required a four-ton truck to haul. Boker was employing a time-honored dissembling tactic; using quantities of dross to camouflage the few nuggets of gold.

Once Boker had the components assembled on the ground floor of the Villa Pagenstaecher, where he had negotiated a set of rooms to serve as headquarters for the reconstituted FHO group's activities, Gehlen and his men embarked on a ceaseless round of work. Their output was prodigious. Their major project was a history and analysis of German Intelligence methods relating to Soviet Intelligence as it operated on various levels in the military. But they also produced reports, based on their files, on Soviet tank production, strength of the Soviet Army, Soviet manpower, an estimate of probable Soviet demobilization policy and much else.

One of the reports Gehlen produced at the 7th Army Interrogation Center, in June of 1945, was titled: Notes on the Red Army—Leadership and Tactics. Among the topics he addresses are Observations on the Russian Character, Development of Russian Principles of Leadership, and Characteristics of Russian Leadership Principles, as well as technical information and analyses. His insights into the Russian character, with which, significantly, he opened his study, are striking and unexpected, referring as they do to Dostoevski, the emotional dualism inherent in the Russian nature, and the overriding importance of the Russians' innate distrust. An impressive document, it is lucid, well-informed, and considered by Intelligence officers to be both objective and of far higher caliber than most other reports being received by the Allies.

"Another important characteristic of the Russian is his boundless distrust toward others, the world and himself. The Russian character is ruled by distrust, in contrast to that of the Western European, whose principle it is to trust the surroundings within his little world. This distrust of the Russians toward their immediate surroundings has led to the well organized security system which has infiltrated into every fiber of state life and on which the present Soviet state is based. On the other hand, this is the reason why the Russian negotiates with others in a very lengthy, careful, and clumsy manner, why he sticks to formalities even when his partner can see no reason for it. In this connection it should be noted that the distrust is often coupled with a distinct inferiority complex and the suspicion that he is not looked upon as a full partner. This distrust, and the inborn intelligence of the Russian, are furthermore the roots of the proverbial Slavic shrewdness. Proof of it are his tendencies to conspire, to be crafty, and to avoid the straight road toward his goals wherever possible."[25]

By mid-July Boker judged the time was ripe to make an overt attempt to gain Philp's full support: he arranged a party at the Villa. Philp was guest of honor at what turned out to be a carefully arranged production of show and tell. First Philp was given an opportunity to meet Gehlen and his men over glasses of wine. Then he, the old artillery officer, was treated to a thorough briefing by the group on Soviet artillery tactics. The evening, the culmination of a campaign which had lasted almost six weeks, was a success. Philp, impressed by the seriousness of Gehlen and his men, and by their professionalism, recommended that Sibert take a close look at what they had to offer.[26, 27]

The next problem which faced Boker was the same one he had met

with Colonel Holters: persuading Army Intelligence not to separate
the documents from the men who could interpret them. The use of
purloined documents as currency to buy preferment, advancement, or
safe haven in the enemy's camp must go back to the most primitive
forms of portable written communication. Gehlen too was using docu-
mentary coin—secrets are an essential part of the baggage defectors
bring with them—and as he talked with Boker he understood how
urgent it was to buy with it the best arrangement he could.

Gehlen's and other German accounts of his "discussions" and
"negotiations" with the Americans make it appear that he had some
kind of power base from which to operate, a degree of leverage with
which to make a deal which would meet his terms. In fact, Gehlen was
a prisoner. He was in jail and powerless. Not only that, since the
German General Staff together with the Nazi leadership, the SS, SD,
SA, Gestapo and the Cabinet had been placed in the category of those
automatically subject to indictment at Nürnberg, he was liable to be
tried as a war criminal. As the survivors of the death camps began to
tell their stories, the Americans were in a hanging, not a deal-making
mood. What Gehlen had on his side were his wits, and the luck to have
found Captain John Boker and through him General Sibert.

The American authorities were interested in Gehlen's papers, not
Gehlen, except just possibly and temporarily as an historian. But
Gehlen made a dramatic claim: his group had more to offer than the
ability to analyze the past and make educated forecasts about the
future, he told Boker. They could provide up-to-the-minute intelligence, current information. The officer in charge of FHO undercover
intelligence operations in Eastern Europe, Major Hermann Baun, had
been able to maintain contact with elements of his network, Gehlen
insisted. If only the Americans would come to their senses, recognize
the threat from the East and move quickly to accept his group as
collaborators, Baun's agents could be reactivated and information
would continue to flow to the West. On the basis of the information
available to him, Boker thought there was a reasonable chance that
Baun's network, or parts of it, had survived and could be resurrected.
But the obstacles in the way of convincing the authorities to work with
Gehlen were formidable. The odds that summer of 1945 that Gehlen
would win American support were slim indeed. Still, he never lacked
persistence.

A lack Gehlen apparently did feel, however, was legitimacy, a
personal problem which led to two extraordinary encounters which, if

they actually took place, are most remarkable for what they reveal of the working of Gehlen's mind.

"We could not work purely as mercenaries for a former enemy . . . I therefore later tried to establish a degree of formal legality for our plans; in the last weeks of the war I outlined the plans to General August Winter, deputy Chief of the OKW [German High Command] operations staff, and secured his blessing for them (since he was the only OKW authority I was able to reach). After the war I chanced to meet Grand Admiral Dönitz in the prison camp at Wiesbaden. Dönitz was formally Hitler's successor as head of state. He also approved my plans.''[28]

This is the account Gehlen gave in an effort to defend his decision to work for his country's enemy. Whether real or manufactured for his German audience, the episodes have elements of the bizarre. The conversation with General Winter, at a time when Gehlen's plans were his most closely guarded secret, sound unlikely on the face of it, despite Winter's confirmation of it seven years later. But to seek, or even to claim to have sought, within the walls of an American prison where Dönitz was a captive, the permission of the man whom Hitler named as his successor to the most infamous regime in modern history, on the ground that he was Germany's head of state and therefore could convey legitimacy, sheds an interesting light on Gehlen.

The simplest explanation is that this was a latter-day attempt by Gehlen to answer the charge that he was indeed an opportunist and a quisling. But it also raises the deeper issues of conscience and treachery. The German General Staff considered itself to be the repository of the finest elements of the German character. Naturally, one of its tenets was an abhorrence of treason, but under Hitler many officers found themselves faced with a profound dilemma: they loved their country but despised its leader.

In this setting the conviction grew that a valid distinction existed between *Hochverrat,* treason against the government, an internal act, and *Landesverrat,* treason against the state, an act of conspiracy with a foreign power. As opposition to Hitler mounted within the Wehrmacht, the decision to take action against him and his government, *Hochverrat,* despite the fact that the country was at war, was considered justified by a deeper commitment to the ultimate well being of the state. However, collaboration with the enemy, the divulging of secret information to another power which would put their country and their fellow Germans at risk, *Landesverrat,* was unconscionable. Gehlen resolved the issue for himself on the ground that what he had to offer the Western powers would strengthen them, and thereby protect Germany, in what he foresaw as the inevitable struggle with the Soviet Union.

In any event, Gehlen above all was a pragmatist. He had something to sell, something he knew the Americans would need even if they did not fully realize it yet. It was his job, now that he had his foot in the door, to close the deal with his potential, but still wary, buyers.

Post Office Box 1142
Prisoner of War in the United States

When the orders came for Gehlen to be sent to the United States, John Boker felt he had been double-crossed. Washington wanted Gehlen, the handful of FHO officers working with him, and their documents sent to Post Office Box 1142, the cover name for the interrogation center at Fort Hunt, Virginia. General Sibert, who had argued in favor of gathering the rest of the unit together and keeping it in Wiesbaden, was equally dismayed.

Once they were in the United States the Pentagon would be in control, not United States Forces, European Theater. And Washington had made it abundantly clear that what they were interested in was paper, not people. Still, Sibert's authority at least had produced the result that Gehlen and six of his staff would go with the documents. It was a serious set-back, and it meant fighting a new bureaucratic war on hostile ground, but it could have been worse.

Large problems loomed ahead, but Gehlen's group was beset with little ones close by. First among them was that seven German Intelligence officers being brought into the United States under the tightest security and secrecy, on a plane provided by Eisenhower's Chief of Staff, General Walter Bedell Smith, could not wear Wehrmacht uniforms. They must find civilian clothes. It took ingenuity, cajolery and arm-twisting, but with Boker's help all seven found ill-fitting but non-issue coats and trousers, and a motley crew they were. They need not have worried about being mistaken for General Staff officers. Colonel Stephanus, the highest in rank after Gehlen, somehow had got hold of a violin case in which to carry his few possessions, so they looked like nothing so much as a bunch of down-at-the-heels musicians as the trim, impeccably tailored Captain Boker led them across the tarmac to the waiting DC-3.[29] The group of German officers was comprised of

General Gehlen, Colonel Stephanus, Majors Hiemenz, Hinrichs, Lütgendorf and Schöller, and Captain Fühner.[30]

That long transatlantic flight had to be a time when even the most
glacially disciplined of men would be besieged by conflicting emotions.
Gehlen admits to being curious, about the United States and what lay
ahead, but makes a point of saying his mood was not one of exhilara-
tion. Probably not. He was in a tricky spot. His most powerful
protector, General Sibert, was back in Germany, and John Boker, the
man responsible for the degree of reincarnation he and his group had
achieved, was a Captain whose relatively low rank would rob him of
his effectiveness once he fell among the senior officer-politicians in
Washington. Above all, Gehlen and the others were prisoners, travelling under guard to the distant land of their captors, there to have their
fate decided by the highest authorities. And no one knew better than
Gehlen how capricious such authorities could be.

Yet even if he was not euphoric, it is still reasonable to suppose
some positive emotions were quieting his anxiety. All Gehlen needed
to do to lift his spirits was consider that despite orders from the
American Commander-in-Chief to turn over anyone of interest to the
Russians, he was not in Soviet hands; nor, although a member of the
General Staff, had he been indicted by the War Crimes Commission;
nor, like so many of his colleagues, was he languishing in prison with
only the bleakest of prospects for the future in his shattered land.

The flight was long, it took thirty-six hours, but the Germans did
have reading matter with them. Concerned that German-language
publications might not be easy to come by where they were going, they
"borrowed" a small library of books from opthalmologist Pagenstaecher's former residence, but left behind a note listing what they had
taken—and signed it. When the plane reached the coast of North
America reading was dropped in favor of rubber-necking from the
windows. To the surprise of the Germans, at a point over the state of
Maine the pilot suddenly reduced altitude and waggled his wings.
Boker knew the pilot was signaling to his girl, but because he considered that a poor reflection on American military discipline, he did not
explain the maneuver to the baffled Gehlen.

The sight of Manhattan, that island of towers, shining and intact, left
these refugees from the smoking ruins of their own desolate and
shattered cities filled with disbelief. For these men whose world had
been war and destruction for five years, New York might as well have
been a mirage. But before the real world was to close in on them again,

in a new and different way, the journey held one more touch of unreality.

When the plane touched down at National Airport in Washington it taxied to a remote, "secure" end of the field, where guards were posted around it. As soon as the door was opened a uniformed official who had been waiting impatiently for the steps to be moved into place strode up them and entered the aircraft. Standing at the door to the cockpit he faced this highly irregular and super-secret human cargo, this captive German general and his band of intelligence officers, and began questioning them.

It was clear that he was a deeply suspicious man and he was demanding straight answers to his questions, but since Gehlen and the others neither spoke nor understood many words of English they turned to Boker for help. Trying his best to maintain his composure, Boker explained that they were being interrogated about what flowers, fruits, plants or seeds they were bringing into the country, and being issued a stern warning that the illegal importation of such products was a punishable offense. The uniformed gentleman was from the Department of Agriculture.

If Gehlen and his group were bemused by this initial contact with American authorities in their native land, they would be dismayed a short time later. After being escorted to a remote section of the terminal where they underwent a brief medical examination, they bade a reluctant farewell to Boker. They had good cause to regret his departure; things took an immediate turn for the worse. Since Boker's arrival on the scene, Gehlen and his group had not been treated like other captured officers. In Wiesbaden they had been singled out, given special privileges, coddled. In the United States, however, they were once again German prisoners of war, to be treated as such. When they left the terminal they were led to a windowless van, a Black Maria, and unceremoniously loaded in. It was stifling; a single, covered ventilation grille did little against the heat and damp of August in Washington. The change from being passengers on the Army Chief of Staff's plane to prisoners in a paddy wagon could hardly have been more abrupt.

Gehlen's wits were still about him, however, and his espionage training did not desert him. Having noted the direction in which the van was pointed as they entered it, and apparently having committed a detailed map of the area to heart, Gehlen, riding blind, engaged in some detective work. He gauged the speed at which they were travelling, timed the stretches of road between turns, followed the directions of those turns and when they arrived at their destination announced they were fifteen miles south of Washington. It was an impressively good guess. They were at Fort Hunt, near Alexandria, Virginia—and whatever pleasure he derived from his successful deduction, it would have to carry him through some unpleasant times.

One section of Post Office Box 1142, or Truman's Hotel—the names, official and unofficial, by which Fort Hunt was known—was the Old Building prisoner compound. Not only was it old, it was ugly, surrounded by barbed wire and guarded by four watchtowers, one at each corner. The Old Building bore no resemblance to the Villa Pagenstaecher. The best that could be said about the accommodations provided for the group was that each member of it had a separate room; an advantage which lost its charm when they realized the doors had no handles on the inside.[31] Although he was not immediately aware of it, a further indignity had been visited on Gehlen and his men: like all the others at Post Office Box 1142, their rooms were bugged.

The Top Secret Fort Hunt Interrogation Center, Post Office Box 1142, and its sister installation on the West Coast, Byron Hot Springs or Post Office Box 651, at Tracy, California, had been established by the Military Intelligence Service in 1942 for the detention and detailed questioning of prisoners of war who might have strategic or technical information of particular value to the Allies. The psychological approach taken to the individual prisoner was left to the discretion of his interrogator, including the decision whether to take notes or record the interviews. The interrogation sessions were the obvious focal point of this intelligence-gathering effort, but in fact information was gleaned by less overt means as well.[32]

As anyone familiar with communications interception will confirm, the monitoring of conversations is one of the most tedious, time-consuming, frustrating, and least cost-effective undertakings imaginable. People, no matter who they are, tend to talk a lot and say little. So the microphones hidden in the ceilings of the prisoners' quarters were switched on at times considered most likely to produce results: usually before, and always immediately after an interrogation. Those were the times a prisoner was likely to discuss with a fellow-inmate what to reveal, what to hold back, what strategy to use with the interrogator and, after the event, to brag, often in useful detail, about his success in outsmarting his less-than-brilliant questioner.

Another common but surprisingly effective device was the use of stool pigeons; that fellow-inmate with whom the prisoner was discussing his interrogation, and perhaps a great deal more, frequently was a plant. Military Intelligence was very cautious about recruiting these informers; they found them useful but had little respect for them. That they were prepared to betray their countrymen made them suspect in American eyes, but as the Occupation Forces were to discover, informing on one another reached epidemic proportions in Germany. "They were always ratting on each other," one former CIC agent said. "They did it under Hitler and they kept right on doing it under us." In Gehlen's case there was no question of using informants, listening in on the group's conversations was all that was needed.

When Boker had left Gehlen at National Airport he had been uncertain about the degree of control he would now have over the group. By the next day he knew the answer: not only did he no longer have any authority over them, he no longer even had official access to them. Not easily thwarted, Boker maintained contact with them nonetheless, but the ground under Gehlen's feet had shifted and left him off balance. The inauspicious note sounded by the Americans' brusque and businesslike reception at the airport had become an ominous theme at Fort Hunt. Gehlen's discovery that their small single rooms in fact were cells, coupled with Boker's precipitous removal, left Gehlen shaken. But, although he could not know it as he sat in disturbing isolation, a new figure, one who would play a critical role in his future, was about to make his entrance on the scene.

At first blush it might not appear that a young Austrian who had fled his country after it was occupied by the Nazis, and both of whose parents subsequently had been killed, would be one to whom any German officer who had served Hitler would one day owe a sizeable debt of gratitude. Yet in fact Captain Eric Waldman, who became an American citizen after enlisting in the United States Army in 1942, was uniquely qualified to deal with this particular officer. An intellectual and a student of German political and military history, Waldman had retained his objectivity about political realities. Despite his own tragic family history, the fact that he was Austrian by birth gave him not only a linguistic and cultural advantage in working with a German, it gave him an appreciation of the depth and strength of the forces at work in Europe. Nonetheless, Waldman had misgivings at first.

It was after one of the regular teletype conferences between the Pentagon and Military Intelligence Headquarters in the former I. G. Farben building in Frankfurt that Waldman learned Gehlen and his group were coming to Fort Hunt, and he would be working with them. As a German-speaker already in the section concerned with gathering intelligence on the Russian order of battle, Waldman was the logical choice for the assignment. He had completed a study of German military forces' tactics, was deep into another on Soviet tactics, and was an experienced interrogator. But when John Boker gave him some of the background and outlined the plan to reconstitute Gehlen's group and put it back to work, under American sponsorship, Waldman was more curious than convinced, and it was with mixed feelings that he first met the General.

Boker introduced them, and as Gehlen looked at Waldman he could not have failed to realize how important it was that he win this man's support. He had learned through his experience with Boker that the relatively low rank of Captain apparently was no bar to effectiveness in this American Army; the question was, would Waldman be willing as well as able to help him? Boker stood by as the two sized each other up. They were virtually the same height, but Gehlen was slight and fair, while Waldman was dark and strongly built, and despite the fact that Waldman was by nature expansive, now he more than matched Gehlen's innate reticence.

"We said goodbye to John Boker, and then Gehlen and I went for a little walk," Waldman says. "I was a bit reserved, to be sure. I was trying to feel him out. Is he a Nazi or is he not a Nazi? Is he a *good* German? A military man with military tradition? Or is he a Nazi?"[33] It took Waldman time to overcome his reserve, but soon he was satisfied not only that Gehlen was not a Nazi, but that they saw eye to eye about the Soviet threat, America's frightening lack of awareness of it, the West's urgent need of information, and much besides. For a second time intellectual rapport between Gehlen and the agent of his captors developed into a personal bond. Like John Boker before him, Eric Waldman became not only Gehlen's close collaborator, but his friend.

Gehlen's status first became an issue at Fort Hunt, and it would continue to cause increasingly serious trouble in the intelligence community for years to come. Technically, the Gehlen group did not belong at Fort Hunt at all. The branch of the Army which controlled the captured personnel and materiel operation there did not have authority over Gehlen; Military Intelligence, G-2, which had brought him over from Germany and to which Boker and Waldman belonged, was responsible for him.[34] It was on this technicality that Waldman mounted his campaign to isolate the group and to improve their living conditions.

Not only did Waldman believe that Gehlen's people should be pressed into service in interpreting their documents, he fully supported the concept of reconstituting the group as an operating arm of American Intelligence in Germany. Before any moves could be made in that direction, however, the jurisdictional dispute at Fort Hunt would have to be resolved. "There was a lot of resentment, and I didn't make any friends," Waldman says, "but they [the officers in charge at Fort Hunt] didn't play by the rules either,"[35] as he discovered when Gehlen moved to new quarters.

After a number of bruising tussles, Waldman managed to have Gehlen's group transferred from their solitary cells to three small cabins in a secluded, wooded area on the sprawling compound grounds, within which they were given considerable freedom of movement. And he got them PX privileges. It appeared that Waldman had won and the commanders of Fort Hunt had relinquished their claim of authority over the group—until what Gehlen calls his "professional mistrust" prompted him to look this gift horse in the mouth. A thorough search of the cabins turned up microphones, hidden with ingenuity and skill, in each one.

"That infuriated me," Waldman says, "I was enraged. It meant not only that they were bugging Gehlen, which they had absolutely no right to do, but they were bugging *me*. I went right over to the Pentagon and raised hell."[36] He went further than that. To demonstrate exactly where he stood, he bought Gehlen a radio which the Germans then played at high volume whenever they wanted to talk in confidence.

At first Gehlen's group worked with Waldman on a handbook of Soviet military tactics, doing evaluations and analysis of various materials. At the same time they were learning about America. Waldman had won for them an unusual amount of freedom, and Gehlen had his first taste of southern fried chicken, as cooked by Mrs. Waldman, at the Waldmans' house in nearby Alexandria, Virginia.

The Germans applied themselves diligently to learning English, and despite Gehlen's complaints about the length of time it was taking them, by January, 1946, they were sufficiently fluent to write graceful thank-you notes to John Boker for the "trinkets" he gave them for Christmas.[37]

"Dear Mr. Boker,

"I want to say you my heartiest thanks not only for your very kind lines, but also for the marvelous Christmas gift. I was very pleased of it. The whole way and the careful choice of the presents, acted according to the characteristic nature of each of us, showed me the spirit which directed the giver. In this sense it should be a good omen for us that our first contact with America is joined with your person and your name. Thus many thanks once more!

"I think you would be interested to hear that my family has moved to another place. Mr. Z who dropped in at the new place some days ago informed me that they are in good physical surroundings with satisfactory food situation, good accommodation, etc. 'They are well, and looked quite radiantly healthy.' You will understand that I was very happy that all the things which have worried me became clear. I was in a considerable disquietude because of the last very depressed letter of my wife before moving, as I know that she is very brave and never does complain. Now, that's all right . . .

"Always sincerely yours,

"R. Gehlen"[38]

At the same time, political events were breaking in Gehlen's favor. "I told him," Waldman says, " 'If the West comes out of this O.K. it won't be because of our smart moves, but the Russians' mistakes.' Then Stalin, who was not the good boy so many Americans thought he was, went on and proved it to everybody." But in Washington, disillusionment with the Soviets took a while to come. Despite the fact that the Russians were causing difficulties over the first meeting of the United Nations; that in Austria and Germany virtually all semblance of cooperation had been sucked into a whirlwind of hostility and aggression; and that the defection in Canada in September, 1945, of the Russian code clerk Igor Gouzenko rang warning bells throughout the Intelligence establishment, on October 1 1945, President Truman suddenly dissolved the OSS.

Even when, three months after getting rid of Donovan's service, and of Donovan, Truman created the Central Intelligence Group, the spirits of those looking warily toward Moscow were not much raised. The CIG's sole function was to coordinate information; there were to be no espionage activities. It was evident Truman did not want a reincarnated OSS. Indeed it is not clear exactly what the President did have in mind, but the ceremony over which he presided at the inauguration of CIG on January 24, 1946, suggests the degree of seriousness with which he viewed it.

"At lunch today in the White House," wrote Admiral William Leahy, Truman's Chief of Staff, ". . . Rear Admiral Souers and I were presented with black cloaks, black hats and wooden daggers . . . 'To

My Brethren and Fellow Dog House Denizens,' '' the President said during the presentation, " 'By virtue of the authority vested in me as Top Dog, I require and charge that Front Admiral William D. Leahy and Rear Admiral Sidney W. Souers receive and accept the vestments and appurtenances of their respective positions, namely as Personal Snooper and as Director of Centralized Snooping.' ''[39]

But then the Soviets made a move which shook the Americans to the core. They blatantly abrogated their agreement with their allies that all foreign forces would be withdrawn from northern Persia [Iran] by March 1946. Instead, in February, 1946, they sent more troops in.[40] Suddenly those in the United States who had been warning against the Soviets gained respect and a new audience, while those in Military Intelligence in Germany who had been quietly working against what they perceived as pervasive communist infiltration gained credibility and support. The decision was made: Gehlen would be sent back to Germany. It was a turning point for him and for United States Intelligence. The enemy of their enemy was to be their friend.

The decision to return Gehlen to Germany did not assure his future, but it did give him a further chance to prove his worth. As a seasoned veteran of military and political wars, he knew his ultimate fate lay in the hands of senior officers, such men as Generals George V. Strong and Edwin Sibert, but he also recognized the debt he owed the two young Captains of German and Austrian background whose maneuvering and manipulation had won him his opportunity. Before leaving for Germany, he wrote one more letter of thanks:

"June 17, 1946.
"Dear Mr. Boker:
  "With our departure for Europe a first period of our work is finished. I feel it is my duty to express you our thanks for your kindness and support once again, we will never forget it. After our return we shall continue our work in the same sense as before, and we will do all to increase our efficiency within the tasks which will be given to us. I hope that the ties of friendship arisen during the past year may further on gain in strength in the future.
  "With kindest regards from all the boys.
  "Very sincerely yours,
    "R. Gehlen"[41]

The long, hot days before his departure were difficult and filled with uncertainty for Gehlen. Boker had explained that he and his group were pawns in a desperate tug-of-war among different branches of Military Intelligence, as was Boker himself. But Gehlen also would be the beneficiary of an atmosphere of doubt and distrust of the Soviet Union which was spreading through the United States, and spreading quickly.

The heroes of Stalingrad, Americans began to recall, were also the allies of Hitler when it had suited them to be. And the Russians, who had fought so valiantly and suffered such huge losses in their fight against Germany, were, after all and above all, communists. The uneasiness which was growing among the American people was indicative of shifting sympathies, but it was a shift back, a return to a deeply felt and long-held fear of communism.

Chapter Four

The Soviet Threat

Although it seemed to him agonizingly slow in coming, in 1946 the vehicle that would carry forward Gehlen's dream of re-establishing a German intelligence service finally arrived. It came in the form of a reawakening in the Americans of the fear they had felt in the wake of the Russian Revolution of 1917. As Gehlen saw it, the Americans had come to their senses and were looking back beyond the war to their own historic reaction to communism.

In the United States, the Revolution and its brutal aftermath sparked a profound distrust of political radicals. This response to the apparent threat posed by the Revolution came in part because in the minds of many Americans there was little or no distinction between anarchists and communists: they were all Reds. Both groups wanted the overthrow of the established order, both were willing to use violence, and the famous anarchist slogan, "property is theft," had a clear collectivist ring to it. On top of that, not so many years before, in 1901, William McKinley, the President of the United States, had been assassinated by Leon Czolgosz, an anarchist, a Red.

Two years after the Revolution in Russia, on December 27, 1919, the growing fear of radicals reached its peak in America. On that day President Woodrow Wilson's Attorney General, A. Mitchell Palmer, issued secret orders which resulted, six days later, in a wholesale attack on thousands of people he had concluded were politically suspect. Between 7 p.m. and 7 a.m. on the night of January 2, 1920, nationwide raids, under the overall control of J. Edgar Hoover, were mounted in which more than 4,000 people in 33 cities were routed from wherever they were, including their beds, and hauled off to jail. Many were arrested without warrants and, despite explicit written instructions, repeated three times, that "no violence is to be used," many were clubbed, beaten or otherwise abused. In Boston, four hundred "radicals" were arrested, handcuffed one to another, and paraded through the streets of the city. Palmer was jubilant, claiming actions such as this to rid the nation of undesirable aliens prevented the spread of radicalism.

The country's people and its press rejoiced with him. Across the country, newspapers joined the chorus of congratulation to Palmer for a job well done, chastising any who might have misgivings on constitutional grounds. "Attorney General Palmer and his subordinates may have committed errors of detail," said the New York Times, "but their purpose and object and efforts . . . to drive from the United States a mob of dangerous aliens are heartily supported by the majority of the American people."[1] This orgy of Red-routing reached a high of sorts that same month when five properly elected members of the New York State Assembly were not permitted to take their seats because they were Socialists.

Most of those arrested in the Palmer raids eventually were released, and American interest in the radical threat waned.[2] Then the terrible tensions in Spain which in 1936 led to the Civil War between the right-wing nationalists and the leftist Republicans, a war marked with horrifying brutality, attracted the sympathy of American liberals. The fascist Falangists were pitted against the Popular Front (an uncomfortable amalgam including Republicans, Socialists, Communists, Trotskyists and anarchists) and both sides received aid from governments siding with one faction or the other. Mass executions by the nationalists and the leveling of the Basque town of Guernica, later memorialized by Picasso, galvanized liberals who fought with the Republicans in the International Brigade and the American Abraham Lincoln Brigade.

The Spanish Civil War ended in March, 1939, with victory for General Franco's nationalists. By then Hitler had pushed the world to the very edge of war, and a romanticized view of the Partisan and communist cause in Spain, as well as anxiety about the implications of fascist aggression in Europe, helped obscure American understanding of Stalin's communism, and the popular view of "the left" shifted.

Nonetheless, public indifference in America to the Terror, the purges in which millions died, and the persecution of "enemies of the state," as currently defined, was difficult to explain, especially in light of the amount of press coverage there was at the time of the Show Trials of the Old Bolsheviks in 1936, 1937, and 1938. In part this apathy may have resulted from the popular and hazy American perception of the Russians which had at its core that they were different from Europeans, and everybody else. The Russians were not considered to be civilized in the same sense as the French or the Germans, so excesses in the Soviet Union were less surprising and therefore less appalling than in Europe.

Still, the stories filtering out of Russia in the following decade were enough to command anyone's attention; during the 1930s the Soviet Union was drenched in blood and reports of it were reaching the United States. Information was available, it was the willingness of the people to accept it which was missing.[3]

Then came the Hitler-Stalin non-aggression pact. Revulsion at what was taking place in the Soviet Union was noticed and quickly grew, but just as quickly halted. Suddenly Americans were at war, and equally suddenly the Russians were invaded, switched sides, and became their allies. Overnight, dismay over Stalin's short-lived alliance with Hitler, as well as fear of communism, were overshadowed by admiration for the heroism and sacrifices of the Soviet people, sentiments which lingered on.

At war's end, revelations of the horrors perpetrated by Hitler's regime further diverted attention from those of Stalin. The eyes of the civilized world were fixed on the obscenities perpetrated by Nazism. Horror at the German acts overshadowed whatever revulsion had been inspired by the arrogant hypocrisy of the Show Trials as well as the barbarism and blatant anti-Semitism of Stalin's brutal, terrorist, but less visible regime. For a time after the war ended, men of other nations, unable to comprehend the barbarity of a people as accomplished as the Germans, could not see beyond the death camps and forgot, or ignored, anti-Semitism as well as the Terror in Russia.[4]

With reports of overtly hostile actions by the Soviets in Europe and Iran, however, American anti-communism quickly took root again. By January 1946, the U.S. House of Representatives Un-American Activities Committee had begun an investigation into subversive propaganda. And when, little more than a month later, on the fifth of March, Winston Churchill made his Iron Curtain speech in America's heartland, Fulton, Missouri, a kind of imprimatur was put on anti-communism.[5,6]

The fate of Reinhard Gehlen was decided in this climate, one which was shifting in his favor. A live threat was rapidly supplanting a dead one, and the growing momentum of that perceived danger would continue to serve Gehlen's interests. What Gehlen and his American supporters wanted was his return to Germany where he and his group would work for the Army's occupying forces, to gather information on the increasingly ominous Soviet actions. But in early 1946 attitudes in Washington, although changing, had not yet hardened. Nazis were still objects of loathing. The Nürnberg trials continued. And the politicians charged with making policy for defeated Germany failed to understand the reality, physical and political, of conditions in that broken land.

The Rising Soviet Threat in Germany

The Germany Gehlen had left in 1945 was, in the words of Chancellor Willy Brandt, a world of "craters, caves, mountains of rubble, debris-covered fields, ruins that hardly allowed one to imagine that they had once been houses, cables and waterpipes projecting from the ground like the mangled bowels of antediluvian monsters, no fuel, no light, every little garden a graveyard and, above all this, like an immovable cloud, the stink of putrefaction. In this no man's land lived human beings. Their life was a daily struggle for a handful of potatoes, a loaf of bread, a few lumps of coal, some cigarettes." It was little changed in 1946.[7]

The population lived in a country whose urban landscape resembled a dead planet; a country under the urgent threat of famine and disease. Water, sanitation, transportation and communication systems were gone. There were no medical facilities, there was precious little food, and no fuel to cook it. But there were people: men, mostly old; women of every age; and children—all in desperate need. And then, suddenly, there were thirteen million Displaced Persons as well. Slave laborers from Russia, France, Poland, Holland, the Balkans and elsewhere, joined inmates released from concentrations camps in trying to make their way home, if one still existed. Destitute and weak, they needed food, clothes, medical care, transportation, and there was none.

As glimmerings of the real situation began to reach them, the policy makers in Washington were in disarray. Some believed there were choices which could be made, but there was really only one course to follow, and while the politicians postured and dithered, the Army acted. Dictated by the simple human reaction of revulsion at the sight of preventable human suffering, and the recognition that a broken, impoverished Europe could not, even if it would, feed and care for Germany, the course was clear. America could and would be both occupier and rebuilder. And it was equally clear to the military men thrust into the position of determining the course of the American occupation that the country would have to be run by Germans. They knew how their systems worked; the Americans could not even speak the language.

America would provide the goods, but the services would have to come from the Germans. Inevitably, those who began running the trains and maintaining the water supply under Allied military occupation were the same ones who had been doing it under Hitler—they were the ones who knew how. A country cannot function without a bureaucracy, and the vast majority of German civil servants had been Nazi Party members. But the American government was committed to its program of denazification—it was one subject on which the politicians agreed. They leapt into it with the single-minded fervor of prohibitionists and a tunnel vision born of horror at the grotesque barbarism of the Hitler regime. From the vantage point of Capitol Hill it seemed simple: Nazism must be rooted out forever, so find all the Nazis and make them pay. But there was more to it than that. The reality was that there were other urgent priorities. The Americans had to act quickly and decisively to deal with an emergency of unparalleled proportions. The occupiers needed Germany's bureaucrats, whether they had been Nazi Party members or not, and if this was compromising American principles then the compromising had begun.[8]

Like members of the Wehrmacht, German civil servants traditionally took the position that they were servants of the state and therefore were loyal to whatever government was running the country. Under Hitler virtually all state employees were required to become members of the Nazi Party; even the faculty of the University of Heidelberg was under Nazi control. To some it was quickly apparent that the denazification program, with its questionnaires that no German with anything to hide was going to answer honestly and that all Germans resented and ridiculed, was ineffective. Out of necessity more and more Nazi government administrators and workers were being "cleared" summarily and brought back to their former posts, despite the fact that it ran counter to the official American position.

United States policy was being further eroded by two significant and incompatible developments: the American Army was disbanding in a headlong rush, and the reality of the Soviet threat against the West was becoming increasingly apparent. Frustrated time and again in his efforts to shake Roosevelt out of his Russian fantasies and bring him into the real world, Churchill had wasted no time in trying to set Harry Truman straight. On May 11 1945, at the time of the German surrender, Winston Churchill had sent a cable to the new President spelling out his fear of war with the Soviets.

Mincing no words in his message, Churchill urged that outstanding issues with the Soviets, such as the status of Poland, the "temporary character of the Russian occupation of Germany," and the future of Hungary, Austria, Czechoslovakia and the Balkans, must be resolved. "If they are not settled before the United States armies withdraw from Europe and the Western world folds up its war machines, there are no prospects of a satisfactory solution and very little of preventing a third World War."[9]

But the United States armies did withdraw, almost overnight. The government was doing what its people wanted, bringing the boys home as fast as ships could carry them, leaving only a skeleton occupation force behind. The American shield on which the Europeans were relying was not so strong as they imagined. Just as Churchill feared, the Western war machines were being packed away, and it became clear within weeks, even days, of Germany's surrender that trying to get things settled with the Russians was going to be risky business, the two sides lurching from one confrontation to another.[10]

The Soviets relentlessly pursued their own ends while the Administration in Washington turned a blind eye and failed to respond to the most blatant provocations. But in Europe the price of peace was rising dramatically; as coup followed coup in Eastern Europe, and Italy appeared headed for a communist takeover, the threat of war increased by the day and fear among the occupiers and the occupied was real. Hostile Soviet moves were being made all the time and everywhere: in January 1946 they occupied Manchuria; then they marched into North Korea; in March 1946 they refused to withdraw their army from Iran; in the same month they massed troops on the Turkish border; and so it went.

Harassment by the Soviets was continual. From 1945 to 1947 they shot down more than forty planes, most of them British, flying over or on their borders.[11] And all the time there was an unremitting stream of highly inflammatory incidents in Europe. Taking stock of their position, American military leaders blanched. In addition to the constabulary, the Military Police, they had two divisions in Germany, while the Russians had—what did the Russians have on their borders? And where exactly did they have it? How war-worthy was it? Above all, what did they intend to do with it? American ignorance of Soviet readiness was colossal.[12]

Churchill's warning of May 1945 was backed by a frightening amount of evidence that World War III might indeed be imminent. Although they were up against the challenge of day-to-day survival, this ultimate threat from their ultimate enemy strengthened the sudden and unlikely alliance between the Germans and their conquerors at the very time their former leaders were being tried, convicted, and hanged. "One of the strangest episodes in the foreign relations of the United States," says Ambassador Robert Murphy, "was our alliance with the German people." Mutual fear was one strand of this new bond.

Looking back it is easy to say that after waking to the fact that their former ally was implacably hostile, the United States overreacted, that the Soviets were in no position to wage war. But the fact is the Americans did not know the degree of Soviet preparedness, a lack which played right into Reinhard Gehlen's hands. As the Soviets provoked more hostile incidents (what Anthony Cave Brown calls "flourishes"), and as the Americans began to appreciate how little they understood Soviet intentions and capabilities, Gehlen's confidence began to revive. And with good reason. All at once, information about the new adversary was at a premium, and compared with many former Nazis being used by Army Intelligence, Gehlen looked benign as well as smart.[13,14]

Not only did Gehlen come with an above-average record with regard to the Nazis, his sophisticated evaluations, like that of the Russian character made after his capture by the Americans, left a strong impression on those who had been in the Soviet Union. It was obvious to them that no matter who he was or where he came from, someone with this degree of insight could be of use to the United States. In July 1946 Gehlen began his journey back to Germany where he would rejoin members of his old command, Fremde Heere Ost, whom the Americans had brought together near Oberursel.

Chapter Five

American Army Intelligence and General Gehlen

General Gehlen Returns to Germany

They called it "Basket" for reasons no one now remembers. But despite its history as an interrogation center, first for the Luftwaffe and now for the Americans, the German nickname for Camp King outside Oberursel was surprisingly appropriate. With overtones of gathering together, of homeliness and security, "basket" was not far off the mark for the Germans in those desolate days of 1945 and 1946. What was being gathered and given a home was a select group of former officers of Gehlen's Fremde Heere Ost. Security and homeliness, however, did not necessarily mean universal harmony.

While Gehlen was at Post Office Box 1142, General Sibert had rounded up the remaining two signers of the Pact of Bad Elster, in which each agreed to offer their joint services to the Americans: Gerhard Wessel and Hermann Baun. They made an ill-assorted pair. Wessel, slim, cool and handsome, was the officer who had succeeded Gehlen in the last days of the war. The son of a pastor in Holstein, he had once been rated by Gehlen as "An outstandingly efficient staff officer of above-average ability . . . [with a] personality suitable for command positions."[1]

No one, certainly not Gehlen, would have made that set of claims

71

for Hermann Baun, Gehlen's former chief of frontline intelligence. (He had been responsible for twice saving Gehlen's family, and his files, from the advancing Russian troops.) Baun, a Volga German, was a temperamental, emotional man, described as having "a covert-action mind." Secretive, imaginative, and impulsive, he thrived in the half-light of the clandestine world. He was careless of details and given to painting with a broad brush, but it was not only his conduct of his professional life which was viewed as irregular; inhabitants of Basket looked askance at the woman who had taken the place of his dead wife and called herself Mrs. Baun. But it was Hermann Baun, not Gerhard Wessel, who had the upper hand at Basket.

Indeed, when he returned to Germany, Gehlen, who had assumed he would be the undisputed chief of whatever they could negotiate with the Americans, would discover that Baun appeared to have gained the upper hand altogether. While Gehlen was in the United States trying to convince his captors that his knowledge and understanding of the Soviets could be of inestimable value to them, Baun was doing the same thing at Oberursel, and he was talking directly to General Sibert. Furthermore, what he had to offer was particularly attractive; his claim to have a network of agents throughout East Germany and Eastern Europe. Shortly after Gehlen left for the United States, Sibert gave Baun the green light to try to contact his agents, and to assemble a group to work with him at Camp King, although what was to happen to that group was far from certain.

While Baun was scurrying along the dimly lit back alleys of clandestine intelligence, Wessel was out in the open. He was working closely with the Americans, trying to find and recruit former FHO hands, and was acting as liaison with the officer directly in charge of his unit.

At the age of twenty-six John Russell Deane, Jr., Lieutenant Colonel, United States Army, with no background in intelligence and little grasp of German, was put in charge of this sensitive and potentially explosive experiment.[2] Many years later, having retired from the Army with the rank of General and enjoying the obvious success of his Washington consulting firm, he looked matter-of-factly at the apparent anomaly of the situation. For one thing, he pointed out, in 1946, if you had been through the war, twenty-six was a lot older than it seemed. For another, he says, "I didn't have to know anything about intelligence. They were the experts in that." He also got a lot of help from the man he considered among the best intelligence professionals in the business, Major General Robert A. Schow.[3]

A West Point graduate, Deane was the son of General John Russell

Deane, who, as Chief of the Military Mission to Moscow with Ambassador Averell Harriman, had worked with OSS's William Donovan to establish contact with the NKVD.[4] The younger Deane had commanded a battalion in Europe during the war and risen quickly through the ranks. He was an Operations man and after the surrender of Japan was slated to be sent there with the Occupation Army. But in November, 1945, while Gehlen was at Fort Hunt, Deane found himself an Intelligence officer at Oberursel instead. He reported to General Sibert and started to look over just what sort of operation he was to command.

Neither the question of mounting an intelligence operation against nominal allies, the Russians, nor the use of recent enemies to man it when their leaders were still on trial at Nürnberg, troubled Deane. Regardless of the reality of the threat of an attack by the Soviets, which he says looked more real in Washington than it did in Europe, he considered it "prudent" to have such operations, even against friends. As far as using Hitler's soldiers was concerned, Deane drew on his experience at Oberursel to illustrate his position.

"At the interrogation center almost all our people were either German-born Jews or first generation American Jews of German descent. Some of them may have gotten some sense of satisfaction, some feeling of power out of being in a superior position vis-a-vis the Germans, but I never heard any one of them complain about working with them. Here they were, Jews, those most directly affected, and they weren't complaining." For one thing, Deane pointed out, they could and did make the distinction between Nazis and non-Nazis, "and those people at Oberursel," he said emphatically, "were not Nazis."[5]

The most significant figure among the Germans was Hermann Baun. Most of those associated with the Oberursel group at the time are cautious in discussing him, but Deane, a direct man, is refreshingly outspoken. "He cooked up a lot of schemes in the time before Gehlen got there. Mainly he wanted to reactivate his old net. I considered him an unsavory type, but he was very knowledgeable and he had a lot of connections. When Gehlen got there things changed for him." But before Gehlen's arrival, Baun was given the go-ahead by Deane to try to re-establish contact with his agents in the East and get the network functioning again. He caused nothing but trouble from the start. Baun was constantly going off somewhere, no one knew where, making contact with someone, no one knew whom, and returning to Oberursel with his financial accounts a shambles. Friction built up, but the possibilities Baun held out overshadowed the difficulties his secretive behavior and apparently disorganized nature presented. He was not held accountable for either his actions or his expenditures.

It may have been at this precise point that the trouble, the big, long-term trouble, set in. The latitude given Baun, a shadowy figure born and raised in Eastern Europe, and the extent to which his secrecy was tolerated by Military Intelligence in these earliest days, left the operation vulnerable from the very start. This, critics claim, was the start of a pattern on the part of American Intelligence, which they label irresponsible, on which Gehlen would capitalize, but which in the end would cost him and West Germany dearly.

"The weather had been magnificent for the entire crossing," Gehlen said of the journey home which began July 1 1946. "Cramped though the confines of the troop transport were, we soaked up the sea air and the sunshine. We enjoyed the good food and spent the evenings on deck watching the films . . . For the other prisoners outside our group there must have been an agony of doubt and uncertainty as to what lay ahead of them. But our own morale could not have been higher: we were coming home to Germany, and we were on the threshold of a great new task."[6]

What Gehlen did not say is they were also bound for France, and worried sick about it. Instead of docking at Bremerhaven, as they had hoped, they were making for Le Havre, and that was not where they wanted to go. The French had been boarding transports like this one from America, and hauling off German prisoners of war they thought might be useful to them. It was Gehlen's fervent hope that Waldman knew where they were headed and would be able to prevent a first strike by the French.[7]

Waldman had left Gehlen behind at Fort Hunt and arrived at Oberursel in June 1946, to scout out the land and take stock of the situation. Shortly before Gehlen's ship was due to dock Waldman discovered their destination and immediately set out to foil any possible "kidnapping" attempt by the French. He flew to Paris, then took a car to Le Havre, where with bluff and bravado he had his charges off the ship and safely in American custody within minutes of the gangplank being lowered.

Eager to hear what Waldman had to say, Gehlen was excited, or as excited as his cool, undemonstrative nature allowed. Driving alone with Gehlen from Le Havre to the airport at Orly for their flight to Germany (the others following in two cars), Waldman brought him up to date, outlining what he could expect to meet at Oberursel. As

Waldman described the situation, it was clear there was a good deal for Gehlen to be excited about. For a start, he would be seeing some familiar faces; Wessel had been busy rounding up, and Colonel Deane securing the release of, former FHO members. Even more significant, although Gehlen's group's main task continued to be the historical one of analyzing FHO documents, was the fact that Baun had been sent out to try to resurrect his wartime net. That meant the Americans were actively pursuing the idea of putting the group to work on current intelligence. For Gehlen there was a dull side to that particular coin, the question of Baun's status with the Americans—but that would have to wait.

Of more immediate importance were the Americans themselves, and Waldman was able to reassure him on that point. General Sibert was still in overall charge of Army Intelligence in Germany, and Colonel Philp, whom they had so successfully won over with their presentation on Soviet artillery, was in command of the entire Interrogation Center. Colonel Deane was the only new American in a position of authority on the scene, and he harbored no illusions about the Russians or Soviet intentions.

"Gehlen was nervous when we first met," Deane says. "He wasn't sure what our relationship would be. He was very proper and correct, but it was obvious he was nervous." Along with uncertainty about his future, there was the difference in rank and the difference in age, not to mention the difference in situation. "But as far as I was concerned," Deane adds, "there wasn't any awkwardness. We had some discussions and it was clear we were seeking the same goals, so the way I visualized it was that he had a company and I had hired his company to do a job. We had mutual respect for each other. Eric Waldman was the one who dealt directly with his people, but when it came to policy I got involved." At least one of his policy decisions had far-reaching consequences: it was Deane who set the wheels in motion which ultimately led to the transfer of responsibility for the group from the Army to the CIA.

In July of 1946, however, what was on Deane's, Gehlen's and Waldman's minds was getting organized, and once again the news for the Germans was good; their families would be permitted to join them. "Mrs. Gehlen was at Oberstdorf with her children and the wife of another officer, so I drove over to tell her and give her a day or two to get ready," Waldman says. "It came as such a surprise to her after so long that she was a little rattled by how sudden it all was. I told her, I said: 'A car and a van will be coming for you Wednesday,' and she said: 'Wednesday? Wednesday? Oh, no. I can't leave on Wednesday. I have a skirt at the dressmaker. It won't be ready.' "[8]

At about the same time Friedel D., a former FHO staff member, received a visit, at the American rest center where she was working. The caller was a woman who did not identify herself beyond saying she had been sent by an old colleague from Gehlen's unit. She told Friedel she was to pack up her belongings and be ready to leave the next morning; there was a job waiting and someone would come for her. There was no mention of who was coming or where she was to go, but it hardly mattered: the Americans were closing down the center where she worked and Friedel was about to be out of a job.

For a German in the desolate aftermath of the war, working for the Americans could mean the difference between destitution and survival, but it did not mean you had to like it. Especially if you were an attractive young woman exposed to the rough behavior of the men of a foreign army. "The American soldiers acted like what they were," Friedel says now, without rancor. "They behaved like an occupying force. Conquerors are arrogant, and they were arrogant. Sometimes the soldiers would push the Germans off the sidewalk, sometimes they would call the Germans swine. Immediately there was friction. But what would you expect?"[9] Nonetheless, the prospect of losing her job was cause for real concern. The anonymous messenger could not have come at a better time.

The next morning a big American car with an American driver stopped at her door. He did not tell her, and she did not ask where they were going: "To be riding in a car—you can't imagine what a luxury it was," she says. "What I remember most as I got in was just a feeling of looking forward to whatever it was that was coming next."

After a short drive to a neighboring town, they stopped to pick up more passengers: Mrs. Gehlen, the Gehlen children, and Mrs. Hiemenz, the wife of one of the former FHO officers who had gone to the United States with Gehlen. "I can't recall now what we talked about, but I know none of us knew where we were going. And one thing I do remember was stopping along the way at an American coffee shop. This was Heaven. We had these big rolls and real coffee. I had had nothing, really, for so long until then. Now there was a big car, and this wonderful coffee shop. Then, when we got to Oberursel, we went through some gates to an area set off behind barbed wire, and there were old friends to greet us." The next day, for all intents and purposes, Friedel, who had been with FHO even before Gehlen took it over, was back doing her old job for her old employers.

Security for the group at Oberursel was obsessively tight. No one outside the gates was supposed to know who they were or what they were doing there in their small compound. On one occasion the officer for whom Friedel was doing a job locked them both into his room until the work was finished. This kind of isolation did more than aid security, it fostered a close camaraderie among the members of the group. "We worked together, we ate together, we lived together in this tight little world. We were a family, really," Friedel says.[10]

German accounts of the earliest days of the Gehlen Organization are replete with colorful anecdotes of senior American Intelligence officers courting Gehlen, offering him inducements to put his unit to work for them, and of the way in which he, steely and uncompromising, set the conditions. "Gehlen's terms whiplashed down the table," runs one version of a supposedly decisive meeting. "Here was the defeated party dictating his terms, a little man with a weak voice, but a man who knew what he was worth."[11]

In fact, intense controversy surrounded the concept of using Germans at all. And, more specifically, the Americans were unsure about Gehlen's value to them, other than as an historian. Even when the decision was made to send him back to Germany and set him up in business again, it was on a limited and experimental basis, and it was the Americans who were making the decisions. "It was always a one-way street," says one former, senior CIA officer. "It had to be that way, and that's the way it was. They provided the expertise and the personnel, and we issued the requirements, provided the logistics and received the product."

That did not prevent Gehlen from immediately setting out to take a firm hand with his own people. Back home amid not only his own countrymen, but his own former staff, and regardless of the circumstances, Gehlen quickly reverted. While making every effort to impress and ingratiate himself with his American captors, on whom everything depended, to the Germans he intended to leave no doubt that he was still their commanding officer, General Reinhard Gehlen of the General Staff. Nor, as time passed and he realized the degree of looseness in American control, did the fact of his dependence upon them stop him from taking advantage of it. He began to build a wall of secrecy between the Americans and the Organization, the bedrock of which was his refusal to divulge the identity of the agents he rapidly recruited. Gehlen's first priority, however, was to take command of his group.

If Gehlen was dismayed to discover a previously unsuspected ambition in Hermann Baun, and the degree of responsibility which had been given to him, he was reassured to find that Baun had been unable to capitalize on it by winning the confidence of either the Germans or the Americans. One organizational plan the Americans proposed for the group was an equal division of labor: Baun would be in charge of Acquisition, intelligence gathering; Gehlen would be responsible for Evaluation. The group, in effect, would be a cart drawn by two horses. It was an idea with a notably short life-span. With the cooperation of Eric Waldman, who firmly believed the group's efficiency lay in having a single officer in charge, and the support of Deane, who had reservations about Baun in any case, Gehlen moved to make himself supreme. The organization chart showed Baun still in charge of Acquisition, but Gerhard Wessel would be head of Evaluation, and above them both was Reinhard Gehlen.

Baun felt betrayed, but he lacked support within the group. He was an outsider, had a reputation as a liar, and proved to be a constant source of friction. In addition, says Deane, there was the social factor. "Not only was Gehlen a General while Baun was a Colonel, Gehlen was a gentleman. He and Baun were of different classes, and Baun felt resentful that he wasn't being accepted as an equal. Those things are very important to the Germans, and you could tell Gehlen had no respect for him. He looked at Baun as a necessary evil." Matters finally came to a head with a controversial episode which may have been engineered by Gehlen as the *coup de grace* for his tottering rival.

In order to finance his effort to reconstruct his network of agents, Baun was given a certain amount of money to work with. The method of dispersal, however, was unusual. The money was kept in a safe to which he had access, and he helped himself—without, as it turned out, keeping accurate records of the amounts involved. Stories began to circulate about the questionable purposes to which Baun was putting the funds, and when they reached Colonel Deane, responsible for the group's financial records, he became increasingly concerned. After one particularly flagrant discrepancy was discovered, Deane confronted Baun, and was not satisfied with the explanation he was given.

Baun ultimately was forced to leave the Organization, and his supporters say he never got over the disgrace. He fell "morally to pieces like a whipped dog. He died an unhappy man, accused of fraud . . . Baun died a miserable death on 17 December 1951."[12] Whatever the truth about Baun—whether (and all these have been suggested) he was an embezzler, or simply careless with money; working for the Soviets, or inadvertently used by them; a difficult personality, a social misfit in a tight Establishment group; or a threat to Gehlen's position and therefore a victim of a conspiracy—Gehlen took undisputed charge of the group, and did it with Colonel Deane's blessing. He had consolidated his position, and no one would threaten it again.

The extent to which Gehlen had reasserted his authority over his group was made explicit at a family affair which took place a few months later. One of the former FHO officers whom Wessel tracked down was Rudolf von Glinski. A sophisticated, widely travelled former military attaché, he had joined Gehlen's unit in April 1945, just in time to help it evacuate. Three months earlier, in January of 1945, von Glinski had been at the War Academy in Berlin, assigned to the Military Attaché's Department, and it was there he first met Gehlen.

"It was at the annual Attaché's Reception in honor of Frederick the Great's birthday, January 27th. It was always the best party in the Army," von Glinski recalls, "and even with the Russians at the portals this was no exception. There were about a hundred people including the Military Attachés of all the other countries. I remember a particularly congenial contingent of Siamese, and after things got going the Hungarians were dancing on the tables. But that came later." Earlier, there were toasts and speeches, including a remarkable one by the Dean of the Corps, the Swedish Attaché. " 'It is important to remember on the anniversary of this great hero,' he said, very dignified and solemn, as was befitting of his position, 'that Frederick turned defeat into victory, just as the German Army will today.' At that moment the Russians were moving in on us, and everyone knew it was hopeless, but the speeches and the toast went on.

"While all that was going on I saw this General with a pale face quietly standing there. The reason he stood out was because while all the other Generals in the room were resplendent in their rows and rows of medals, this General, who of course was Gehlen, had only a single decoration around his neck, and it wasn't one given for combat. It was the Kriegsverdienst Kreuz, the War Merit Cross, something on the order of a Good Conduct Medal. What he looked like, really, was a University professor, not a soldier, in spite of the uniform. It was that which made him noticeable; he was so unsoldierly."

By late April, 1945, when von Glinski joined it, Gehlen's unit was disbanding. He was unaware that Gehlen had already gone into hiding with his files. He simply reported and waited to be told what to do. What needed to be done right then was to find spots well off the beaten track where supplies, and people, could safely be deposited. The "supplies" were to be buried; the people, in this case women staff members, were to be found places close enough to the hidden material so they could keep an eye on it. Even now von Glinski says he does not know what the "supplies" consisted of, perhaps food, but CIC records of uncovering caches of gold, some of them huge, suggest he was dealing with something even more precious. (In one brief operation alone, the Americans recovered almost eight tons of gold bullion hidden by the Germans.) Whatever it was, whether gold, more documents, or food, von Glinski headed off to find secure hiding places for it.[13]

Von Glinski had quickly won a reputation for daring and imagination and was high on the list of former FHO members Gerhard Wessel set out to find. When he tracked von Glinski down in a garret in Marburg, north of Frankfurt, von Glinski seized the opportunity to rejoin his former comrades. In doing so he joined a strongly cohesive group. As Friedel said, it was a family, really. Indeed, no family could have followed von Glinski's subsequent courtship of Friedel with more intense interest, and at their marriage Gehlen, fully in command now, relished the role of *pater familias*.

Because of the secrecy surrounding their activities and whereabouts, Friedel's and von Glinski's parents were not present, so the role of Father of the Bride was assumed by Gehlen. His toast to the couple, accompanied by champagne acquired by von Glinski, whose skill at blackmarketeering had made him a highly effective purchasing agent for the group, provides an unusual insight into the private Reinhard Gehlen.

"When I speak to you here, now, in order to give expression to today's festive occasion, I am doing so in a triple capacity. First, so to speak, as representative of the absent father of the bride, second, as your former Commanding Officer and, finally, as your present boss.

"I assume the first task without official assignment. However, I feel certain that even without an express mandate I am acting in accordance with the wishes of your esteemed father by expressing his joy and good wishes at today's celebration. I need not outline his thoughts and felicitations in greater detail since you are well aware of them from his letters. If he were here, I am sure that he would address the ties between both families. In this sense, may your thoughts salute your relatives, particularly the mother of the bridegroom, and your close friends who cannot be here with you today.

"I now turn to my second office as your former C.O. In this

respect I am recalling the days when you, dear bridegroom, in such efficient manner took a hand in all those preparations which eventually got you stranded in a mountain hut near Kufstein together with two of our Wacs [sic] assigned to that particular operation. Already then, a few days after the armistice—if I remember correctly—one of my agents, whose keen hunter's eyes nothing escapes, reported that: 'Something is stirring between Miss D. and Mr. vG. This may very well lead to an engagement.' I greatly rejoiced at this good news at the time and was disappointed when reports received in America implied that the initial seemingly successful offensive had developed into protracted static warfare. It appeared just as difficult to foresee the outcome as to determine whether the strategic goals of the attacking party had changed.

"In my third position as your present boss I found myself faced with an uncertain situation which conveyed the general impression—though based on insufficient intelligence—that these two political powers now were confronting each other with benign neutrality. Renewed reconnaissance provided no exact results—as usual—but turned up some indications which, upon careful scrutiny, led us to suspect well-camouflaged, suspicious preparations by one of the parties. Thus, in the initial phase, repeated reconnaissance missions across the iron curtain were noticed between House Two and House Three, until eventually a shrewdly disguised regular courier connection was successfully established.

"Counterintelligence directed toward this operation could trace these courier missions in only a few cases. Subsequently, installation of a line of acoustic signal communication between House Two and House Three (by the way, the whistle code could not be broken) as well as the covert smuggling of courier shipments under the code-name 'flowers,' were construed as particularly alarming symptoms. It had to be suspected that, in reality, these were explosives intended to disintegrate and break down the anticipated resistance from within.

"Finally, information from the political sector indicated that in negotiations conducted in strict secrecy the opposing party appeared quite receptive to the arguments for political cooperation. Thus, the treaty concluded on September 7, 1946, which is being ratified today, for an intimate political alliance in connection with a mutual aid pact and consultation agreement could no longer surprise the intelligence community.

"But joking apart, all of us are very happy that you two have found each other and we are delighted to celebrate this event with you today.

"First of all, however, let me express our good wishes. We wish you with all our hearts a very long succession of years of joint happiness and mutual effort to accomplish what we should regard as the purpose of life: The development and formation of our own personality toward the rarely achieved goal of ultimate perfection and harmony. As is true for all human beings, you too will not be spared disappointments and adversities. However, on the course just indicated you will find the key to render subordinate the incomprehensibilities of one's own fate and to free one's self from a petty view of the world. Our wishes include many other thoughts which, in part, have already been expressed individually by each of us. All of these shall be incorporated in our joint toast to you: 'Long live the bride and groom . . .' ''[14, 15]

Back on his own ground, but working for the Americans, Gehlen flourished as never before. With a keen eye for an advantage, he had always made the most of every opportunity, even in the face of the Nazis' iron discipline. Now, under the loose control of benevolent captors, amateur soldiers who could not even speak his language, Gehlen found himself in a situation ripe for exploitation. Suddenly he had even more authority over his countrymen, and commanded even greater respect from them than before. A General Staff officer, supported by and bearing the seal of approval of the Americans, Gehlen was a man of real stature among the Germans.

It is particularly difficult for Americans, products of the world's only true melting pot, to appreciate the often subtle, but critical social distinctions which exist in other countries. Americans tend to find them both anachronistic and silly. This lack of understanding was more prevalent in the 1940s, before air travel brought hordes of Americans to Europe, than now. And the class distinctions among individual Europeans were more significant then, as well, before the Americanization of the continent. One result of this cultural ignorance was that most of the Americans who were dealing with him did not really understand Gehlen, or appreciate the reaction of his fellow-countrymen to him.

While the Americans were looking at Gehlen solely as an Intelligence asset, Gehlen was looking at a far broader picture. He was looking at the position and role of post-war Germany in a new Europe whose political landscape he knew would be dominated by the relationship between the Soviet Union and the United States. And he was also looking hard at the part he and his organization would play in it. Under the circumstances, then, it was Gehlen's good fortune to have Deane, who was sensitive to the political climate of Soviet-American relations, as his first American commander. And he was lucky to have had John Boker and then Eric Waldman who, because of their backgrounds, understood the cultural forces at work, on his side.

An intelligent student of history and an astute politician, Gehlen knew how wide the intricate web of German influence was spread through Europe, and the role played by the Abwehr in its deployment. He understood the subtleties of political relationships and the long-range importance to Germany of re-establishing them. If he was the one to initiate the process, so much the better. Further, as a product of post-World War I Germany, which saw itself as victimized by the Versailles Treaty, Gehlen saw at first hand how its military leaders had secretly rebuilt its armed forces under the noses of the Allies. The lessons were clear: first and most important, the Americans could be manipulated; second, elements of the Officers Corps must be, and could be preserved. The General Staff were the nation's surviving aristocracy, its natural leaders, and one day, sooner rather than later, Germany would once again need an army. In the long run it could do Gehlen nothing but good to be the one to take on the job of providing them with a life raft.

"It was important at the time to get as many officers as possible off the street," Gehlen's closest aide, Heinz Herre said. In rapid succession former members of the General Staff joined the new unit, and many of them would once again become the leaders of Germany's armed forces. Gehlen's former superior officer Adolf Heusinger would become Inspector-General of the Bundeswehr; Joseph Moll would be Inspector of the Army; Heinz Günther Guderian, son of the former Chief of the General Staff, one day would become Inspector of the Armored Corps. Gehlen helped preserve what would become the core of Germany's military leadership, an act which would win him support later on.[16]

When Gehlen and Waldman settled down and went to work the aim was to develop information on the Russians, but that was a goal so broad it allowed for simultaneous action in widely different areas, some of greater and more immediate interest to Gehlen than to American Military Intelligence. Although entirely dependent upon the Americans, now it was indeed Gehlen's Organization—henceforth it would be known simply as the Organization—and its activities were directed toward goals which, as he saw it, served the best interests of his employers, his country and himself. With the Americans so compliant, Gehlen's drive and ambition reasserted themselves. That resurgence marked the end of an era for the Organization; the first of several transformations through which it would pass.

The Organization: Expansion, Operations
Captain Eric Waldman

A job with the Organization, on any level, was highly prized. A German would be working with and for his fellow countrymen, but with all the advantages, material and otherwise, of American support. "The German people have a characteristic that was very apparent after the war," Deane says. "When they're down they're servile; when they have a little power, then they're arrogant." Gehlen agents had a degree of power and they flaunted it, behavior which earned them the undying enmity of, among others, the American Constabulary, and the Counter Intelligence Corps—both of which would fight back.[17]

Such power as Gehlen's agents possessed came directly from the special authority Deane had been given by the head of the American Military Government, General Lucius Clay. Deane and Waldman carried identification cards stating that they represented the General personally, and were to be given all consideration—as well as whatever it was they were after, from gasoline or nylons to a prisoner being held in custody. That those controlling the Gehlen Organization, which was quickly dubbed "that bunch of Nazis," had been granted this unique privilege infuriated other arms of the American military.

But in the early days, operational intelligence, such as information about the Soviet order of battle—the units comprising a military force, their type and equipment—was the top priority. What Washington wanted was military intelligence and operations were set in motion to collect it. Agents were sent to the East where they spied out troop concentrations and made contact with local people who might let slip a word here or there.[18] But infiltrating an agent into the East meant giving him a credible identity so he could travel from one place to another. Throughout Germany, movement was restricted and the occupation authorities could demand to see one's papers at any time. Since the Americans running the Gehlen operation ordained that it was Top Secret, and the identity of its operatives was kept from other

American authorities as well as everyone else, there had to be a way to establish false identities which could withstand American as well as enemy scrutiny. The one they came up with was virtually fool-proof.

Deane obtained quantities of blank official American Prisoner of War Release documents, entered the agent's operational name and fictitious background, then signed the papers. With that one document the agent could get the rest of the papers he would need. "As a general rule," Waldman says, "you shouldn't forge more than one document. All the others should be real. This way, if we wanted to get a man into Dresden, in the East sector, we released him as POW Heinz Schmidt, or whatever, from Dresden. With that piece of paper he could get all the others he needed, legitimately, so he could get back 'home.' It worked beautifully."

While the main thrust of the operation was the collection of military intelligence, Gehlen and Waldman were also pursuing other, political objectives which took them, among other places, to Italy, Switzerland, and Spain.[19]

By the end of the war, the relationship between German and Spanish Intelligence had spanned thirty years and the reservoir of good will was wide and deep. Times, however, had changed, and with them politics. Fascism was out, and in the employ of the Americans as he was, Gehlen would have to be discreet in re-establishing contact with the Spanish. He would have to use caution in dealing with the Germans there, as well. Spain not only had been teeming with German agents during the war, it was a haven for those on the run after it was over. And SD men had been sent there and elsewhere to go undercover and prepare to cause trouble for the victorious Allies.[20]

Presumably Gehlen was aware of such schemes and on his guard. Original contact with the Spanish government was made by Waldman and Gehlen in meetings with the military attaché in Bern, who made arrangements for them to fly to Spain for discussions with the chief of Spanish Military Intelligence. In the course of their conversations the Spaniard said it was his government's wish to cooperate with the United States and hoped the Americans would recognize that Spain could become "a stationary aircraft carrier" in Europe for the Western powers. Cooperation of various kinds did follow. As far as the Organization itself was concerned, Spain provided a large and completely equipped bolt-hole in the event of war or some calamity which required its evacuation from Germany. Plans for an emergency evacuation of the Organization to Spain were worked out to the last detail, including assignments of personnel to specific buses.

The Organization in its turn demonstrated a cooperative spirit by helping General Franco repay an old debt. The Spanish Intelligence chief gave Waldman and Gehlen an intriguing insight into wartime history by telling them it had been the German Intelligence chief, Admiral Canaris, who had persuaded Franco not to submit to German pressure and join the Axis. As a friend of Spain, and convinced that ultimately Germany would lose the war, the old Admiral looked to the future and consistently argued in favor of Franco's maintaining his government's neutrality. Now, the Spanish G-2 told his visitors, Franco wanted to show his gratitude by offering Canaris' widow a home in Spain, and a life-long pension. The Organization was happy to help: Frau Canaris was swiftly and efficiently spirited out of Germany and into Spain.[21 22]

A sidelight on this visit was the selection of aides assigned to Waldman and Gehlen by the Spanish. On November 20, 1948, Waldman was elected a Knight of the Sovereign and Military Order of Malta, among the highest honors that can be bestowed on a layman by the Catholic Church; with meticulous attention to detail the aide chosen for him by the Spanish was also a Knight of Malta. Gehlen's aide was a Captain who had served in the Blue Division, the Spanish unit which had fought with the Germans against the Russians; an illuminating example of the realpolitik of the new, postwar Europe.

Another critically important stop for Gehlen and Waldman was the Vatican. The part played by the Catholic Church is a thread that runs through the fabric of the story of espionage during and after the Second World War. Yet its role is so complex, so shadowy, so filled with intrigue that any comprehensive picture of its activities may well remain impossible to draw. Isolated incidents emerge from time to time which create new controversies or rekindle old ones, while serving to demonstrate again that as the most wide-spread, tightly knit organization on the face of the earth, it is an intensely attractive vehicle for those who—for whatever reasons—hope to gain access to just such a secure, and sophisticated international network.

The help given by organizations and individuals directly connected with the Church to Nazis who were wanted for questioning by the War Crimes Tribunal is well documented. So, too, is the fact that after the liberation of Rome in June 1944 the Vatican supplied the OSS with reports from the new papal nuncio in Japan, providing useful intelligence for aerial bombardment there.[23] Intelligence agencies recruit informants from the Vatican just as they do from any nation's government. In 1945, the American OSS in Rome paid a Vatican code clerk

$100 a week to turn over summaries of papal nuncios' intelligence reports world-wide, only to discover he was giving the identical material to the Russians.[24] Now Gehlen would join the other intelligence services in turning his attention to Rome. In this, as in so much else, Waldman was invaluable. Gehlen was not a Catholic, but not only was Waldman a Catholic, he was a Knight of Malta. When Gehlen wanted a private audience with Pope Pius XII—"it concerned a business matter, even now I cannot say more," says Eric Waldman—Waldman was able to arrange it within a day. And it is likely that his entree facilitated another kind of appointment and one which doubtless proved extremely valuable to the Organization over the years. Gehlen's half-brother, whose cover name was "Giovanni", was given the post of Secretary to the Director of the Knights of Malta.[25]

Getting an agent where he was supposed to go was the first step, the second was getting the information. But then came the all-important matter of getting that information back to those who needed it. To do that all the standard espionage techniques of the time were used. Radios were smuggled into enemy territory; telephones had false listings; messages written in code and secret ink were passed by couriers, left at letter drops, secreted in cigarette packs and newspapers, even sent through the post. But occasionally Gehlen's agents, suffering an attack of originality, struck out on their own and came up with something straight out of farce.

Potsdam sits on the east bank of Lake Glienicke; its opposite bank is in the West sector, and over it is a bridge then guarded by Russian soldiers. For a spy, crossing from one bank to the other in the conventional manner was risky. It meant being stopped, questioned, having to produce identification and a credible purpose for the journey—in both directions. Crossing from one bank to the other in the conventional manner was not risky, however, for a swan. So Gehlen's men trained one of the local aquatic beauties to paddle serenely from shore to shore, graciously accepting the pieces of bread thrown to her by the Russians who had no idea that under her wings were plastic bags stuffed with secret messages.

In a more serious vein was an operation mounted against the Czechoslovak intelligence network in West Germany, probably the most important effort made by Gehlen's organization during the Waldman era. In the aftermath of the war, in 1945, two significant events took place in Czechoslovakia. Large numbers of Sudeten Germans, long-time residents with close ties of family and friendship there, were expelled from the country; and the Czech government, under Soviet direction, established a school for spies in Prague. Before long graduates of the espionage academy were being infiltrated into West Germany, where they bought the services of the Sudeten expellees with the usual coin, promises of reward and threats of retribution.

An extensive network was quickly formed and information started pouring into Prague: names and addresses of American Intelligence officers; activities of the Counter Intelligence Corps; names of Czechs working for United States Intelligence; leaders of political groups in D.P. camps; troop movements, and so on. There was no end to it, and the reach was long. In one case the wife of a Bavarian government official stole reports on refugee matters from her husband's files and sent them to Czechoslovakia in Bavarian Ministry of the Interior envelopes. The assaults were coming from all sides.

Then in the summer of 1948 there was a break. Former members of FHO, Sudeten Germans still in Czechoslovakia and in touch with Gehlen Organization agents, sent word that there had been a shakeup in the Czech Intelligence department, code named "Tomicka," which had responsibility for West German operations. On April 1 a Captain Ottokar Feifar had replaced the previous chief of the department, Captain Janda, and there was reason to believe Feifar was ripe for defection. Two Organization men were assigned to ferret out every piece of information they could about Feifar; his professional life; his personal habits and weaknesses; his friendships and family ties. By autumn they were ready to act. Feifar was approached and was more than ready to defect, agreeing to pass on everything he knew in return for his freedom in the West and resettlement in the United States.

Feifar was even better than his word. He took his colleague Captain Vojtech Jarabek into his confidence, and Jarabek too decided to defect. On the night of November 8, 1948, Feifar and Jarabek made their escape. Travelling by car to a point not far from the border, they abandoned it and struck out on foot, making for a point where they reckoned they could cross undetected. Once in the American zone they were met by members of the border patrol who had been alerted to watch out for them.[26]

At about that same time, the daughter of one of the defectors was boarding the Orient Express in Prague. Into the lining of her handbag, for delivery to her father in West Germany, was sewn a piece of paper with the names of some twenty spies working for Czech Intelligence in the West—one of whom, although she had no way of knowing it, was travelling on the same train. Frantisek Klecka, a thirty year old Czech, had been a student of philology and a pianist living in Vienna before the war. He was also a dedicated communist who, when he realized he was wanted by the Austrian police, had fled to Moscow where he was given foreign intelligence training. At the end of the war Klecka was sent by the Russians back to his native Czechoslovakia and found a job that was highly prized by the espionage network, that of waiter on the Prague-Munich-Paris express.

Klecka, who had no idea who she was, met the girl in the dining car; he was her waiter. As the train approached the German border where Czech frontier guards would board the train, she became increasingly nervous, afraid the incriminating document would be discovered. Leaving her seat, she asked her waiter, Klecka, if he would keep an eye on her bag until she returned, which she did not do until they were safely in Germany. Klecka did as she was asked, and nothing more; it did not occur to him to search her bag. As a result, shortly after the girl handed over the list of names, Klecka himself was arrested.

He was among more than forty men and women picked up by American Military Police immediately after Feifar and Jarabek's defection. The arrests began at once in order to prevent Czech headquarters in Prague from alerting its agents in Germany and allowing them to escape. The espionage trials began in February 1949, and Klecka's, held on the 17th, was the first. He was sentenced to twenty years' imprisonment.[27]

Although this rash of arrests, followed by five separate trials, did not put a stop to Czech Intelligence operations in West Germany, it did put a crimp in their style. The Feifar-Jarabek incident is one example of a successful positive Intelligence operation by the Gehlen Organization, but there were not many, and its useful life in that area was brief. American Intelligence officers repeatedly assert that outside of visual observations and POW interrogations in the earliest postwar days, the Organization's greatest value to the United States lay in its counterespionage capability.[28] [29]

Friction and Change

The question of the limits of the Organization's usefulness to the American intelligence effort came to the fore in the autumn of 1946 when Colonel Deane was approached by the military attaché of an Eastern Bloc nation. The attaché offered to turn over to Deane his embassy's cable traffic in exchange for safe passage for himself and his family to the United States or South America should he be recalled by his government. Declaring that his motives were ideological, he did not ask for money or any payment other than escape to the Western hemisphere rather than a return to his own country.[30] Deane, recognizing that if the attaché was what he claimed this was a major opportunity for the Americans, also concluded that this was something he definitely did not want to take on. It could constitute a dramatic expansion into the area of politically sensitive intelligence. He consulted General Schow, who agreed. In his opinion the Army, and certainly Deane's Gehlen unit, was in no position to assume such a delicate operation.

Among his own people Gehlen was the undisputed chief, a reincarnated General Staff officer, but at the same time, he was on trial with his American backers. While he worked hard to demonstrate his efficiency and determination to cooperate, he was scrambling to expand his operation and get it securely entrenched. But he did not realize just how insecure his position was. Elements of Military Intelligence, citing both political and security objections, were becoming increasingly strident in their opposition to American support of the Organization, and even Colonel Deane, although he favored keeping it and putting it to work, decided he would have to go out and look for new owners for this mongrel group of his. The overture from the Eastern Bloc officer was the catalyst. Such an apparently attractive offer needed close scrutiny, but by those professionally equipped to evaluate its political implications.

The Central Intelligence Group, linked with the Departments of State and War, and endowed with a large cadre of bright and able former members of OSS, was the lap into which Deane wanted to drop the Gehlen unit. Despite its limited charter, the newly formed CIG appeared to offer a broad intelligence capability, and in Deane's view Gehlen's group, properly controlled and supervised, might well be a vehicle for operations such as that proposed by the Eastern Bloc officer. It would solve a good many problems if CIG would take them over; so, in the late autumn of 1946, Deane travelled to the United States.

At the old sandstone Naval Medical Building which served as the CIG headquarters he met with General Hoyt Vandenberg, the head of the group. Vandenberg heard Deane out and then suggested he go up to New York and discuss the whole matter with some old hands at this sort of thing. So Deane knocked on the door of a Manhattan town house and settled down to sell the Gehlen Organization to former Army Intelligence officer William Jackson and the OSS's Allen Dulles.

During the war, while Gehlen was striving to hold back the engines of war which would bring defeat to Germany, Dulles, at Herrengasse 23 in Bern, Switzerland, had been speeding those engines on. The Bern flat, which overlooked the Aare River, was large, comfortable, accessible, and well placed for his purpose. It had a large garden at the back through which nighttime callers could come unobserved, and it was Dulles' hope when he leased it that he would have many visitors. Short of hanging out a shingle proclaiming that here were the offices of OSS, he did what he could to let it be known in the relevant quarters that the Americans had an intelligence presence in Switzerland and he was it. So he kept his garden dark and his rear door open.

The flat's American tenant had been gently reared in a quietly distinguished family which would boast three Secretaries of State. Well-connected, well-educated and widely travelled, Allen Dulles was not at first glance the sort of man who one day would inspire *Pravda* to this atypical flight of literary fancy: ". . . should [he] arrive in Heaven through somebody's absent-mindedness, he would begin to blow up the clouds, mine the stars and slaughter the angels."[31] But for Dulles, espionage was a huge competitive game. He was, perhaps, the last of the great romantics of Intelligence, one for whom the tools of the trade were secrets and mysteries, and he reveled in it.[32]

Sitting with Jackson and Dulles in New York, Deane pulled out a diagram, in code, of the composition of the Organization. Preoccupied with security as, ironically, they always were, the Germans had created an intricate drawing disguised as the schematics of the electrical system of a big house. As the three examined the diagram Deane explained his position and put forward his arguments in favor of a CIG takeover. After considerable discussion it was agreed that CIG would at least take a first-hand look at the apparatus and then make a decision.

Several months later CIG's Samuel Bossard arrived at Oberursel and took up residence. "From that moment I never had the opportunity to be lonely," says Eric Waldman. Like a shadow with eyes, Sam Bossard stuck close to Waldman, watching, looking, peering into every cranny of the operation. "He went with me all over the place to see what the Organization was like. He went into the field with me and saw my contacts, we drove all over the place. I carried on my work normally except that Sam Bossard was right next to me the whole time."

Not only did Bossard follow Waldman around, he studied reports, held exhaustive interviews with the chiefs of the various arms of the

Organization, and compiled reams of information for the report he was to write. He had ample opportunity to do a thorough job; he stayed more than three months. At length Bossard completed his study and submitted a report to CIG. On the basis of it and other information the decision was made that CIG would not take on the Gehlen group. It was still Military Intelligence's baby. And the only trained intelligence officer among the handful of young American soldiers in charge of this burgeoning organization of German Intelligence professionals was Eric Waldman.

There was no job description for Waldman's work with Gehlen. Adviser, implementor, agent—sometimes disguised as an interpreter, sometimes as a criminal investigator—Waldman's was a free-wheeling assignment. In one pocket he carried forged identity papers, in the other the magic card that required the representative of any American organization to honor Waldman's request, regardless of what it was. If there was any doubt about what it was he asked, they were to do it first and then ask questions. Being forced to release Germans picked up for violations, especially in connection with black marketeering, was a particularly bitter pill for the American occupation authorities to swallow.

The Organization, whose size Gehlen was increasing with great speed, was strapped for money; what it was alloted by the Army couldn't begin to meet its needs and the black market became its major source of income. The system was as slick as it was unscrupulous. The Army spent its allotted money on buying supplies, which special Organization units sold on the black market. Then, after completing the sales, the American Army Criminal Affairs Division confiscated the goods, claiming they had been illegally traded on the black market, and repossessed the property—which was subsequently resold on the black market. This profitable recycling operation became a matter of survival after the June 1948 currency reform when the new Deutsche-marks were issued—Gehlen says after that they got 70% less in actual buying power—and it was the black market which kept the Organization solvent. At the same time it added fuel to the growing fire of resentment of Gehlen's Germans.

"Our supply of American dollars was extremely limited," Waldman explains, "but if we gave our people who ran the agents in the field dollars and they exchanged them on the black market we multiplied our income ten times, at least. And there were other things, of course. Cigarettes were currency. We could buy a carton for eighty cents; sold on the black market they brought many, many times more than that.

And there was penicillin. My great concern was with penicillin. Giving East German physicians penicillin to treat Soviet officers—for a price. But if we had an agent who was not only using a cover identity but was on an operation that involved working the black market, he was much more easily compromised. And the Army hated to have to turn them over to us. Of course it got to be well known that we would get our agents released.''

From the start, friction between American military personnel and Gehlen agents in the field had been widespread and constant, but at Oberursel itself—until the advent of Deane's replacement, Colonel Liebel—that had not been the case. The tone had been set by Deane who, understanding that his assignment was to see that the operation worked smoothly, dealt with Gehlen on the basis of mutual respect. And by Waldman, who fully supported the undertaking and worked hard for its success.

In the field, American and Gehlen agents were stepping on one another's toes and the clash went beyond professional rivalry and concerns about security, deep into the well of mutual postwar resentment. Relishing the power they had over Americans who challenged them on their missions, while choosing to ignore the fact that the power was granted to them by other Americans, Gehlen agents frequently went out of their way to be antagonistic. They enjoyed humiliating the Americans who questioned them by demonstrating they carried more weight with the American's own commanding officers. For their part many Americans, enlisted men and officers, reacted with bitterness, anger, and frustration when a German civilian not only tried to pull rank, but succeeded.

Furthermore, Gehlen's agents, they charged, used all kinds of strategems to undercut American Intelligence. During interrogations they would warn the prisoners not to talk with the Americans because ''the Americans and the Russians were still working together just as they had during the war. Whatever the prisoner told the US intelligence officer would be relayed back to the Soviets,'' they claimed. Not only that, the Gehlen agents said, if they did talk to the Americans their lives would be in danger because a communist agent would be sure to kill them once they were released. Cooperation was not the watchword, and side-effects of this friction, some long-term, would manifest themselves on both sides, infecting Oberursel itself after Deane left.

Deane had no wish to remain in intelligence. He agreed with Gehlen that it was a dead end for a military man, and in any case—unlike Gehlen—he had no great interest in it. By mid-1947 he had managed to persuade Washington that he would be more valuable to his country elsewhere, and he was replaced by Colonel Willard K. Liebel, which, in the opinion of many who were there, was unfortunate.

Colonel Liebel arrived in the fall of 1947 and the atmosphere at Oberursel underwent an abrupt change. Where relations between the Germans and the Americans had been harmonious, now there was acrimony and confrontation. The Colonel had little use for Germans and made no bones about it. The Americans had won the war, the Germans had lost it; the Americans were calling the tune and the Germans were going to dance to it.

What Colonel Liebel found when he arrived at Oberursel was a group which to a large extent had been given its head, and he was determined to rein it in. It is questionable whether bringing this burgeoning organization under the sort of military control Liebel wanted was still possible—some in the Intelligence community say it should have been broken up with only a few elements being retained—but if it was possible, he was not the man to do it. Liebel did not have the respect or backing of Waldman and the few other Americans who worked closely with Gehlen, either. The more authority he attempted to exercise over the activities of Gehlen's agents the more Gehlen balked, and the natural cohesiveness among the Germans only became stronger.[33]

"None," Waldman says, "and I must emphasize *none* of Gehlen's officers in those days when I was there were Nazis. While I was with him, until March of 1949, regardless of my relative youth and low rank at the time, he and I had a very good understanding. He would always take me along when he was going to interview someone. I'm speaking here only of the high-ranking people he was considering for his staff, not the low-level people who were out in the field; he didn't hire them directly anyway. The reason he took me, he said, was that he thought I had good *Fingerspitzengefühl*—a feeling in my fingertips—about people.

"I made it absolutely clear from the beginning that I would have nothing to do with an SD man," Waldman says. "I would not work with one. For example there was Walter Schellenberg who wanted to join us, and I said 'absolutely out. I don't work with SD people.' On the top level we had nobody from the SD. I am afraid to say that after I left things changed. They said they were short on personnel and were under pressure—anyway later on they did take them on. But I always said no. First for personal reasons, I would not work with a Nazi, and second I said they can always be blackmailed. And they were.''

But Gehlen had always had his own agenda, which was of little interest to American Army officials. As a German he cared deeply about the future welfare and political direction of his own country. As an ambitious, politically astute and subtle man he recongized a great opportunity to realize a dream and make his mark. Liebel's insensitivity to the situation made it virtually inevitable that the Germans would close ranks even more tightly and curb whatever disposition there was toward openness.

Students of history might have understood that the Germans had been in this position before, as recently as 1918, and appreciated their skill at manipulating their conquerors. And they might have recognized their pride, patriotism, and determination. But the American military was preoccupied with overwhelming and immediate problems. It did not have the luxury, even if it had had the interest, to analyze the inner dynamics of this group which was assembled to do a job for them. The Americans needed information about what was going on in the East, and they needed it at once.

In addition to this lack of American sensitivity to the interests and ambitions of the Germans under their command, there was a lack of experience. American field officers were in charge of a group of German Intelligence professionals, and regardless of the reputation of German Intelligence during the war, they were professionals and the Americans controlling them, with the exception of Waldman, were rank amateurs at espionage. They were military men seconded to do a job in occupied Germany. If all the elements are totted up—pressure to get a specific job done, lack of experience, lack of understanding of the people with whom they were working, and more—it would have been surprising had Gehlen not gathered the reins in his own hands.

For Gehlen, by contrast, had insight into the politics of intelligence in the United States and recognized that there were changes in the wind. His own record demonstrated that he was a master at manipulating even the most difficult situations to his own advantage, and he kept a weather eye on developments in Washington. When he had been in custody in the United States, he had seen OSS dissolved and military intelligence apparently ascendant. But there followed the establishment of the Central Intelligence Group, which, despite its inauspicious inauguration, signaled significant changes to come and with them a shift in power. He would have to keep his nose to the wind, no matter how difficult his situation, and he did.

His own position was difficult; although he continued to work in harmony with Waldman, his relationship with Liebel was miserable and offered little prospect of improvement. In addition, by mid-1947 the Organization was pushed for more than money; it was growing at such a rate the Oberursel quarters were badly cramped and it was clear they needed more space. Colonel Liebel, who was uncooperative in many areas, was helpful in this one. So when Waldman proposed they consider moving south, to a suburb of Munich called Pullach, the Colonel agreed.

The Pullach compound has become a legendary site in Germany. In a small town forty kilometers from Munich, it sits on the banks of the Isar River, completely surrounded by high walls, and has its roots deep in Nazi history. Originally belonging to Rudolph Hess, it became the headquarters for Hitler's most trusted lieutenant, Martin Bormann. Immediately after the war, for a brief time, it was headquarters for American postal censorship. Inside the walls when Waldman first visited it were the Bormann mansion, some twenty small family houses, a number of barracks, a mess hall, garage, clubhouse, and a swimming pool. It was, as Waldman said, "the perfect place."[34]

On the 6th of December, 1947, the Organization moved into its new home, and there was rejoicing all around. With the move coming so close to Christmas, the new quarters were dubbed by the Germans "Camp Nicholas" in the saint's honor. Relief from the serious problem of overcrowding was one reason for rejoicing; another was that staff members were not merely encouraged, they were required for security reasons to move their families into the compound with them. But there was a further significant factor at work as well. The move to Pullach was a move away from Oberursel and the powerful American military presence there. Liebel, Waldman and the handful of Americans on their staff were at Pullach and were in charge, but the Germans far outnumbered them. Whereas the Gehlen group at Oberursel had been a German "family," here it would quickly expand into a community, thereby altering its character.

The Bormann house, the largest in the compound, was the hub of the operation. On the ground floor were Liebel's and Waldman's offices; on the floor above were Liebel's quarters, and above that, under the eaves, was a warren of little rooms. On the ground floor of a smaller house, across the road from the American headquarters in Bormann's house, Gehlen had his office. Over the front door of the Bormann house was a stone eagle. It had originally been a full-fledged Nazi symbol, a German eagle holding a swastika in its claws; the

Americans had removed the hooked cross from its grasp, leaving the mighty bird empty-handed.

This takeover of the Pullach installation meant giving the compound a cover identity as headquarters of a large business which had a network of regional offices—a fiction that was not far from fact. The combination of the Organization's new-found domesticity and the necessity for secrecy also meant turning it into a self-contained village. A kindergarten and school were established. There was an infirmary, and a small PX was installed so the "villagers" would not have to venture far outside the walls. All the inhabitants lent a hand; wives of both German and American personnel served as secretaries and staff assistants. This physical isolation not only reinforced the tendency natural among Intelligence people—who are seldom really comfortable outside their own milieu—to band together, it brought with it the intimacy of small town life, with all its advantages and disadvantages.

As Gehlen settled into Pullach with Waldman's help, he continued the rapid expansion of the Organization. Through an elaborate recruiting system more and more agents were acquired, and there was less and less real possibility of investigating their backgrounds. For one thing, the Germans did not have direct access to the records held at the Berlin document center; to do an identity check they had to go through the Americans. It was on this issue that the sharp differences between Liebel and Waldman became critical. Liebel demanded that he be given the identities of all Gehlen's agents, but Waldman, on the grounds of security, supported Gehlen in his refusal to obey Liebel's order. It was a decision that would have far-reaching consequences. After Waldman's departure from Pullach, Gehlen stepped up the pace of recruitment, a process which became increasingly suspect.[35] At the same time, the secrecy inherent in any espionage activity now became increasingly directed at Gehlen's own sponsors, the Americans.[36]

At headquarters, with Waldman at his elbow, Gehlen may have been careful to avoid former SD men, but further down the line the Old Boy network of former Nazi Intelligence agents was hard at work. Not all American—or British, French or Russian—Intelligence officers took Waldman's stand on refusing to use former SD men. (Nor, to his ultimate regret, did Gehlen continue the Waldman policy after the Americans officially left Pullach.) As long as they were not actively engaged in trying to resurrect Nazism, many French, British, American (and Soviet) Intelligence officers saw the practical advantages in using SD agents. They were experienced, knew their way around, were presumed to be anti-communist, and were eager to expunge the past and curry favor with the occupiers.

Indeed, at the time the Organization was making its move to Pullach, the British had two former SD officers working for them who would soon be in Gehlen's Organization, and one would write the most damaging chapter in its history.

But at that point Gehlen's primary concern was building his organization, and as it grew it became increasingly vulnerable. Information-dealing was a major German industry, but free-lancers made a precarious living at it, and a berth in the American-sponsored Organization was a plum. Recruitment meant sudden riches relative to the poverty that gripped Germany; meat, milk, lodging—even parcels of food and soap for one's relatives—could be had. There was no shortage of candidates and some of the best turned out to be servants of another master. Among the many ironies in the Gehlen story is the fact that despite his preoccupation with false identities and cover names—every member of the Organization had an alias by which he was always addressed—in the final analysis security was the Organization's weakest link.

For Gehlen, building the Organization did not simply mean expanding agent operations. As always, he was looking to the future, and what he saw emerging—assuming there was no war with the Soviet Union—was a partnership with the United States and the other Allies, one in which Germany would be the strongest of the European partners. Already figures were appearing, men who would take leading roles in a German government to come. Prominent among them was Konrad Adenauer, who had already begun to make his mark before the war and before the emergence of Hitler.

A former President of the Prussian State Council and Bürgermeister of Cologne, Adenauer lost both offices under the Nazis, and was arrested twice, in 1934 and again in 1944. In 1945 the British restored him as Bürgermeister of Cologne, but quickly removed him as being too obstinate. His political career continued, however, and in 1947 he was leader of the Christian Democratic Union (CDU), which would be a ruling party in West Germany for years to come. A confirmed anti-communist, he viewed rapprochement with the Soviet Union as letting down the West's guard and permitting the Finlandizing of Western Europe. To avoid that he was willing to pay the price of long-term rivalry and tension.[37]

Just as Gehlen knew there would have to be a new German army and had moved quickly to rescue prominent Wehrmacht officers and bring them to the safe temporary haven of his Organization, so now he began to reach out to these emerging political and business leaders of the new Germany.[38] He would need their support to legitimatize his Organization and bring it into a German government, and that doubtless was his primary motive in setting out to cultivate these men.

But he also saw that there were political divisions among the people and that parties were forming. He had no desire for a leading role in the political drama to come. As always, he preferred to work behind the scenes and manipulate the characters out front. His was a position uniquely well suited for the task. In time he might be able to help build bridges between the Germans and the Americans, but first he had to gain credibility and establish himself with those who would be running Germany. Unlike the Americans, who historically tended not to appreciate its significance, the Germans understood the value of intelligence as a weapon in the armory of national defense—and also grasped its wider political potential. It is wise to be friends with the man who holds the secrets, and in Germany that man was Reinhard Gehlen.

But while Gehlen was moving quickly and adroitly to establish himself in the emerging new Germany, his relationship with the representative of his American supporters, Colonel Liebel, was deteriorating. This precipitous decline was hastened by the American's gift for the gratuitous insult. On one memorable occasion he informed Generals Gehlen, Winter, and Heusinger that the German General Staff was "nothin'." After a series of increasingly unpleasant confrontations, the higher authorities finally recognized that Liebel was the wrong man to develop and work with a German unit, and in August 1948 he was transferred from Pullach.[39]

Word of Liebel's impending removal had reached Pullach some weeks earlier, as Waldman was leaving on an assignment in Switzerland. There, in Lucerne, he encountered Colonel Russell ("Rusty") Philp, who had been in charge at Oberursel when Gehlen and John Boker were there. After he listened to Waldman's account of the situation at Pullach, Philp joined Waldman in pulling some strings, with the result that he was appointed as Liebel's successor. An easygoing military man who had formed a high opinion of Gehlen already, Philp took over the group in December 1948.

"At Basket," Friedel von Glinski said of Oberursel, "we were like a family, but Pullach was different. It grew so quickly, it was so big, the atmosphere was no longer the same."

Change, in fact, was thick in the air. The international tensions that had culminated in the Soviet blockade of Berlin and the subsequent drama of the 1948 airlift established the Cold War as a fact of life. A German government was in the making, and in 1947, under the National Security Act, the Central Intelligence Agency had been established. Relations with Germany were shifting, and that fact, together with the creation of a new centralized Intelligence agency with overall responsibility for foreign operations, precipitated another look at the United States Army-sponsored Gehlen Organization.

Part Two

The Gehlen Organization Fully Established

Chapter Six

The CIA and the Organization

The Actual Terms of the Relationship
James Critchfield

Once the morally arguable and politically risky decision to employ Gehlen was taken, his unit quickly established its usefulness to the Americans. Through personal sightings, interrogations of returned German prisoners of war, and analysis of communications intercepts, Gehlen's agents were able to provide timely information on troop concentrations and movements. At a time when the danger of war appeared very real, the Organization gave the Americans valuable operational intelligence they otherwise would not have had. It was after the threat of a shooting war receded and the struggle with the Soviets became the Cold War that the Organization's failure to live up to its promise in the area of strategic intelligence, providing insight into what the enemy planned to do with what it had, became increasingly important.

It was then too, that the American relationship with Gehlen became more complex and problematic. Gathering intelligence for the Americans was not all Gehlen's burgeoning group was doing. From the start Gehlen had the Organization moving along two paths. One was directed toward satisfying his American sponsors' needs by supplying them with information, the other at anticipating the needs of the future German state he had no doubt would emerge, and establishing his claim to play a significant role in its political life. Skillful at exploiting situations and manipulating men, Gehlen was able to move quickly down both roads, but with mixed long term results. In racing to build up his Organization, Gehlen acted out of twin desires to prove his value to the Americans and have in place a functioning Intelligence agency which a future German goverment would be virtually compelled to adopt.

That Gehlen provided a safe haven for former members of the General Staff, although it was clearly a move down the path of his German ambitions and one which would have been greeted with outrage by the American public had it been informed, it had its advantages for the United States. In taking into his Organization and giving "dignified employment" to prominent former military figures, Gehlen was helping to preserve the core of the new army Germany was certain to have one day. He also used some of these officers, regarded by their countrymen as Germany's elite, to establish contact with those who would become the country's political leaders. This provided the Americans with a valuable window on and connection with significant elements in the evolving German state.

As control of the Organization was shifted from the Army to the CIA the importance of and interest in the political aspects of Gehlen's activities increased. The transfer of responsibility from the Pentagon to the CIA was an act of major importance, it could not have happened without approval of the highest ranking members of the administration in Washington. What the politically astute Gehlen, trapped in a deteriorating relationship with Army Intelligence, saw in this was more than a new lease on life, a new stability. He recognized the potential for broad new opportunities.

In September 1948 James Critchfield's beat-up old black Chevrolet rolled into Pullach and pulled up at the front entrance of Martin Bormann's former headquarters. Thirty-one years old, strongly built, and in the uniform of an American Army Colonel, Critchfield got out and walked briskly to the door. There he was greeted by a slight, fair-haired German in his late forties who had the coldest, bluest eyes the American had ever seen. The German, introducing himself as Dr. Schneider, and Critchfield, calling himself Marshall, shook hands and went into the building. As they sat down to drink coffee—tea for the Doctor, as Gehlen was called universally—the two men openly sized each other up, knowing neither was what he appeared to be.[1,2]

Of the two, probably "Dr. Schneider" was the less convincing. In uniform he had an unexpectedly professorial air, but now, in mufti, he looked very much like an officer out of uniform. "Marshall," however, was entirely at home in his disguise as an officer; he had only become a civilian of sorts, a short time before.

"Herr Marshall," as James Critchfield would be known to the multi-national force of Intelligence officers in Europe at the time, had been in the ROTC program at college in the United States when war broke out. Commissioned as a Second Lieutenant, he discovered to his own surprise that he was a born soldier, that nothing in his life gave him more satisfaction. He had ample opportunity to find out. He served on the Mexican border with the last horse-cavalry unit in the United States Army, then as a tank commander in North Africa, Italy, France and Germany. Before embarking from Italy for the H-hour landing in Southern France on August 15, 1944, he took command of a battalion of members of the Texas National Guard 36th Division which, with battle streamers of the Alamo and St. Jacinto flying, led the assault on the beaches.

From that moment he and his men were in constant combat. In the hard, seemingly endless campaign, they tried to close the trap on the 19th German Army in the south, but were unable to crack the line until late December. Later, in Pullach, he would work closely with General Kühlein, whose troops Critchfield had faced on the Rhine Plain that Christmas.

There were other ironies. On May 4 1945, just before the end of the war, Critchfield led a column of tanks along the road which passed directly below the hut in which Gehlen was hiding. Not many days later Critchfield was sent to accept the surrender of the First German Army at their headquarters in Kufstein. With another American at his side and a white flag flying from his jeep, German military police let him in, and Critchfield took his place at the table with six senior German officers. Five of them he would meet again—when they were all associated with the Gehlen Organization.

With the war finally over, Critchfield, the youngest full Colonel in the American Army, came home. But a year later he returned to Europe. The United States zone was overrun with refugees from the Polish and Russian armies as well as displaced persons of every kind. All of them were destitute. American supplies of food, clothing, fuel, medicine—everything, in fact—were all that saved the lives of millions during that cruel winter of 1946–47, among the most bitter on record.

It was then that he began hearing whispers about Operation Rusty. No one really knew anything, it was all very vague and sinister. "We were picking up these spies," says Critchfield, "and when we'd search them we'd find American money, hundred-dollar bills sewn in the lining of their coats. They'd tell us they were working for the Americans, that all we had to do was check it. So my standing orders were: 'cut out the linings, take the money and throw them back across the border.' "

Among the Americans struggling with the array of post-war problems was the chief economist in occupied Austria, Eleanor Lansing Dulles. She met Critchfield and wrote home to her brothers John Foster and Allen about him, suggesting his talents might be put to better use by the State Department or the newly born CIA than by the Army. So, when Critchfield was given orders in 1948 to return to the United States for reassignment, Foster Dulles asked if he would stop by and see him. Dulles, at that time an advisor to Thomas E. Dewey in his presidential campaign against the incumbent, Harry Truman, said he would be interested in having Critchfield's views on the situation in Eastern Europe. Equally interested was Foster's brother Allen, who, although a partner in his brother's law firm, Sullivan and Cromwell, was about to return to intelligence work, with which he had kept a close connection since the demise of the OSS. It was shortly after that meeting in 1948 that James Critchfield joined the CIA.[3]

His first assignment was not long in coming. He was to go to Munich and set up a major operations base against the Soviet Union.[4] The job of visiting Pullach, which Critchfield was to do in whatever time he could steal from his primary task, was given to him in part because no one else at the Agency wanted it. Some avoided it because they considered it a high-risk assignment in terms of advancement in the Agency, others because they objected to a resurgent German Intelligence service with a predominantly military character. "The Agency was full of senior officers far better qualified than I for the job, but the whole subject was so controversial they decided to give it to the new boy on the block. Me," says Critchfield.

The Gehlen Organization was a constant irritant to the American Intelligence community. Military Intelligence had asked the Central Intelligence Group to take it over, and they had declined. Army Counter Intelligence was openly hostile to it, and everybody recognized that American sponsorship of it was a political hot potato. Finally, in September 1948, the CIA and the military agreed to make a joint study of Gehlen's organization and decide its fate once and for all. Should it be broken up? If so, which elements of it should be retained? And which service should be given control of what function?

Chosen to conduct this investigation, which lasted from September to December, 1948, and write a report, were Critchfield of CIA and Colonel Charles Bromley of Army Intelligence. As it turned out, Colonel Bromley was involved for only a short time; the bulk of the work was done by Critchfied. And every step of the way he was met with the determined opposition of Colonel Philp.[5]

In their first meeting, Critchfield told Gehlen only that he had come to visit and learn about the Organization. He did not say who had sent him, but Gehlen knew he was from CIA and was as eager to have the Agency take over as Philp was reluctant. As a result the Germans were more eager than his fellow Americans to give Critchfield the help he needed. The investigation took almost two months, and when it ended he filed his report in a long cable to CIA headquarters. The thrust of that 2,000 word message was that history had overtaken them. The Organization existed. It already employed a staggering 4,000 Germans, and was not subject to being carved up and parceled out to various American interests, as had been suggested. The genie was indeed out of the bottle and there was no shoving it back in, even if that was what Washington wanted. As Critchfield saw it there remained two options: eliminate it or control it.

In analyzing how American interests would best be served, Critchfield stressed the potential political value of the Organization to the United States. He pointed out that since sooner or later there would be an independent Germany, they would be better off identifying and controlling, as long as possible, the inevitable German intelligence service. It must be accepted that this Organization into which Gehlen had gathered men of potentially great influence was going through a rapid transition which would eventually give it a German character. But, Critchfield argued, it was to the benefit of the United States to have a hand in shaping the direction of its growth.

Critchfield concluded by saying that in reality the CIA had no choice but to take over the Organization. Not only did it exist, it had grown exponentially; Military Intelligence was merely sustaining, not controlling it; it bore the seeds of both benefit and mischief to the United States; and it behooved them to find out what the Organization really was all about. Once they had done that, Critchfield added, CIA could decide what to do with it.

The reply to his telegraphic tour de force was a terse cable saying: Stay there and wait. Not long after, another message came for him. This one, in effect, said simply "stay there."

Critchfield's report had been read and his recommendation approved at the highest levels of government, and now he was asked to remain in Germany and carry it out. He was to take over American control of the Organization with the specific task of finding out exactly what it was doing and where, whom it was using, and was to make a recommendation about what CIA should do with it. He was given two years to complete his study.

In the months between December, 1948 and CIA's formal takeover of the Organization on July 1, 1949, months during which Philp is said to have fought a rear-guard action to have the decision reversed, Critchfield began gathering his staff. He reached out for people he knew had had intelligence experience in Germany and Austria, several of them OSS veterans, all German-speaking.[6, 7]

Eric Waldman was caught in the transition of the Organization from the Army to CIA. There were those in both Intelligence organizations, some from the "They're a Bunch of Nazis" camp, some less antagonistic, who believed the Army had been far too lax in its administration of the Gehlen group. Pointing out that since Gehlen had been brought back to Germany in 1946 there had been only one American officer with intelligence training assigned to the group, Waldman, and that he was Austrian by birth, they suggested he might have lost his objectivity. Since the Army was no longer in charge of the Organization, Waldman had no choice but to leave Pullach, although there was the possibility of his returning as a CIA officer. When he understood the nature of the controversy surrounding him, however, he picked up the scholarly ambitions he had put aside when he joined the Army, left active service, and accepted a post in the Department of Political Science at Marquette University.[8]

In July 1949 Critchfield officially took over as chief of the Pullach base, although he and the CIA group remained under military cover. Critchfield returned to military status as a Colonel of Armor, and to all outward appearances had simply replaced Philp as commanding officer of the military unit. He and the seven other CIA officers, who had been relegated to a chilly hut in what was referred to as the compound's Siberia, eventually moved uptown to the Bormann mansion.

There the business of establishing new ground rules began. That meant long, thorough and detailed discussions with Gehlen. Legend has it that these discussions in fact were flaming rows, but it is a characterization that does not fit the personality of either man. Although both were strong and determined, they were also low-key and soft-spoken. Large areas of disagreement lay between them and both knew they had no choice but to bridge those differences. But each recognized that if they did indeed share a common goal they would have to work closely and at least reasonably comfortably together to achieve it. Although for months each meeting between Critchfield and Gehlen was a tug of war, it would be misleading to say the relationship was confrontational; it was more subtle than that.

Authority and money were the most pressing matters on that early agenda—volatile issues which had their roots in such fundamental questions as responsibility, trust, and nationalism. There was no disagreement on what for Gehlen was the most critical point. The Organization ultimately would become German. Allen Dulles, Richard Helms, Gordon Stewart, those at CIA most intimately involved with the decision to take Gehlen on, all understood that in the fullness of time his Organization would become a part of a new German government. But that was in time to come, and it was clear Gehlen did not fully appreciate that regardless of what might lie in the future, right now it was Critchfield and the Americans, not Gehlen and the Germans, who were in charge.

Much later Gehlen would declare haughtily: "My admiration for the individuals on that early CIA liaison staff is boundless: they recognized that their own parent organization was considerably younger than ours, and clearly regarded their job as being to learn as much from us as they could."[9] This interesting perspective on the relationship left former members of that CIA liaison staff bemused. CIA, in fact, had turned the Organization down once, and they finally took it on, on a trial basis, because of Critchfield's argument that it was the lesser of two evils. As for learning from them, one member of the original staff observed: "It would have been more accurate to say we clearly regarded our job as being to learn as much *about* them as we could."

Few questions had been asked about the details of this by now sprawling organization while it was run by the Army; now Critchfield wanted a complete accounting, including full, specific information about operations and sources. Gehlen balked. It was a matter of trust, he protested. The CIA should have faith in him and trust him not to do anything that was not in the interest of the Western alliance. Critchfield replied that if Gehlen meant what he said there was no reason for him *not* to reveal everything. Trust must run two ways.

The arguments, muted in tone and style, ranged from the practical to the philosophical. The CIA was responsible to Congress and the White House, and therefore was obliged to present detailed information on its operations, Critchfield said. To release details of sources and operations would be irresponsible behavior on the part of a chief of Intelligence, Gehlen countered. And always the argument returned to the same point: whatever had gone before, now Germany and the United States were ploughing the rough seas of the postwar era in the same hastily-built craft and they, together with the Western allies, must pull together if they were to outstrip the Soviets.

"First and last," Critchfield says, "Gehlen was a political animal. He had a broad vision of a unified Europe linked with the United States and strong enough to resist the Soviet threat." That there would be a sovereign German state sooner rather than later Gehlen had no doubt, and he meant to play an influential part in it, regardless of the party in power. So it was with those large aims in mind that he and Critchfield, always avoiding confrontation, engaged in their subtle maneuvering for control of the Organization. Before long, Gehlen, if all went according to his plan, would be in a position to present to the new government a large, functioning *German* Intelligence service, with him at its head—and there was the crux of the problem.

For Gehlen, an alliance with the United States, even accepting aid from the United States was one thing; but being a creature of the Americans—the victors and the occupiers—was another. He always wanted to be able to say he had withheld many things from Critchfield and the Americans; he needed a political image he could live with. As far as the Organization was concerned, he needed to promote the concept that the American relationship with it was a trusteeship arrangement, that the United States was holding it in trust for the German government to come.

"We were candid with each other; we understood each other; we developed mutual respect;" Critchfield emphasizes, but that did not mean there was mutual trust. "There was no simple face value acceptance on either side, and for us there was an element of 'Can you really trust the Germans?,' but we shared a commonality of interest that was broad," Critchfield says. "Common interests diverge when national purposes diverge, but at this point our goal was the same. What we had, essentially, was an agreement to exploit each other, each in his own national interest."

There was no single agreement hammered out between Gehlen and the CIA. As Critchfield describes it, it developed out of many understandings, not unlike common law. "Our personal relationship and that between our organizations was a living thing," Critchfield says. "There were a number of interlocking contracts made, but they weren't worth anything if they weren't honored. So it came back to a matter of trust—it was everything, but it was nothing."

The negotiations continued in long sessions between Gehlen and Critchfield, attended by Heinz Danko Herre, who was Gehlen's right hand and who, Critchfield says, "acted as marriage counselor, rushing between us for years."[10] Agreement was reached that in exchange for its support CIA had certain, but not all, rights. CIA would supply the requirements; the Organization would run the operations. A CIA officer would be assigned to the German agent running a department, and CIA would get all reports—which went to a combined German/American reporting center—and all evaluations. The sticking point, however, remained: Critchfield continued to insist on being given the names of the Organization agents, and Gehlen continued to refuse.

Since false identities, listed by number and pseudonym, were given to all members of the Organization, unless Gehlen chose to tell him, Critchfield had no direct means of discovering the real names of those who worked for him. This was a matter of critical importance to the CIA which, among other things, was concerned that the Organization might be harboring both Nazis and Communists. Since Gehlen would not furnish them with the names of his prospective recruits, or his agents, no check could be made by the Americans.

The issue was of such significance that by the time Gehlen reluctantly agreed to make a gesture toward cooperation and turn over the names of his top 150 officers, the small CIA liaison staff had taken matters into its own hands. Finding itself in the bizarre position of having to spy on the Organization of which it was the sole support, the CIA broke out the tools of its trade. By combining the power of the purse with an appreciation of the orderliness of the German mentality, insisting that all projects be discussed with them before they were initiated, and fostering personal ties with their opposite numbers, the Americans gradually winkled out the secrets of what the Organization was up to and who Gehlen had working for him.

Using an intricate system of checks and cross-checks—travel authorization requests, expense reports, operational assignments, and so on—the CIA began to build up a German personnel dossier. And the Germans didn't like it. "[The Americans]," Klaus Ritter, one of Gehlen's field office directors complained, "are insisting on more and more information on what we are doing, in more and more detail, down to the very lowest levels . . ."[11] The CIA's security concerns—possible Soviet penetration and, to a far lesser extent, the presence in the Organization of Nazis—were approached as two separate and distinct problems. A link between the arch-anti-communist Nazis and Soviet espionage was not considered.[12]

Critchfield maintains that Gehlen's use of Nazis was never a serious problem. "When we got the facts there weren't more than four or five names that troubled us. I discussed it with Gehlen and it wasn't a big issue." Events, however, proved him wrong. Although their numbers were not large, the problem presented by the Nazis in the Organization was real and serious, and would have far-reaching consequences. As would Gehlen's whole approach to security.

In part the failures in security resulted from intellectual arrogance. Unlike members of any other intelligence organization, Gehlen and his staff were so confident of their ability to evaluate the information that came in that they were convinced they would have no difficulty spotting false or planted material. It was an attitude that courted disaster. Although there was a heavy General Staff presence, Gehlen now was not dealing with the Army but with an odd gang of assorted types many of whom, at the end of the chain, had only the sketchiest bona fides. He gave sensitive positions to East German refugees,[13] relied on poor screening techniques, and refused to use a polygraph.

Basically Gehlen relied on the Old Boy network of the General Staff, officers he knew, who were leaders and free of the worst stigma of Nazism. But in recruiting for the Organization these former officers used their friends who in turn used theirs, forming a chain which became increasingly weak as each new link was added. It was inevitable that as the Organization's activities expanded, former members of the SD would be recruited.

Former Nazis, said one member of that early CIA liaison team, were the skeleton in Gehlen's closet. The Nazi question, however, became much more than a personal embarrassment for him, or even indirectly for American Intelligence. By the time it became apparent at a later date that the Old Boys of the Nazi network within the Organization were the same unscrupulous lot that they had been under Hitler, irreparable damage had been done. But in the meantime a familiar argument was used: sometimes the ends justify the means—or do if those ends are achieved.[14]

A Joint CIA-Organization Operation

When the end was an opportunity to get priceless information about the new Soviet cipher system, CIA was not terribly finicky about the means it was prepared to use to achieve it. Not even an Otto von Bolschwing.

Von Bolschwing, a tall, patrician-looking descendant of an aristocratic Prussian family, had taken up with bad company during the Nazi era. In the mid-1930s he was an advisor to Adolf Eichmann, administrator of the Final Solution, and then became chief of the SD for Romania. There he was in liaison with the virulently anti-Semitic Iron Guard. He was such a partisan supporter that he aided the Iron Guard's abortive attempt to overthrow the Romanian government of Marshal Ion Antonescu.

That effort earned for the Iron Guardists a lasting place in the history of anti-Semitic atrocities. During the pogrom which accompanied the coup attempt, synagogues, houses and stores were destroyed; more than six hundred Jews were slaughtered—some literally butchered; and four hundred more were never seen again. Antonescu was able to put down the revolt, but its repercussions, although dangerous for von Bolschwing at the time, helped him on the way to a bright new life after the war.

The failed Iron Guard coup was viewed by the Nazis as an action designed to undercut Hitler, and as a result von Bolschwing was brought to Berlin, thrown in prison by the Gestapo, and not released until 1943. He also had taken as his second wife a woman who was part Jewish, an act he, of all people, must have known could only lead to trouble with the Nazis, and by February 1945 he had been expelled from the SS. With these credentials, within a few months of war's end von Bolschwing was working for United States Intelligence, and in 1950 he told them he had a source with information on a new Soviet cipher.

During the war, the fragmentary remains of a partially burned Russian code book had been recovered in Finland.[15] Using it, American cryptanalysts mounted a major effort to crack the Soviet code. The Armed Forces Security Agency, later the National Security Agency (NSA), collected—as it still does—all Soviet communications traffic, and with endlessly painstaking work progress was made, but it was slow. Finally, in 1947 there was a shocking breakthrough which not only provided additional incentive, if any was needed, but also a new source against which to check what had already been pieced together. The cryptanalysts had deciphered the text of a cable from Prime Minister Churchill to President Truman. The Russians had a spy so strategically placed, apparently in the British Embassy in Washington, that he was able to obtain the complete text of a private message between the two world leaders and forward it to Moscow.

Checking through copies of communications handled by the British

Embassy, the code-breakers acquired more pieces to the puzzle of the cipher, and along the way found conclusive proof that there had been massive hemorrhaging of ultrasensitive material to the Soviet Union from both the British Embassy in Washington and the Manhattan Project in Los Alamos.

The legacy of the Soviet cipher system was a rich one. Breaking it led to the uncovering of the spies Klaus Fuchs and Donald Maclean, and pointed to Guy Burgess and Harold "Kim" Philby. In one of the most notorious of the ironies with which the field of espionage is replete, the British Intelligence officer assigned to work with the Americans on tracking down the spies whose cover names appeared in the Russian messages was that same Philby. Whether he had manipulated the assignment or whether it was his by chance, the result was that the Soviets were able to follow every move the FBI made in uncovering their network. And Philby was able to gauge just how well they were reading the signs pointing to him.

In 1948 the Soviets, having been tipped off by William Weisband, an American informant in the Armed Forces Communications Agency, that their cipher had been broken, abruptly changed their whole system, leaving the Americans once again faced with an impenetrable code. By 1950, the CIA's mouth was watering for any information about Soviet ciphers, so in the spring of that year, when word of a possible lead came into Pullach from an Austrian subunit of the Organization run by Otto von Bolschwing, the CIA bit hard. Gehlen was operating in Austria with people who were semi-independent, and over whom he exercised the kind of loose operational control that created security hazards and invited exploitation of various kinds. One of those who found it served his own purposes to contact the Americans directly was von Bolschwing. His group in Austria submitted reports on its operations to the Americans in Salzburg, and when one dealing with Soviet ciphers arrived, the CIA intended to pursue it alone.

This is what happened. Count Friedrich Coloredo-Wels, an impecunious bon vivant of illegitimate birth, whose charm at the age of sixty-five still won the favors of any number of well connected and well-to-do ladies, said he had been approached by a Russian officer who had put forward an interesting proposition. The Count, who lived in the Soviet sector of Vienna, had made friends with a number of Russian officers, and was a frequent visitor to Soviet headquarters in the Imperial Hotel on the Ringstrasse. One of those officers at the Imperial, Major Ivan Galkin, the Count said, had asked his help in contacting the Americans.

Galkin claimed he wanted to defect and offered to make a deal. In exchange for safe passage to the United States and $25,000 (it is unclear whether he or the CIA set the figure), he would "borrow" some new Soviet cryptographic equipment from the cipher office at the Imperial and "lend" it to the Americans for a few hours—long enough for them to examine it. The equipment consisted of a machine, about the size of an electric typewriter, and a book roughly the size of a mid-sized city telephone directory. The Count, who may well have known von Bolschwing personally and in any case was aware of his connection with the Gehlen Organization and American Intelligence, passed this offer on to him.

The Americans' first concern was whether the proposition was legitimate or a Soviet trick. Vienna in those days was second only to Berlin as the world center for espionage, and with that distinction came another even more dubious. So frequently did intelligence operations in Vienna erupt in violence that it was dubbed "the shooting gallery." Nonetheless, even if the offer relayed by von Bolschwing was a trap, the bait was so enticing it could not be ignored. A report on the overture was sent by pouch to CIA headquarters in Washington, which fired back an urgent reply: no effort was to be spared or time lost in following this lead.

A member of the Pullach liaison team, who was fluent in German and was in touch with the CIA liaison officer in Bad Reichenhall who received reports from von Bolschwing's group, took charge of the operation. He had an initial meeting with Count Coloredo-Wels at which plans were made to meet over dinner in Munich to map out a course of action. By the end of dinner, at which Peer de Silva was present, skepticism had replaced the Americans' enthusiasm. Not only were there too few hard facts, the debonair Count was looking more and more like a slippery customer. The next day a cable was sent off to Washington recommending contact with the Count be broken and the whole project shelved. Headquarters sent back a heated reply pointing out the overriding importance of obtaining information on the Soviet cipher system and ordering them to pursue this lead to the limit.

The Count, it was clear, was willing to spin the negotiations out, but the Americans wanted the situation brought to an immediate head. The Count was told to inform Major Galkin that his terms would be met. He would be brought to the United States, and they had $25,000 in cash ready for him. As soon as the Count reported that the Russian had named a date and a place, a small Austrian village on the edge of the Soviet zone, Grieskirchen, and a time—they would have no more than three to four hours—the Americans got to work.

They set up a safe house across the railroad tracks which separated the American from the Soviet zone and procured the most sophisticated photographic equipment. A Navy man, who was an electronics expert from the National Security Agency, had a state-of-the-art tool kit with which he could dismantle and reassemble anything, and he was prepared to do just that while the machine's parts were also being photographed. When everything was ready, the waiting began. The mechanical wizard fiddled with his exotic tools; slight adjustments were made to cameras and lights; and feelings of pent-up anticipation reached their peak. Then the mood gradually started to deflate as the minutes and then the hours told them as certainly as the spoken word that no one was coming.

The operation had been a bust, and the Americans on the spot were prepared to write it off. Washington, however, was not ready to let the matter drop. The description of the apparatus sounded authentic, and where there was smoke perhaps there really was fire. The key was Count Coloredo-Wels: what exactly did he know? So, when the Count agreed to come to Munich from Vienna, Washington sent out what was called the Pelican Team to interrogate him.

Led by a doctor whom de Silva describes as being the next thing to a quack, this team used a combination of sodium pentathol and hypnosis as a means of getting the truth out of a subject. But all it got out of the Count was the contents of his stomach—the drug made him violently ill. Disgusted by the Pelican approach, de Silva brought in a polygraph operator who hooked the Count up to his machine and ran him twice through the same series of questions. The verdict was, "This guy's lying like a rug." He knew nothing about Soviet ciphers, and he had no contact with anyone who did know anything about Soviet ciphers. Furthermore, he had been an informant for the Soviets.

Faced with the polygraph results, the Count admitted it had all been a fraud, an attempt to supplement his uncertain income as an aging gigolo. Warning him that if he made any further attempt to contact any Allied Intelligence service the Americans would see to it the Russians were informed that he was in reality working for the United States, they gave him train fare back to Vienna and sent him on his way.

In this episode of the Cold War von Bolschwing had a peripheral role. The key player was the enterprising and, by the standards of the profession at the time, only moderately unscrupulous free-lancer,

Count Coloredo-Wels. But the larger issue is the use and therefore the protection of a man like von Bolschwing who, in this instance, had been co-opted from the Gehlen Organization. Suppose the outcome had been different? Suppose von Bolschwing's contact with the Count had led to the all-important breaking of the Soviet code? Do you treat with demons in fighting the Devil?

Apologists for the practice of using people like von Bolschwing claim that the Americans looked only at his documented anti-Nazi activity, his imprisonment and his expulsion from the SS, suggesting American Intelligence may not even have been aware of his association with Eichmann or the Iron Guards. Knowledgeable CIA officers, however, do not deny that with the files that had been accumulated it is altogether unlikely United States Intelligence was not in possession of all the facts and, for what it is worth, von Bolschwing himself says they knew his history.

"This post-facto business of criticizing government because it employs people whose characters are not admirable is sheer hypocrisy," says Ray Cline, former Deputy Director of Plans at CIA. "You don't seek these people out, you seek out avenues to vital pieces of data, and in many cases, whether you're dealing with the Mafia, the drug trade or Soviet intentions you are going to find your best access to what you need to know among the crooked, the cranks, the disaffected, the criminals. You can't allow yourself to say 'I won't get a piece of information vital to the country because I don't like the guy.' American Intelligence has no predilection for people like this, but it does have a vital interest in the national security."

Another former Intelligence officer sees it differently. "If you are going after the Mafia you get a Mafia guy to come over to your side. To name names, inform on his bosses and testify in court against them. It's the same with any criminal organization from Murder Incorporated to a drug ring. That's what the Federal Witness Protection Program is for, that's the informer's payoff; immunity, a new name and a new life. That's what we do with Soviet defectors, too. If we're lucky enough to get some high-level KGB officer we're not going to turn him away because he was involved in some expensive operations against us. He has too much vital information that affects our current national security.

"But a Nazi war criminal is a different story, unless he's informing on other Nazi war criminals or has some specific highly valuable information only he and no one else can provide. Then all right, you use him just for that. But you don't just put him on the payroll and hope he'll turn out to be useful. There's a line you have to draw."[16]

Tug of War Within the CIA

Although the Gehlen Organization had the approval of those at the top—General Bedell Smith, Allen Dulles, President Eisenhower— there was no unanimity within the CIA about supporting it. Indeed bitter, deeply ideological debates raged for many years, disputes encompassing such issues as German anti-Semitism and an historical commitment to the Weimar Republic. But there was also a group of purists in the Agency who prided themselves on their high standards of tradecraft. For them the role of the professional was everything. They made a fetish of defining and redefining and codifying the purist doctrine of international espionage. This group had close sympathies with the British, with MI-6, was an Old Boys' club in its own right, and was critical of what it saw as the Gehlen Organization's lack of professionalism. So, although the opposition within the Agency tended to originate with those who had come out of OSS and fancied themselves the true professionals, the reasons for it varied.

In the early 1950s this anti-Gehlen sentiment within the CIA was galvanized when the Defense Department, on the basis of information received from Army sources, began to voice its own grave concerns. The result was the formation of a commission which conducted a major investigation of the Organization's activities. By this time the positions were polarized. There were those in CIA who believed the whole investigation was directed at discrediting the Agency's work in Germany. Critchfield gathered all his evidence, which included extensive material from the Army files, and presented a picture of mismanagement under the Army which so shocked the commission members that the investigation was hastily broken off.

Proponents of continued support for the Organization, like Critchfield, took a pragmatic view which went beyond intelligence in its purest sense. Critchfield is the first to admit that Gehlen, in his words, "wasn't interested in tradecraft. He didn't give a damn about intelligence operations per se." Although espionage and counterespionage were his business, Gehlen also saw the Organization as a vehicle toward political ends. He had woven politics throughout the fabric of the Organization, and if he was using it as a vehicle then there were those in the CIA, Critchfield among them, who wanted some control over the direction it was taking. When responsibility passed from the Army to the CIA, Critchfield found that a newsletter, "Orientierung" (orientation or information), composed by a group of former General Staff officers, was being disseminated among the German staff. Concerned that the content was slanted and unsure of Gehlen's real motivation—a resurgence of German nationalism was not something to be encouraged—Critchfield put an end to it.

But Gehlen's concern and support for the senior General Staff members he had rescued was unflagging. He had foreseen that Germany would have its own army eventually, and as it turned out it was to be sooner rather than later. The outbreak of the Korean war in June 1950 meant the United States would reduce the size of its armed forces in Europe in order to concentrate them in the Far East. The significance of that did not escape the military men at Pullach. It was under Gehlen's auspices that a meeting was held that year at which the conditions were set for German rearmament. At a hunting lodge north of Frankfurt, General Halder, former Chief of Staff of the Army, addressed a group of his former colleagues and laid out the terms. Among other things, they would insist that the Germans be treated as equals in NATO, which had been formed in 1949, and that they were to serve in German units, not be used a cannon-fodder in another nation's army.

CIA's ties to the Organization allowed the Americans broad access to, and a measure of influence over, the plans of Germany's future leaders. A decade later Karl Carstens, State Secretary of the German Chancellery in the 1960s, would say: "There was . . . established in the early days a partnership with the Western secret services which was not without influence upon the subsequent political and military co-operation between the Federal Republic of Germany and its allies."[17]

The military men Gehlen had "saved for Germany" were also his political front line, the bridge-builders between then and now, and he quickly organized those possessing the best credentials in terms of German society into the Special Connections Unit, number 35. With General Horst von Mellenthin at their head, they did a vast, detailed study of all aspects of the emerging postwar German society, and then targeted those individuals who they believed would be among the most influential in government and industry. Members of the unit then made contact with them in order to establish a personal relationship. It was natural that von Mellenthin and his people should make these contacts; they were experienced at operating at the highest political and social levels, so it was easy and acceptable for them to forge these new relationships.

Military occupation of Germany ended in 1949 and was replaced by the Allied High Commission. Although not yet a sovereign state, West Germany was permitted to hold free national elections for a Federal Parliament, and Konrad Adenauer formed its first postwar government on September 12. Gehlen's campaign to develop "special connections" was mounted early and carried out with such efficiency and thoroughness that Gehlen was able to do what he did in 1950. On September 20 he met Adenauer for the first time and came to an understanding with him. Twenty-four hours later he had another cordial meeting, this time with Dr. Kurt Schumacher the head of the party opposing Adenauer, the Social Democrats (the SPD). "Gehlen," Critchfield says, "was a consummate political operator." But for the purists in the Agency the real question was not what contributions his Organization had made in the past or its political potential, but, What kind of an Intelligence professional is he?

Questions of ideology and professionalism were not the only nor the most important issues creating divisions within the CIA. The Gehlen Organization was caught in the struggle between two armies of the Agency's Clandestine Service: the Office of Special Operations (OSO), charged with intelligence gathering; and the Office of Policy Coordination (OPC) which ran covert operations.

Frank Wisner, a Southerner given to orotund phrases, was named chief of OPC in the summer of 1948. He was a lawyer by training, but it was his experience as OSS chief in Romania during the war which shaped the rest of his life. When the fighting was over Wisner returned to the New York City law firm of Carter, Ledyard and Milburn, but by early November of 1947, shortly after the establishment of CIA, he was back in Washington as Deputy Assistant Secretary of State for Occupied Areas. Ten months later he was handed the leadership of what turned out to be a hornet's nest, the three-month old OPC.

On June 18, 1948, National Security Council Intelligence Directive NSC 10/2 had given birth to the covert action arm of the CIA's Clandestine Service, OPC. It was intended to be a team of skillful covert political operators standing in the wings ready to act if called upon. But this generally cautious approach was soon confounded by the appointment of Frank Wisner, who brought the untried OPC out of the gate like a rodeo rider.

From the start the OPC fit awkwardly into the Intelligence structure. Its control was not given to the Director of CIA but to a special State and Defense Department panel. The Director of Central Intelligence was not even in the direct chain of command. Frank Wisner had been appointed by the Secretary of State.[18] This gingerly handling of the OPC reflects the anxiety with which the sanctioning of peacetime covert political activities was viewed by the National Security Council. It did not take much imagination to see where establishment of such a group might lead.

In 1975, Ambassador George Kennan expressed the view prevalent in the late 1940s. "We were alarmed at the inroads of the Russian influence in Western Europe beyond the point where the Russian troops had reached," he said, and of particular concern were Italy and France. In the wake of the Communist coup in Czechoslovakia in February 1948, the CIA mounted a successful campaign in Italy which led to the defeat of the Communists and put the Christian Democrats in office. It was a turning point for the future of Europe and won credibility and support for such action.

It was a time when there was a boom in operations. "The Berlin blockade made many officials in Washington hit the panic button," says Harry Rositzke, then CIA station chief in Munich. "Everyone thought the Soviets were plotting war and that we had to have an early warning of their plans if we were to survive. The advent of the Korean war was, at first, believed to be a diversion so the Soviets could take the rest of Europe. It was conspiracy-time in Washington and the CIA took the brunt of it [sic]." At one Pentagon meeting an Army colonel demanded that CIA "put an agent with a radio on every airfield between Berlin and the Urals," Rositzke continues. "I agreed that we needed agents equipped with radios in various locations inside the Soviet Union if we were going to get any early warning of a Soviet attack on western Europe, but how to get our agents there? That was the hard question."[19]

Sending in spies by parachute was CIA's answer, but early warning of an attack was not the only goal. Late in 1949, after the Soviets had tested their first atomic bomb, OPC began pushing a "liberation policy" based on the conviction that, with active American help, anti-communist revolutions would occur behind the Iron Curtain. Relations were established with partisan groups—with emigrés from the Ukraine, Poland, the Baltic States, Yugoslavia, Albania and elsewhere—and it is reasonable to assume that wartime contacts in Romania proved useful. Remnants of the criminal, but unequivocally anti-Soviet Iron Guard were likely targets for recruitment.

"All of us were engaging in this quite tricky business of infiltration at this time," says former senior CIA officer Howard Roman. "There were, for instance, the very complicated air drops into Russia itself. It was a terribly hard thing to do logistically and technically, and it caused us no end of headaches. You had to have airplanes, you had to have guys who were willing to do it. They might turn out to be Russian agents—they usually did."[20] Furthermore, any genuine ones were not on a level of Soviet society to be of any value: "The ordinary Russian isn't privy to what is said in the councils of State," Richard Bissel, a senior CIA officer said. "He doesn't know the design of a war head on an intercontinental ballistic missile. He doesn't know if there's an air base a hundred miles down the road."[21]

Given the circumstances, it would have been surprising if OPC had not wanted to appropriate and exploit Gehlen's Organization, which by this time was spread out across Europe. But it was the other branch of the Agency's Clandestine Service, the Office of Special Operations (OSO), which had responsibility for Gehlen. Richard Helms, who in 1946 had been in charge of OSO's Foreign Division M responsible for Germany, Austria and Switzerland (and who later would become Director of Central Intelligence), was chief of OSO and Pullach was one of his Special Operations bases.

Both OPC and OSO were clandestine services, but beyond that they had little in common. OSO's mission was intelligence collection, the gathering of information by clandestine means; OPC's was active political intervention, covert action directed at influencing the internal affairs of foreign nations. In purpose as in style, the two were poles apart, but since they were operating on the same ground there was competition for resources and personnel, and with that came an increased danger to security.

The tense, suspicious relations between OSO and OPC grew out of the generic difference between espionage and covert action. Behind it all, however, was the old distrust of the OSS from whose veteran ranks most of the OPC officers were drawn. The OSO was doubtful of both the judgment and loyalty of OPC members, whom they suspected of dangerously left wing political leanings.[22] But the OPC was riding high and was engaged in rampant empire building. Testimony to the success of that effort is the fact that the number of officers in OPC grew from 302 in 1949 to 6,000 in 1952.

For years it has been asserted that OPC took over the Organization and used elements of it in its covert operations; that Gehlen agents were part of OPC's "private army." So prevalent has this notion become that some veterans of the CIA's liaison operations with the

German government, including at least one officer who spent many years at Pullach and later devoted considerable time to a study of Soviet disinformation, believe it was deliberately planted by the Soviets to discredit Gehlen and the CIA. Eric Waldman also denies this allegation. He states that he had no contact with any member of OPC, and would have been aware of any overtures to the Organization from that quarter.[23]

There is no framework of substance on which to build the argument that the Organization became part of OPC and its operations. Nor is it a move which would have been in Gehlen's own long-term interest, since doing OPC's political work would have fatally compromised his Organization's carefully nurtured intelligence-gathering function. That was the vehicle which would carry him into a position of influence in the new German government, and Gehlen had demonstrated that he was a master at planning for the future.[24]

That does not rule out the possibility that some Organization members moonlighted for OPC. Recently released Army CIC documents confirm that some Gehlen agents, including a few in positions of responsibility, were for sale. One was Ludwig Albert, a former Gestapo member. He sold Organization secrets to two Intelligence services, the American CIC and the East German State Security Services (SSD). Others sold them directly to the Soviet KGB. Some Gehlen operatives did free-lance for other interests, but such transactions, among individual entrepreneurs, obviously do not reflect a policy of official Organization cooperation.[25] It was Richard Helms' OSO, not OPC, which, on Critchfield's advice, took control of the Gehlen Organization—and its clandestine activities were limited to intelligence collection and did not include covert political intervention.[26]

As East-West tensions mounted, the disputes swirling around the Organization, intense as they were, did not seriously threaten its continued support by the CIA. The Americans needed every possible source of information about activities in the East as they became increasingly engaged in the Cold War, which by 1952 had the world at the brink of World War III.

Chapter Seven

The Cold War

The Bitter Chill: Ambassador George Kennan

A dramatic demonstration of the depths to which Soviet-American relations had sunk by spring of 1952 can be seen in an incident which began in London on the afternoon of June 26. Peer de Silva, who had been Critchfield's deputy in Pullach, walked into Claridges to meet the newly appointed American ambassador to the Soviet Union, George Kennan. His mission was to convince Kennan to overrule the State Department's repeated refusals to allow CIA to place an officer of the Clandestine Services on the embassy staff in Moscow. After a long discussion, Ambassador Kennan rejected the CIA's request, and this, says de Silva, "was a great disappointment to me. However," he goes on, "during the conversation I had noticed that the Ambassador was very tense and nervous. He was pale, his hands trembled, and he seemed to have much on his mind. At the end of our talk, he said there was something he wanted to ask of the agency." De Silva and the Ambassador were alone in the hotel's writing room, and Kennan paced slowly up and down as he explained what was on his mind.

"There is something you must do for me," de Silva quotes the ambassador as saying. "I have here a letter [addressed to Pope Pius]. I have a very pessimistic view of our immediate future with the Soviets, particularly at the diplomatic level. I want you to get this letter to Allen Dulles and make sure it is passed, by secure means, to the Pope in Rome. I fear," Kennan continued, "that there is a good possibility that I will wind up someday before long on the Soviet radio. I may be forced to make statements that would be damaging to American policy. This letter will show the world that I am under duress and am not making statements under my own free will. The letter to the Pope will let him make public my position and the true situation there."

Surprised as de Silva was by what Kennan had said, he was wholly taken aback when the Ambassador went on: "I understand that CIA has some form of pill that a person could use to kill himself instantly. Is that right?" Realizing Kennan was in earnest, de Silva confirmed that CIA did have what it called "L-pills," L meaning "lethal." Small wire-mesh covered glass vials containing cyanide, they could be put in the mouth; death would occur within seconds of being crushed. The Ambassador then asked if arrangements could be made to send him two L-pills by diplomatic pouch, and de Silva said he would relay the request to Dulles when he reached Washington the next day.

When de Silva handed over to Allen Dulles the Ambassador's letter addressed to the Pope and repeated the conversation of the day before, "there was a long silence in the director's office . . . Obviously this was a shock to those present, but it was agreed that these things could not be denied him. I was authorized to get the necessary items and pouch them to Moscow." All this took place in June of 1952. In September, Ambassador Kennan, who together with his family had been subjected to barely veiled hostility and lived in enforced isolation from the Russian people, discovered that his study in Spaso House, the Ambassador's Residence, was bugged—at that time an unprecedented violation of international conduct. This discovery, which Kennan describes as unfolding like a "strange and sinister drama," took place the night before he was to leave Moscow for a conference in England. His description of the atmosphere at Spaso House that next morning conveys in a few sentences the terrible weight of what he calls the "psychically impregnated" air of Russia in which he lived during that "difficult and nerve-wracking summer."

"The atmosphere of Spaso House was heavy with tension. I had thought it best to close and lock, temporarily, the room where the [listening] device had been found. The Soviet servants, their highly trained antennae positively humming with vibrations, sensed serious trouble, and cast terrified glances in the direction of the locked door, as they passed along the corridor, as though they suspected the place to contain a murdered corpse. The faces of the guards at the gate were frozen into a new grimness. So dense was the atmosphere of anger and hostility that one could have cut it with a knife.''

Against this backdrop, the Ambassador met reporters later in the day at Berlin's Tempelhof Airport on his way to England. It was an encounter which would so infuriate the Soviets that they would see to it he would not set foot in Russia again.

"The reporters were indeed there, at the airport," Kennan recalls. "They asked the expected questions. I reeled off the prepared answers. But then one young reporter . . . asked me whether we in our embassy had many social contacts with the Russians in Moscow. The question itself annoyed me. Had the man been born yesterday? . . .

" 'Don't you know,' I asked, 'how foreign diplomats live in Moscow?'

" 'No,' he replied. 'How do they?'

"I should of course have let it go at that. But there welled up in me, at that point, the whole dismal experience of the past four months, ending with the experience of seeing my little boy's playmates chased away from him, lest they be contaminated by his proximity. Being again in Germany, I was reminded at that moment of the five months I had spent in internment as a prisoner of the Germans, in 1941–1942 . . . There, too, we had been, officially, 'the enemy.'

" 'Well,' I said, 'I was interned here in Germany for several months during the last war. The treatment we receive in Moscow is just about like the treatment we internees received then, except that in Moscow we are at liberty to go out and walk the streets under guard.' ''

The press conference in Berlin took place on September 19 1952. On October 3 the Soviet Foreign Office presented to the American chargé d'affaires a note which, in effect, called Ambassador Kennan a liar, demanded his immediate recall from the Soviet Union, and labelled him *persona non grata*.[1]

After Ambassador Kennan's return to the United States, de Silva paid him a visit, in the course of which he asked what had happened to the L-pills. "He told me, with a curious smile—an obviously much more relieved and composed man than when I had last seen him—'I have already flushed them down the toilet.'

"At the time and in the years since," de Silva concludes, "I have always thought that the actions of Ambassador Kennan were the actions of a very brave man. During the early 1950s the CIA was aware that the Soviets were experimenting with drugs intended to destroy a person's natural inhibitions and controls. The topic was frequently discussed in the agency and in the State Department. In the cold-war atmosphere of the time, Kennan saw himself as a likely target for a Soviet effort along this line. An extremely competent and knowledge-able scholar of the Soviets, he held no illusions concerning the kind of actions they might take if they felt their interests required it. Neverthe-less, he went back to that environment of danger and was prepared to take his own life rather than let himself be used by the Soviets in a manner degrading or shameful to the United States."[2]

Operation Hacke

The cold war raged in the United States as well, with the Americans inflicting far more wounds upon themselves than the Soviets, primarily through the investigations of Senator Joseph McCarthy. In the United States, the Nazis had been replaced by the Communists as the prime enemy, although Nazis still ran a close second. Nearer their home base in Europe, however, Nazis continued to make the most excellent copy. Rumors of the Gehlen Organization's existence, leadership, personnel and activities had been rife from its inception, but they had been only whispers, titillating gossip. As far as the public was concerned at least, the Organization's cover remained intact. Then, on March 17, 1952, the London Daily Express printed an explosive article by Sefton Delmer, dateline Bonn: "Hitler's General Now Spies For Dollars," ran the headline.

"Watch out for a name which is going to spell trouble with a capital T," Delmer begins. "It covers what in my view is some of the most dangerous political high explosive in Western Europe today. The name is spelt Gehlen and it is pronounced Gale-enn. Ten years ago this was the name of one of Hitler's ablest staff officers . . . Today Gehlen is the name of a secret organization of immense and ever-growing power . . . As he expanded, plenty of former Nazis, S.S. men and S.D. men (Himmler's Secret Service Organization) crept into his staff where they enjoyed full protec-tion. Today Gehlen is the head of an espionage organization which has agents in all parts of the world . . . The danger of the organization lies in the future. For Gehlen's network already today has become an immense underground power in Germany . . ."

Copies of the article flew among American Intelligence offices in Germany. The Office of the Coordinator and Special Advisor (Intelligence office) of the U.S. High Commission sent a copy to Army Counter Intelligence. The American liaison officer at the German Office for the Protection of the Constitution (BfV) had a copy, as did the 7714 Engineer Intelligence Group and, to quote one memorandum: "DAD," the cover name for CIA, "is already painfully aware of the publication of the article." Old friends were heard from, too. Walter Holters, who had been interrogated by John Boker in 1945, appears to have stayed in touch with American Intelligence because on March 31, 1952, he sent the following note from Essen:

"Dear Mr. Weittenmiller: By chance I read the annexed paper. Assuming that C.I.C. will take an interest in such irresponsible and dangerous press reports I send you this article. Gossips can cause much damage and should be fixed for good. Hoping that you enjoy the best of health I send you my kind regards."[3]

Holters was not alone in his anger at Sefton Delmer, his story struck many in American Intelligence more as the first salvo in an all-out attack on the Organization than a reporter's one-day press sensation. Delmer was a good friend of the controversial Otto John, President of the BfV (roughly the German equivalent of the American FBI), with whom Gehlen was enmeshed in a fierce rivalry. John's sensational "disappearance" to East Germany two years later, followed by his equally sensational public repudiation of the West, reinforced the conviction that in "exposing" Gehlen, Delmer had been acting as an instrument of the KGB. (Later, Otto John threw everyone's theories into confusion by reappearing in West Germany claiming to have been kidnapped and brainwashed—and proclaiming that his old friend Delmer had rescued him.[4]) In any event, regardless of the motive, a light had been thrown on the shadowy General Gehlen and his connection with the Americans.

Delmer's article also signaled the start of a Soviet-orchestrated East German assault on the Gehlen Organization which began shortly after the story's appearance. Dubbed Hacke, literally "hoe," the operation was designed to expose, discredit and destroy the Gehlen Organization while at the same time sowing discord between Germany and its allies. It was the culmination of careful preparation involving penetration of the Organization by East German agents. Among them was Henry Troll, the colorful author of detective stories, mysteries and tales of adventure. His books had been staples at lending libraries since long before the war.

Troll, whose real name was Hans Joachim Geyer, joined the Nazi party in 1928, and had done very nicely in his chosen calling, living with his wife and three children in Falkensee, a fashionable suburb of Berlin. But when the war ended he suffered a setback. Falkensee fell into the East Zone of Berlin and the new communist government evicted him and his family from their luxurious villa. He landed feet first, however, continuing his prodigious production and finding a generous West German firm to publish it.

His faithful readership was intact, and he was living in comfortable circumstances. But apparently there was something missing from his life. His most famous literary character was the detective John Kling, and perhaps Geyer, now in his middle years, wanted to live some of the thrills he experienced only in his imagination. Whatever the reason, in 1952 Geyer became a member of the Gehlen Organization with, and this must have pleased him, a real alias: Grell. He worked in East Berlin as an investigator for one of Gehlen's most active branches, 9592 in West Berlin. Then came the East German uprising of June 1953 and in its aftermath a tightening of security there. Overnight Geyer/Troll/Grell abandoned his family in Falkensee and fled to West Berlin, where he was given a desk job at Gehlen's West Berlin branch office.

This, it turned out, was unfortunate for the Organization since Geyer, either under threat or because he had found that being a simple spy did not fulfill whatever it was he was searching for, had become a double agent. As far as the Soviets were concerned, his position would have been hard to better: he had the trust of the head of the branch; as part of his job he read the reports of informers and agents; he was responsible for the security of the files; and, since he had a duplicate key, he had access to the strong room. Using his Minox camera, every night when the office was empty he photographed reams of sensitive material, including cipher keys and a list of the names of all sixty of the branch's informers in East Germany. Each morning a courier spirited what Geyer gave him over to the East Zone.

There is no telling how long this outpouring of Organization secrets might have gone on had Geyer not let his thriller-writer's imagination run away with him and lead him to try to add something extra to an utterly prosaic assignment. In the middle of October 1953, the head of the branch asked Geyer to take on the job of finding a new secretary for the office. Representing the firm as a large West German industrial corporation he put an advertisement in the paper. Thirty-four girls responded, of whom he decided to interview five. It was here that he got into trouble. Instead of setting up the appointments in an office rented for the occasion, Geyer, carried away with the moment and assuming his John Kling persona, arranged rendez-vous with the girls in a run-down café off the beaten track. His air of mystery, his reluctance to describe the work of his supposed firm, and his persistent questioning about her family and personal life led one applicant to the conclusion that he was recruiting for the white-slave trade. She immediately reported him to the police.

There had been a recent rash of such cases and the police took the girl's suspicions seriously. At ten o'clock on the morning of October 29, 1953, two officers from the vice squad rang the doorbell of Geyer's apartment and, when there was no answer, asked the landlady where he worked. She quite honestly told him she had no idea, which only deepened the mystery. When Geyer returned an hour or so later, she told her tenant "the police" had come by, and Geyer panicked. Convinced he had been discovered, he threw films and papers into a suitcase, locked the door of his apartment, jumped out the back window, and fled across the border to East Berlin.[5]

Within hours Gehlen agents were being rounded up all over East Germany; more than three hundred had been picked up by nightfall. Key people, including an editor of the important Berliner Zeitung, found themselves in custody. The next day their faces, as well as reproductions of some of the documents supplied by Geyer, were spread across the pages of the communist press, which gleefully reported that "the biggest American spy ring yet had been smashed."
On November 9, 1953, Geyer starred at a press conference whose real message, however, was delivered by Colonel Hans Bormann, a counterespionage officer of the East German Intelligence Service (SSD). His people, Bormann announced, were extremely well informed about the Gehlen Organization: they knew the names of Gehlen agents, their assignments and methods of communications; furthermore SSD informants supplied advance notice of specific Organization operations.

Gehlen, his staff, and the CIA liaison officers might have tried to comfort themselves by claiming that Bormann exaggerated. But four days later an operation which was a serious and sensitive one, even if it did sound like something out of Boys' Own Spy, was broken wide open and the agent in charge kidnapped by the SSD. As those at Pullach knew all too well, this was not an isolated incident.

On the night of November 13, 1953, just after Geyer's press conference, former Wehrmacht Major and reliable Gehlen agent Werner Haase went to an isolated spot on the Landwehr Canal which separates West from East Berlin. With him was a colleague, Heinze, and they were on a communications mission. With heavily reinforced security all along the border, passing messages by courier was riskier than ever, so Haase and Heinze were to lay a telephone cable across the canal. Waiting on the East Berlin side, ready to pull the cable onto the shore was another Gehlen agent, Beutel.

What took this operation out of the mainstream of espionage adventure and gave it a dusting of farce was the method by which this daring maneuver was to be accomplished. One end of the cable was to be attached to a small, motorized model boat which would make its way across the water to the waiting Beutel. Presumably the toy boat was intended in part to lend an air of legitimacy to Haase and Heinze if someone should stumble on them, although it would be interesting to know how these two grown men intended to explain playing with a toy boat on the edge of the canal in the middle of a late November night. As it happened there was no time for explanations. Tipped off in advance—some say by Beutel while others point the finger elsewhere—an SSD [East German] team had crossed the border, hidden in the bushes and overpowered Haase and Heinze as they launched their ill-fated operation and abducted them to the East Zone.[6] The East German authorities claimed Haase and Heinze had been caught red handed on the East side of the canal, charged them with espionage and brought them to trial.

Operation Hacke was having its effect, it would not be long before such tattered cover as remained would be stripped from the Organization. At the same time, a dangerous Nazi-Soviet connection within the Organization would come to light. It would be a doubly disturbing revelation because the means by which it was revealed raises serious questions about loyalty and responsibility among those charged with protecting American national security.

American Army Intelligence's Operation CAMPUS

At the end of the war the Americans' immediate preoccupation was to prevent a resurgence of Nazism, and there was some reason for concern. Pockets of fanaticism did exist. Small groups of conspirators were banding together, drawing up schemes to restore the Third Reich by bringing back Nazi leaders who had escaped from Germany to South America. Elsewhere attempts were being made to form *Feme* organizations, clandestine assassination squads in effect, to liquidate Germans who were collaborating with the Allies by identifying former members of the SS.[7]

But these were the acts of fringe groups. By any objective assessment Nazism was dead and these pockets of resurgence were merely the twitching of a corpse. Nonetheless, as responsibility for their own local affairs gradually was returned to the Germans, the Americans' sole test of a German's political health was a record free of the taint of Nazism. And what, they reasoned, proved that better than having been imprisoned in a Nazi concentration camp?

One group of Americans, however, viewed the question of political coloration from a different perspective. They were a small, bright band of Army Counter Intelligence Corps officers who remained in Germany after the war and who, working closely together, provided continuity in the work begun during the war. Led by Thomas Wesley Dale, a huge man from Mississippi with a command of two dozen languages, a brilliant mind, and an overpowering personality that earned him as much enmity as his intelligence won him respect, they were considered, by themselves and others, The Experts.[8]

Well-educated and skilled linguists, they were committed to the proposition that the war was only an interlude in the communist campaign of expansion. In a corps where a system of postings rotation brought into positions of authority a series of field officers with no background in intelligence, these strong-minded civilian professionals quickly became an elite, and left themselves open to charges of being arrogant, personally abrasive, dangerously independent and paranoid.[9]

They were not alone in doubting that the Germans as a people were psychologically suited for democracy, believing that they responded best and most comfortably to strong authoritarian and highly structured leadership. But as they saw it, the real danger was from the left rather than the right.

In the wake of the Russian Revolution, communists had done their best to get into positions of political influence everywhere. Throughout the 1920s and 1930s the Party worked aggressively to take over the world. In Germany their efforts collided with those of Hitler, who had the same idea, with the result that thousands of communists were interned by the Nazis. This tactic achieved its goal of removing the immediate Bolshevik threat, but at the same time it brought militant believers together in the concentration camps.

There they had ample time and opportunity to form committees and study-groups in which they drew up detailed plans for establishing communism in post-war Germany, and that meant infiltrating their people into government administrations at every level. As far as Tom Dale's group was concerned, the Americans were playing right into the communists' hands when being interned in a concentration camp—which housed common criminals as well as political enemies—was equated with political reliability. Although this approach put them at odds with the American authorities, Dale's team was not deterred. They simply went underground.

Dale's team secretly designed and directed a vast, sophisticated, clandestine and unsanctioned intelligence operation called CAMPUS. Aimed at the emerging German government, conceived and carried out without the knowledge, let alone the approval, of the authorities in Washington, CAMPUS trampled all over the other American intelligence agencies' turf. Operation CAMPUS threw its net wide. A partial list of CAMPUS subject headings reads like a directory of German government security offices, their leaders and individual agents. Particularly prominent on the list were the CIA-supported Gehlen Organization and Reinhard Gehlen himself.

A mixed bag of motives lay behind the creation of CAMPUS, among them a conviction that the CIA had no real control over the Gehlen Organization if it did not know who was working for it. A member of Dale's group remembers telling CIA officers that if Gehlen would not give them his personnel dossiers the situation was hopeless. Worse than hopeless. "One of the biggest mistakes the United States ever made in intelligence" he says, "was taking on Gehlen. In wartime his outfit was not that effective, and with the passage of time he did not learn. His methodology was antiquated; his communications primitive and his security nil. He was subject to penetration from day one."[10]

More was at work than professional disdain. Internecine struggles beset the American intelligence services, battles which took place behind a facade of unanimity of purpose, since the various agencies were expected to cooperate. Liaison officers from the different branches were assigned to one another's offices. Permanent representatives of Army, Navy and Air Force Intelligence were stationed at Pullach, while CIA had reciprocal arrangements with them.[11] But that did not curb the strong current of resentment of the CIA which ran through the other arms of American intelligence. Individual CIA officers, many with degrees from Ivy League universities, often appeared elitist and imbued with a sense of their own and their agency's superiority. Army Intelligence considered this attitude to be as offensive as it was unjustified. Army Intelligence, older at the game, maintained that it had broader experience and richer resources.

Being part of the occupation army, Army Intelligence was not saddled with keeping its identity a secret. Because of its high visibility and accessibility, Germans had been pouring into Army Counter Intelligence offices since 1945 to denounce or inform, as had East bloc refugees who either hated the Soviets, wanted money, or both. As Allen Dulles had discovered in Switzerland during the war, it pays to advertise; if no one knows you are there how can they find you? Another factor which may or may not have contributed to the effectiveness of Army Intelligence—one which its officers were unwilling to discuss, but which is well-documented—was its coldly pragmatic recruitment policy: the record shows its willingness to hire war criminals.[12]

Other elements contributed to this uneasy situation. One was a legacy of doubt in the minds of old Army CIC hands about what was widely perceived to be the leftist coloration of CIA's parent, OSS, and the lingering suspicion that it was an inherited characteristic. Another was the widely held and ill-concealed opinion among CIA officers that military Intelligence, including CIC, was bumbling, amateurish and clumsy. On those last points CIA was in for a surprise.

Despite the presence of CIA liaison officers, the 66th CIC Detachment succeeded in keeping its huge CAMPUS operation secret, and one way they did it was by enforcing tight control over their mailing list. Reports closed with notes such as these: "Neg. for you HQ pass this report to G2 or any other Agency . . ." meaning they were not even to be forwarded to Military Intelligence headquarters.[13] So tight was the security around CAMPUS, in fact, that there is reason to believe the CIA was still unaware of certain information about the Gehlen Organization which had been acquired by CIC through CAMPUS until some twenty-five years later when the material cited in this book was released through the Freedom of Information Act.

What exactly did the elaborate, super-secret Operation CAMPUS discover about the Gehlen Organization? Among much else, that not only was it harboring former hard-core Nazis, but they were busily forming into a clearly defined group. As will be seen, it was an Old Boys' network with a dangerous twist to it.

Gehlen had his own reasons for not wanting Nazis in prominent positions. He had his image and that of his Organization to consider. It was not a frivolous concern. The German General Staff was the bedrock on which his organization was built. The military had ruled Germany, one way or another, for generations and he had every reason to believe political power would rest there again in the future. Being accepted as a member of that elite company had allowed him to slough off his bourgeois origins; it had brought him a measure of credibility, legitimacy and entrée into the traditional ruling class.

At war's end, Gehlen was the one who found the vehicle, and the resources, to rescue his comrades, many with distinguished pedigrees which reached deep into the German past. With an eye to the future of Germany, as well as his own, he meant to help them and to win not so much their gratitude as their respect. Having Nazi thugs around could only to him harm. The men whom Gehlen held in such high regard had nothing but contempt for Hitler's barbarians.

But Gehlen faced a dilemma. If he was to succeed in his ambitious undertaking, he had to produce results, and he had formidable competitors. Getting results, however, meant using the most effective material available: experienced Intelligence agents, many of whom were just the sort of SD thugs he would have liked to avoid.[14] One solution for Gehlen was to turn a blind eye, keep them at arm's length and avoid direct responsibility for their employment. Another was secrecy. So long as no one, including the Americans, knew who was working for him, his Organization could exploit the experience of the unsavory types. But Gehlen's dilemma was compounded because this strategy in itself held hazards for his reputation. Security begins with recruitment, and an Intelligence chief who fails to exercise tight control in that critical area is unlikely to inspire confidence in himself or his organization.

Later, when scandals rocked the Organization, Gehlen would argue that there had not been many; that they had been hired by those down the line; that they had done little harm. The German public was unconvinced. "It seems," the *Frankfurter Rundschau* editorialized, "that in the Gehlen Headquarters one SS man prepared the way for the next and Himmler's elite were having happy reunion celebrations." The damage done by these men was so profound, with ramifications so widespread, that it would take years to try and clear the rubble.

Today former CIA officers put a distance between the Agency and Gehlen's "Nazi problem"; this, they say, was a German organization run by Germans. True, CIA paid the bills, set the requirements, received the reports, and had a formidable presence at Pullach, and Allen Dulles did take a particular interest in it, but as far as personnel questions went . . . The CIA officers stationed at Pullach, in effect, give a shrug of the shoulders, but it is an uncomfortable one. Later than it should have, however, it became abundantly clear that indeed there was a "Nazi problem," and it was not just a German concern.

The CAMPUS documents reveal much about the hard-core Nazi

Party members who found work within the Organization. They also make clear that more than enough was known about them to have alerted those responsible for recruitment to the Organization, even without access to the Allied-controlled Berlin Document Center. Take, for example, the cases of Hans Sommer and Friedrich Heinrich Busch.[15]

Busch was six feet tall and slender. His hair was flecked with grey and his blue eyes were set off by his ruddy complexion. Unhappily for the overall effect, though, two of his teeth were missing. But his appearance did not much interest the Nazi Party, which he joined in 1931 when he was twenty-six, nor the Gestapo, of which he became a member three years later. What was of concern, and an obstacle to advancement, was his membership in the Protestant church. In 1936 he was offered a commission in the SS on condition that he renounce this religious affiliation, a step he willingly took.

When war came, Busch worked first as assistant Gestapo chief in Innsbruck, then as senior SD officer in Paris. After Germany fell he was arrested by CIC Detachment 907 on 26 July 1945. Apparently he was released, then re-arrested by the 907th CIC Detachment on 30 March 1946. Having once again been let go, a bulletin was issued in January 1947 by the 7708 War Crimes Group that he was wanted for participation in the murder and torture of an American. He was taken into custody, in March 1947, and a warning was issued by the 7th Army Judge Advocate's Section that he was of war crimes interest and was not to be released without its approval. This notice was followed almost at once by a request for his extradition to France on a charge of torture and murder of French citizens in Paris.

At that point Busch disappeared from view and no charges were brought against him. When he reappeared in March, 1954, he was already a member of the Gehlen Organization and of the circle of former SS men within it.

Among Busch's co-workers in the Gehlen Organization's Vera-strasse office in Stuttgart was a younger man who was well-spoken and polite to the point of obsequiousness. Hans Sommer—alias Hans Herbert Paul Senner, Hans Stephen, and Paul Gautier—had also spent some time in France.[16] Moving rapidly through the ranks, he went from SD chief in Nice in 1943 to an undercover post as German Vice Consul in Marseilles in 1944, from which he directed espionage and sabotage. But it was in Paris that he would be best remembered, for instigating anti-Semitic demonstrations and blowing up synagogues. Wanted at the end of the war for the pursuit and torture of Jews, Sommer escaped to Spain, where he flourished as a free-lance spy-master and document forger until 1949. At that point he was expelled from the country, at the request of the British Embassy, and he returned to France, making frequent side trips to Germany. Within months Sommer had joined the Gehlen Organization where he immediately began recruiting new members from the ranks of former SD colleagues, among them a man who would leave an indelible mark on the history of the Organization, Heinz Felfe.

These portraits of Busch, Sommer and those of many other SS alumni who found homes in the Gehlen Organization appear in the CIC's secret CAMPUS files. But the exposure of a nest of unsavory Nazis in the Organization is not all that is of interest in the CAMPUS papers. They also show that the Nazi problem was intertwined with that of Soviet penetration. To the apparent surprise of some, the Nazis revealed themselves as unprincipled scoundrels who could not even be counted on to work against the communists.

CIC's own reports of its incestuous spying operation reveal even more than the presence of Nazis and communist agents in the Gehlen Organization. To find one arm of American Intelligence engaged in an independent, top secret operation which involved spying on a sister service is deeply disturbing in itself. But there also is strong evidence pointing to a deliberate failure to alert CIA, or indeed any other authority, to the real and immediate danger of communist penetration of the Organization, which was a subsidiary of United States Intelligence. In order to protect their own overall CAMPUS operation, the Americans running it allowed suspected Soviet penetration agents to continue their work. Only in the looking-glass world of intelligence could there be such a distortion of objectives and responsibilities.

In the wake of the 1953 assault on the Organization by the East Germans, Operation Hacke, Gehlen himself, of course, became painfully aware that a tide of classified information had rushed out of his organization and into communist hands. The loss of hundreds of his agents, and the public spectacle of former Organization operatives such as Geyer naming names and telling tales was intolerable. Gehlen had to act. And this time it was he who turned to secrecy. Keeping CIA's liaison team wholly in the dark, he initiated a top secret internal investigation to find out who was responsible for the leaks. It was into this German inquiry that the American Counter Intelligence Corps' Operation CAMPUS had tapped. By not informing CIA, or any United States authorities, about the progress or findings of Gehlen's investigation, the CIC found itself in the anomalous position of conspiring to keep Gehlen's secret.

This was unfortunate in many ways, not least because an alarming picture quickly emerged. Of the three Organization offices in the Stuttgart area, only that in Verastrasse had remained unexposed by the East Germans in their 1953 propaganda onslaught. Five agents in that office, Hans Sommer, Karl Schuetz, Walter Vollmer, Friedrich Busch and Heinz Felfe were all acquainted, all former SD agents, and all had unsavory backgrounds. As Gehlen's investigation progressed and was surreptitiously monitored by the Americans of CIC, it became apparent that this whole group of Nazis was also working for the communists and was led by one man, Heinz Felfe.

Despite compelling evidence that what was by then called the "Felfe Complex" was feeding information to the communists, CIC continued to hold its silence. But in 1955, while Gehlen continued to reject, or ignore, the suspicions his own investigators were raising, and the CIC still kept its dangerous information to itself, one American Army officer decided to take matters into his own hands.

Major General Arthur Trudeau, graduate of West Point with a Master of Science degree from the University of California, was an engineer and a soldier, but a soldier first. A gifted battlefield commander, he was decorated repeatedly during his career for personal bravery, and compiled a distinguished record in both the Second World War and in Korea. So it was surprising that this soldier-engineer, who was also an out-going and out-spoken man, would become Chief of U.S. Army Intelligence (G-2). Intelligence was not his calling, any more than it had been that of then-Colonel John Russell Deane before him. Nonetheless, in November 1953, the year the East Germans launched their attack on the CIA-backed Gehlen Organization, Trudeau was assigned to Washington and became G-2.

Trudeau never made any secret of his strong anti-Soviet sentiments, protesting that the United States had been playing with fire in allying itself with the Soviet Union during the war. Later he urged an aggressive post-war posture designed to keep the Soviets from pursuing what he saw as their ultimate goal of world domination.[17] What Trudeau learned about communist activity in West Germany, where he had been commanding General of the 1st Constabulary Brigade from 1948 to 1950, and especially about Soviet infiltration into the Gehlen Organization, disturbed him deeply. By nature a man of action, Trudeau decided something had to be done.

In May, 1955, Germany regained its sovereignty. At this point,

Konrad Adenauer, the first Chancellor of the Federal Republic of Germany, intended to make the Gehlen Organization, its overt ties to the CIA cut, an official arm of the government. Since the new West Germany was to be a member of NATO, its intelligence agency would share the secrets of all the other Western allies, including those of the United States. That was too much for Trudeau.

Some months before, he had told the German Ambassador in Washington that he was eager to discuss the mutual intelligence concerns of the United States and Germany with a representative of the German Army. So, when Trudeau got a call telling him that the German Ambassador had a guest staying with him, one who was highly placed in the German government and with whom he might like to discuss his security concerns, he jumped at the chance. When Trudeau arrived at the Embassy he was escorted into the garden. The highly placed gentleman turned out to be Konrad Adenauer.

Startled at finding himself with the Chancellor, who was curious to know what was on his mind, Trudeau began to express his grave reservations about the Organization. On the basis of information passed to him, Trudeau confided, it was his belief that if Gehlen's Organization was actually integrated into the German government, not only Germany's but all NATO's secrets would go directly to Moscow. In making specific points, Trudeau referred to a handful of 3 × 5 cards he had brought with him. Adenauer listened attentively and then reached out for the cards. "I suppose if I had it to do over I might not have handed him the cards," Trudeau said thirty years later, "but under the circumstances I felt I had no choice. I had told him what was on them."[18]

The cards, even more than his direct approach to Adenauer, were Trudeau's downfall. The Chancellor, when he got back to Germany, turned them over to his State Secretary, Hans Maria Globke.[19] Globke, Gehlen's ardent supporter, handed them over in turn to the CIA's James Critchfield at Pullach, and asked for a report. "They contained unedited, unevaluated extracts from various Counter Intelligence Corps and other military Intelligence reports," Critchfield recalls. "They had derogatory information about Gehlen personnel. I had a lot of information about the people and the cases mentioned, and I gave a detailed account of each one."

Critchfield cabled the text of his report to Washington. The men of CIA were very angry, and echoes of that anger could be heard three decades later. Allen Dulles was so persuaded that Trudeau's accusations were groundless, and so outraged by what the General had done, that he went to the Pentagon and insisted that Trudeau be asked to explain why, on his own initiative, he had taken unevaluated information from the field and handed it over to a Head of State. In July of 1955, Trudeau was called into the office of the new Chief of Staff of the Army, General Maxwell Taylor. Together they went to see Secretary of the Army Wilber Brucker, who had the 3 × 5 cards in front of him. Brucker told Trudeau that Allen Dulles had informed President Eisenhower's Secretary of Defense, Charles Wilson, that he had lost all confidence in Trudeau because of the incident. Brucker then demanded a written report from him.

"I gave him a full report," Trudeau says, "and in it I said I recognized that Allen Dulles might have lost confidence in me, but that I wanted Brucker to know I had also lost confidence in Dulles and the CIA." Within days Trudeau was replaced as Chief of Army Intelligence and was on his way to the Far East.

A year later, on April 1, 1956, the Gehlen Organization became the Bundesnachrichtendienst (BND), West Germany's Federal Intelligence Agency, and Reinhard Gehlen was made its chief. Trudeau's efforts had failed. Eventually, although it was too little and came way past the time when it could repair the damage done to his career, Trudeau did receive something which could pass as an apology, although just barely. CIA director Allen Dulles asked the American Ambassador to Korea, where Trudeau had been posted, to tell the General that he, Dulles, felt he had acted too hastily on the advice of subordinates.[20]

Although Germany had achieved sovereignty in May, 1955, it would take until April 1956 before Chancellor Adenauer had his way and the Gehlen Organization was integrated into his new, young democracy. Members of the government wrangled bitterly over whether it should be taken on at all, and if it were, to which branch it should be answerable. Tirelessly, Gehlen had cultivated allies and held off foes, and in the end his efforts would pay off. But his enemies did not go down without a fight. One of their most potent weapons was Gehlen's, and the Organization's, intimate connection with the United States. For his part, Gehlen struggled to portray himself as a loyal German and a patriot who had worked with the Americans in order to rebuild the country into a strong, democratic society. But his detractors still insisted that he had been a tool of the CIA. Ironically, however, it was not Gehlen's intimacy with the CIA which finally crippled and humiliated him.

Chapter Eight

Heinz Felfe: Traitor Within

The Nazi-Soviet Connection

There were strong pressures on Gehlen and his organization from the Soviet bloc, allied governments suspicious of the breadth of his operations, and critics within West Germany itself. But it was one man, Heinz Felfe, who ultimately would do more to damage Gehlen than all the other forces combined. Like other former members of the SS, Felfe was recruited for the Organization by a former colleague, but in this case Felfe was invited to serve two masters. His recruiter was his old friend and co-worker, the deceptively unprepossessing-looking Hans Clemens, also known as the Tiger of Como.[1]

Despite his thick eyeglasses, the roly-poly Clemens was so short-sighted that when reading a document he held it only inches away from his nose. As a young man what Clemens had read most was sheets of music since he had hoped for a career as a pianist. But during the war he abandoned the gentler world of music for the SD where he cut a considerable figure. It was in 1944, while serving Himmler in Northern Italy, that he gained the title Tiger of Como for issuing the order to shoot 350 helpless Italians, men, women and children the Germans had been holding as hostages. Captured in April, 1945, he was tried for the horror at Como, but the court found him not guilty on the all-too-familiar ground that he was acting on the orders of his superior officers.

By January, 1950, Clemens was in Cologne and his marriage was in

143

disarray. Neverthtless, his wife Gerda travelled from Dresden in the East Zone, where she still lived, to tell her husband about a job opportunity. A colonel in Russian Intelligence named Max, with whom Gerda was having an affair, was interested in meeting Clemens to discuss the possibility of working together. Clemens, undeterred by the personal aspects of the situation, considered it an interesting idea and went back to Dresden to meet Max. The Russian's proposition was simple. Clemens was to go back to West Germany and make contact with former Nazis, SS and SD men, who were working for Western Intelligence.

By June, 1951, Clemens was not just making contact with agents of Western Intelligence; he had joined the Gehlen Organization. Willi Krichbaum, a former SS colonel and Gehlen's District Representative at Bad Reichenhall, hired Clemens and gave him an assignment that could not have suited him better. "My task," Clemens said later, "was to report ex-SD men who were without a job; they could be employed once more." Indeed they could. With their names going to both Gehlen and the Soviets, their days of penury were over.

Clemens had excellent connections in the Nazi world. A native of Dresden, he had joined the Party there in 1931 and, within five years, had become head of the regional SD office. By 1938–39 his co-workers included fellow-Dresdeners Heinz Felfe, a career Intelligence officer, and Erwin Tiebel, a former Senior State's Attorney.[2] When the war ended Tiebel moved West where he was able to capitalize on his experience as a member of Nazi Intelligence by becoming an agent of the British. In March, 1948, he was in Cologne where he was reunited with his old friend, Heinz Felfe.

Felfe had been captured by the Canadians and interned in a British/Canadian POW camp.[3] After his interrogation he was released, whereupon he joined forces with Tiebel in working for Messrs. Cutter and Brown of British Intelligence.[4] By the end of 1949, however, the British were running out of money and first Tiebel, then Felfe, had to look elsewhere for support. Tiebel was hired by a construction company where he openly pursued a successful career, while at the same time joining the clandestine ranks of Soviet agents. Felfe worked as an interrogator at a refugee camp until 1951 when Hans Clemens, now both a Gehlen agent and Soviet recruiter of former Nazis, made contact with his former comrades-at-arms. The old Dresden circle was finally closed.

Knowing Felfe's qualities at first hand and recognizing that he had just the stuff the KGB was looking for, Clemens decided to introduce his prize recruit to his Soviet masters himself. Together, he and Felfe drove to a villa in Karlshorst where they were treated by the Russians, Felfe bragged, to a banquet where the champagne flowed like water. After the festivities, Felfe and Max got down to cases and discussed the possibility of doing some "East-West business." It would be the start of a long and fruitful collaboration.

Shortly after Felfe's return to West Germany Hans Sommer, the polite, soft-spoken former SD officer who had specialized in anti-Semitic terrorism in Paris and was by then a Gehlen agent, contacted Felfe and proposed he too become a member of the Gehlen Organization. When Felfe reported this development to Max at their next meeting on October 18, 1951, there was cause for more celebration. To mark the start of their new careers, Felfe and Clemens took a brief vacation together, and while they were away they did not forget their new friend. They sent Max a postcard saying simply "It is taken care of." And so it was: Felfe became a member of the Gehlen Organization, through whose ranks he would make a dizzying ascent.

He started his remarkably long and successful career in the notoriously short-lived double-agent business at an out-station, but quickly moved to the counterespionage department of the Organization office in Karlsruhe. He was bright, able and outstandingly well-informed, and it was not long before he was brought to Organization headquarters in Pullach. There the startlingly high quality of his work attracted Gehlen's favorable attention, and Felfe soon became a glaring refutation of the Doctor's self-proclaimed gift for sizing up a man.

The Trudeau affair, which came to a head in 1955, may have been fortunate for Felfe since, officially at least, the CIA, angry and on the defensive, had proved to its own satisfaction that Trudeau's accusations of Soviet penetration of the Organization were unfounded. Unofficially, however, CIA counterespionage specialist Clare Edward Petty was not so sure. In his view there had been too many incidents, too many "disappearances" and "kidnappings" into the East Zone. Furthermore, Petty was well aware of the events of February 15, 1954.

That afternoon a man in his early thirties, black haired and round-faced, walked into American Military headquarters in Vienna, announced he was a Russian fleeing from the Soviet Zone of Austria, and wanted asylum. To convince the officer on duty to take him seriously, he identified himself as the Chief of Soviet internal counterintelligence in Vienna, Major Peter Sergeievich Deriabin—alias Smirnov, alias Korobov, alias Konstantin—of the KGB. The American did pay attention, and in time Deriabin provided an abundance of information to the CIA.

In Moscow it had been part of Deriabin's job to handle the recruitment of agents for work in Austria and Germany. The favorite KGB hunting ground was among prisoners of war being held in Soviet camps. Especially rich pickings came from those who had informed against their fellow-prisoners while in camp; those so desperate for release that they would agree to do virtually anything; and former members of the SD who were available for hire by anyone. Although they were alert to the possibility that he was a disinformation agent, when Deriabin said there were two Soviet agents in the Gehlen Organization, code named Peter and Paul, the CIA listened. The trouble was, however, that he could give no solid leads to their identity, so any investigation was hobbled before it could get underway.

Then, in December of 1955, a captured Gehlen agent was put on public trial in East Germany. At this point Clare Petty recognized that certain sensitive information which came out in that case could only have come from a source high in the Organization. Now there was more reason to take Deriabin's shadowy Peter and Paul seriously, and now, too, there was at least a chance of discovering who they were. By laboriously tracing back those who had access to the facts exposed at the East German trial and by scrutinizing each individual, Petty finally narrowed the field to two: one was Heinz Felfe, the other has never been named publicly.

Both men, it was noted with particular interest, had been to the United States recently on one of the periodic orientation trips arranged by the CIA for senior members of the Gehlen staff. But immediately after the most interesting part of the tour, and before going on to the so-called tourist attractions, Felfe had suddenly returned to Germany, pleading illness. A small incident, but a telling one. It was an action that was out of the ordinary by a man who didn't really fit into the Gehlen Organization. For a start, Felfe was both socially inferior and intellectually superior to most of the others at Headquarters, and he knew it. But more significant: he was pushy in his working relationships, he always wanted to know more.

Early in 1957 Petty wrote a report detailing his suspicions and the reasons for them, but leaving out the suspects' names. It was privately passed to Gehlen. Later, at a meeting arranged to discuss it, Gehlen did not flinch when he was given Felfe's name. He agreed that the matter looked serious, and immediately set up a small working party to pursue Petty's line of investigation. But he did not tell the Americans, then or ever, that he had ordered just such an investigation of the same people three years before the CIA officers came to him. Nor did he tell them that his group, too, considered Heinz Felfe a prime target, or that he had chosen to ignore their warnings.

At that juncture, however, Gehlen must have taken another close, hard look at Felfe. But rather than a Soviet mole, perhaps what he saw was his best agent being attacked by others who were jealous of him. Because Felfe was Gehlen's best, the one who produced more and better information than the others. He had proved his bona fides by exposing at least one highly-placed agent of the KGB and was running the extremely sensitive, and for Gehlen personally important, LENA operation.

With Soviet help, Felfe had quickly established his credentials by producing valuable and authentic intelligence, including minutes of secret meetings held by the government of East Germany and advance information about Soviet intelligence operations. And he became famous for his map of the interior of the Karlshorst headquarters of the KGB, which was so detailed that it even showed which lavatory was used by which senior officer. As further evidence of the quality of his information, and in order to dispel any possible doubt about where his own loyalty lay, little by little, one clue at a time, he fed the Organization the information which ultimately led to the revelation that the editor of the magazine "Die Deutsche Woche," C. A. Weber, was a Soviet agent. In the curious world of intelligence, considering one of its agents worth offering up may be the ultimate tribute a secret service can pay to the value of one of its agents.

But it was Felfe's handling of the remarkably productive LENA case, in which Gehlen had invested so much, which made him invaluable. With so much at stake, even the possibility that Felfe was working for the Soviets may have been too much for Gehlen to contemplate. Journalists are particularly attractive targets for recruitment by intelligence services of all nations, but an East German one who travelled frequently to the West would be especially high on the Soviets' list. They wasted no time in recruiting one such newsman, code named Lena, setting as his primary objective the penetration of West German Intelligence. When Lena made contact with a Gehlen field station in Northern Germany, the Gehlen people also saw the possibilities he presented for gathering information about the East Germans, and were equally eager to recruit him for their side. At this point, Felfe entered the picture.

As a counterespionage officer for the Organization, it was his business to uncover and thereby foil Soviet espionage efforts against the West German government. But the best trick of all was not just to uncover the opposition's agent, but to recruit him yourself. That way your side, knowing what the enemy was after, would discover which areas were of particular interest to them and how much they already knew. On top of that, you could feed them misleading information. That is what Felfe claimed to have done with Lena. Suddenly, and early in his career, he appeared to have that plum, a double-agent case, when in fact he had recruited a KGB colleague.

So successful did the Lena operation appear to be, and so skillful his handling of it, that Felfe shot up in Gehlen's opinion, and his reputation was made. The possibilities for exploitation of this remarkable source were so great that Gehlen went to Chancellor Adenauer, briefed him on it, and requested coordination with Bonn about what material could be provided to Lena for transmission to his Soviet handlers. It was necessary to know two things to run this operation effectively: what the Soviet requirements were, and as much as possible about these topics so a decision could be made about what should be fed to Lena for Soviet consumption. What is more, Gehlen's man would have to have total access to the information held by each Ministry involved in order to pass on material which was convincing— some of it would have to be accurate—but which would not jeopardize the national security.

Gehlen's bold request was vigorously opposed in many quarters. What he was asking was that all the government's secrets—about defense, international relations, the economy, everything—be made available to his Organization. And some of it would be deliberately given to the Soviets. A number of Ministers dug in their heels. But Gehlen was not through. With his ally Globke, Adenauer's powerful State Secretary, as a middle man, a plan was worked out. Gehlen went to Bonn, taking Felfe with him, and a "build-up" committee was formed. This committee would review all the information from the Ministries, all the secrets, and then a decision would be made about what could safely be fed to Lena. Felfe was made Chairman of the committee. Virtually all West Germany's secrets were his for the taking.[5]

Caught in the crossfire between American Army Counter Intelligence and the Gehlen Organization, Felfe had been dodging bullets successfully for years. Each group had its own reasons for not pursuing its findings: Army Intelligence for fear of exposing its extensive, and illegal, intelligence operations against the West German government; Gehlen because he prided himself on his instinct, what he called his "nase" about people, and because he had too much invested in Felfe and could not bring himself to suspect his by now invaluable agent.[6] Now that the CIA finally had Felfe in its sights, however, the picture changed. Here was a group with no motive, conscious or unconscious, for looking past Felfe, one in fact with every reason to track him down.

With the help of their agile agents who had infiltrated the Organization, Soviet Intelligence knew that for years Felfe had been safe. They were aware that American Army Counter Intelligence had its suspicions about him, but was doing nothing about them, and knew that the same applied to the Organization itself. Further, and of much greater significance, they were aware that Army Counter Intelligence had not passed its suspicions on to the CIA. But when the CIA independently came to suspect Felfe, the Soviets had to consider his days as a productive agent numbered. The Felfe story, as it unfolds from here, suggests that the KGB may have been kept informed of the new developments. There is sharp disagreement on the point among CIA officers involved in the case, but some, citing a gradual shift in Soviet tactics geared to meet the altered circumstances, believe that the KGB began to prime Felfe as an explosive with which to blow up the Organization.[7]

Gehlen had chosen to disregard the danger signals put up by his own staff as well as the CIA, attributing them to a combination of anti-Nazi paranoia, professional jealousy, and personal dislike of Felfe. Having made his decision, Gehlen did not look back. Instead, he continued to assign Felfe to the most sensitive counterespionage operations. Among them was one Felfe could hardly have bettered had he proposed it himself, which he may have done; operation PANOPTIKUM was an investigation to uncover the means by which the KGB was attempting to infiltrate the Organization. "By this time Gehlen really didn't have an option," says a former CIA officer close to the Felfe case. "If it turned out Felfe was a KGB agent then the LENA operation, for which Gehlen had gone out on a limb and which left him totally exposed at the highest levels of government, would mean the Soviets had West Germany's most closely-guarded secrets. Gehlen, and his organization, would be bankrupt." Gehlen, then, was committed to Felfe.

Felfe had worked himself into a position where he could lay bare some of the most important secrets not only of West Germany's intelligence agency, but of the West German government and of NATO. By the time he was finished, he had succeeded in crippling and humiliating German Intelligence on a scale comparable only to the damage done by Kim Philby to the British. So extensive is the inventory of material Felfe handed over to the Soviets that the sheer bulk of it defies comprehension. By his own testimony Felfe gave the KGB some 15,000 photographs and 20 microtape recording spools, but that was not all by a long shot. The information included: lists of Gehlen Organization agents at home and abroad; cover addresses of informants; internal reports regarding current operations; communications reports; and monthly counterespionage reports. That does not count what he acquired from the files in his own counterespionage division—information he had been able to alter to suit the Soviets' purposes—nor what he picked up by asking questions. Felfe was an inveterate asker of questions and a good listener.[8]

While Felfe was going ahead at full speed; while Gehlen was keeping his head in the sand; and while CIC, which had been ordered to stop, apparently paid no attention and went on with its operations against the West German government; the CIA was keeping track of Felfe. His aggressiveness continued, but his target often appeared to be the CIA rather than the KGB, and he made good use of the resources at his command. If he got wind of a possible area of CIA interest he could ask for a name trace, a tactic which would inevitably betray an operational sensitivity if there was one. If the reply to his request for information on a certain person was a starchy "we can't give you that information," he knew he was most likely onto something.

Felfe's questions frequently seemed oriented to Soviet, rather than German interests. After the crash of a Soviet plane on West German territory, the German authorities secured it and stripped whatever was of interest for analysis. Yet Felfe came around asking the Americans what bits and pieces had been recovered, betraying curiosity about how much the Americans, not the West Germans, had learned. Most disturbing, however, was an incident that took place late in 1955 under the nose of Felfe's American opposite number on the CIA counter intelligence team.

It was unusual for a member of the Organization Headquarters staff to go to Berlin; it was too exposed and involved too much risk. Personal approval for the trip had to be given by Gehlen. Felfe had no trouble getting permission for this journey, however, since he was being taken to the CIA station in Berlin. It was a singularly worthwhile outing for Felfe. In the course of his visit he found out, among other things, exactly what information the CIA actually had about the Soviet compound at Karlshorst, as compared to what he had told them.

Immediately after that meeting Felfe went off on his own, without his CIA escort, for some four hours. This was viewed as a serious lapse in security since, as a senior officer from Headquarters at Pullach, Felfe was considered vulnerable to kidnapping. When Felfe finally rejoined him, his CIA escort said later, he had so many explanations for what he had been doing, including producing the ticket stub for a movie he claimed to have seen, that the American thought it was "strange." All encounters between the CIA staff at Pullach and their German colleagues were recorded, and Felfe's behavior on this outing to Berlin would prove of interest as the net finally tightened around him.

Gehlen's belief that Felfe had been singled out as a possible double agent in part because he rubbed his colleagues the wrong way was not entirely unreasonable. Nobody liked him much, and he did not seem to care. His air of disdainful superiority made his invitation to Charles Wheeler of the CIA liaison staff all the more interesting.

Wheeler was at Pullach from 1955 until early 1960 as a member of the liaison team's counterespionage section, of which he became chief in 1958. Since Felfe was head of the Soviet division of the Organization's counterespionage department, Wheeler saw him from time to time in the course of their work. In the autumn of 1955 Felfe had developed a skin problem, an uncomfortable, unsightly and stubborn affliction for which he had been unable to obtain relief. Wheeler suggested he get another opinion and drove him to McGraw Caserne, the American installation, to be examined by American military doctors. That evening, when Wheeler returned Felfe to his apartment building in Munich, Felfe surprised him by inviting him to come in.

This was a relatively uncommon event between a German and an American at that time, especially since their professional relationship was not particularly close, and their social contacts had been limited to a few formal occasions when the German and American officers gathered with their wives. Like virtually everyone who described Felfe, Wheeler emphasized his coldness. "He was respected for his ability, he was very professional at his job, but nobody really liked him. Not even his fellow Germans. His own chief, the head of the German counterespionage department, didn't like him," Wheeler said.

Wheeler found that Felfe lived very comfortably. The apartment was twice the size of one a German holding a comparable position would be expected to have at that time. The building, a solid, well-built one, was in a good section of Munich, and Felfe's apartment was on a corner, one flight up. It had two exposures, high ceilings and large rooms which were expensively, although not lavishly furnished. As Wheeler describes it, the furnishings were "substantial, they were in acceptable good taste as it existed in the German middle class at the time. The style was middle class *gemütlich*. I did notice he had a very good radio."

Felfe's wife Margarete Ingeborg was there and immediately went off to make tea. Like other wives of the Germans in the Organization, Mrs. Felfe did not frequently mix socially with the Americans, but when Wheeler did see the Felfes together it appeared to him that they were "harmoniously married." From his style of life it was clear Felfe was comfortably well off. He had two children, a daughter and a son of whom he was extremely fond. He talked proudly about the boy and mentioned he was sending him to a private school. When Wheeler observed how expensive private schools were, Felfe said he was willing to make any sacrifice for his son's education, and then referred to a generous aunt in the United States.

After they had had their tea and made small talk, Felfe brought out a picture album, "It was a typically and very German thing to do," Wheeler says. "Felfe had a huge number of pictures of Dresden, a place he clearly loved. Included in the albums were "five yards of pictures of Dresden in ruins," Wheeler says, and Felfe began talking about it. "As he slowly turned the pages he became more and more overwrought about the city's destruction; the artistic and cultural devastation as well as the human loss. He became intensely emotional, to the point that there were tears in his eyes. Mrs. Felfe tried to calm him down, to divert him, change the subject. She made more tea. But he continued to rail against the Allies for what they did to Dresden."

Wheeler is convinced that regardless of how much of the time he was playing a role, there and then Felfe was sincere. The destruction of Dresden was a deep, unhealing wound. Wheeler learned later that the Soviets had taken him through the devastated city in the late 1940s, after his release by the British.

This singular visit did not lead to a noticeably closer relationship between Wheeler and Felfe, but they did remain on friendly terms. Even during the painful period when Wheeler knew who Felfe really was, and Felfe was unaware that he was under suspicion, Wheeler kept up the facade while studying the man. "Felfe was no ideologue," Wheeler says. "He had no interest in the Soviets or the Soviet system. Part of why he did what he did was money, of course, but there was the sheer pleasure of the work itself. It's a not uncommon phenomenon in the business; the corruption of the tools of the trade. And it was also an ego trip. There was the satisfaction of manipulating two powerful political forces. Being a penetration agent is heady stuff."[9]

On February 15, 1960, as a farewell present to Wheeler, who was leaving Pullach, Felfe sent him a picture book of Bavaria, and with it a letter. The book, Felfe said, was to be "a reminder of our work together, for which I am most thankful. Heinz."

Belated CIA Interest in Heinz Felfe

The chain of events which ultimately led to Felfe's exposure began one day in March 1958 when the mail was delivered to the American Embassy in Bern, Switzerland. Addressed to Ambassador Henry J. Taylor was an envelope postmarked Zurich. There was nothing about it to excite any interest or suggest that it and its contents would preoccupy some of the CIA's finest for many, many months. But that envelope contained another, this one addressed to J. Edgar Hoover, and with its opening—the Ambassador passed it on to CIA rather than the F.B.I.—the mechanism was triggered which in time would snare Felfe and at the same time destroy the credibility of Gehlen's organization.

Typed in German, and signed "Heckenschütze" [Sniper], the letter offered to give the Americans information about communist espionage activities, and on both sides of the Atlantic it provoked a flurry of activity. Paper and type were minutely examined while Howard Roman, a senior CIA officer and a linguist, studied the contents. At the same time an elaborate communications system was being put into place. Messages were placed in the Personals column of a Frankfurt newspaper, a post office box was rented in West Berlin, a letter drop established at a public lavatory in the Tiergarten, and an emergency telephone number assigned.

The letter had no spacing between paragraphs, but was written in good colloquial German. Nonetheless, Roman concluded from Sniper's awkward use of the language that he was Polish, and so far all the evidence seemed consistent with that. Still, CIA was on its guard: Sniper could be a deception agent prepared to give them enough genuine information to win their confidence, and then feed them the misleading material the Soviets wanted them to have. "How much truth is the enemy willing to tell you," Howard Roman asked, "in order to set you up for the big deception?"[10]

The letters were few and far between to start with, but then the rate picked up—over a period of thirty months there were fourteen. The operation was codenamed BEVISION, BE being the geographical designation for Poland while VISION was an arbitrary word produced by computer, and every letter from Sniper was dissected, discussed, examined and re-examined by the CIA officers handling the case, each of whom came up with a different interpretation. So opaque were some of Sniper's missives that when an advertisement for a hoola hoop innocently found its way into Sniper's box at the post office, Roman said, "some of the CIA's best minds spent weeks trying to catch his drift."

The great bulk of the information sent by Sniper was of little or no interest to the Americans. For every ounce of gold there was a pound or more of dross. But the shining nuggets were worth the frustration of sifting through all the rest. Not that even his most important leads were welcomed by CIA. Indeed, one pointed squarely at the likelihood of a KGB mole within the top ranks of the Agency. The Soviets, Sniper said, had warned Polish Intelligence that a Polish case officer in Switzerland was going to be approached for recruitment. This did, in fact, represent the American plan, not yet executed, of which only a very few top CIA officers were aware. Of course it was possible that the leak had come from a penetration of CIA's communications, but there was no comfort to be found there, either. The news from Sniper was so fresh that the KGB had to have passed on the information to the Poles within two weeks of Washington's decision to carry out the plan. With intelligence like this, however unwelcome, Sniper caught the full attention of his audience.

Early in this nerve-wracking correspondence, in the autumn of 1958, Sniper also alerted the Americans that Polish Intelligence was receiving summaries of Gehlen Organization reports—and the Poles were being given them by the Soviets. Deriabin's warning four years earlier about Peter and Paul, coupled with the CIA's lingering, inconclusive investigation of Felfe took on heightened importance, but still there were no hard leads. In fact, there was no concrete evidence that the material Sniper said the Soviets were passing on to the Poles actually had come from within the Gehlen Organization; it might have originated elsewhere.

The CIA requested more information, and Sniper gave them some specifics. The summaries he had seen were distillations of classified briefing papers, on one of which the English words "Mutual Assistance" had appeared. This was a clue which set at least one investigator's blood racing, because it could refer only to a single document, a plan conceived by a senior liaison staff officer as an item on the agenda for a meeting to be held between Allen Dulles and General Gehlen. "Mutual Assistance," discussions of future cooperation between CIA and the BND, had taken place only in Germany and did not appear on Washington's version of the agenda. It looked very much as if the Soviets indeed were getting material straight from the Organization, and from the heart of it at that.

The Americans shared material from Sniper's letters with the British who had a sizeable stake in it. The British found, once again, that they were harboring more Soviet moles. It was Sniper who led them to Gordon Lonsdale, in reality a Russian named Colon Molody, and ultimately to George Blake.[11] However, the CIA did not discuss its leads into the Gehlen Organization with the British; the Americans considered it a matter between themselves and the Germans. But they did not inform Gehlen about Sniper's letters either. "He was still inside," one CIA officer said, "how could we risk it?"

The break in the Felfe case came in an account by Sniper of a conversation he had had with General Gribanov, the chief of KGB counterintelligence. Gribanov, Sniper wrote, had bragged to him that of the six Gehlen Organization officers who had gone to the United States on one of the CIA's orientation tours in 1956, two of them were Soviet agents. There they were again, Deriabin's Peter and Paul. But now the CIA attached other names to them, and one of them was Heinz Felfe. At last the CIA had the hard lead it had been waiting for, now they could act. Operation UJDROWSY, as the Felfe case was known, could come to life.[12]

In December 1960, the telephone number the CIA had given Sniper in case of emergency suddenly rang; he wanted to come out. Preparing for his eventual, and for all he knew precipitous, departure from Warsaw, Sniper had squirreled away film of hundreds of documents he had photographed with his Minox. Howard Roman estimates he had copied some three hundred pages, including organizational tables and the names of hundreds of Polish agents. Sniper picked Christmas time to make his move. The holidays would cover his absence and give the CIA man in Warsaw time to empty the drop. (That drop, a hollow tree stump, was fabricated by the CIA, sent to Warsaw through the diplomatic pouch, and "planted" on Sniper's route from his office).

After Sniper's call, Howard Roman flew from Washington to West Berlin where Sniper was to make the crossing. There was a collective sigh of relief when Sniper (bringing his mistress rather than his wife) arrived in the West and introduced himself as Michal Goleniewski.

Highly placed in Polish Intelligence, Goleniewski also had been working for Soviet Intelligence, reporting to them on his own service—a
position which had given him access to considerable information about
Soviet operations. Relieved to find not only that Sniper was not a
mythical figure created by the Soviets to distract and confuse them, as
some in the CIA believed, but that he was alive, healthy and ready to
cooperate, the Americans swept him off to debrief him—a process
which took several years.

It took time, but the CIA was able to piece together enough information to confront the anomalies which appeared in Goleniewski's
letters. Why, for instance, had he shifted the weight of his reporting to
Soviet matters? One answer was that without rousing his suspicions,
the Soviets had discovered and then exploited Goleniewski's secret
correspondence with the Americans. Before writing his first letter,
Goleniewski had been dropped by the Soviets as an agent, a circumstance which may have embittered him and contributed to his decision
to defect. His earlier letters, then, were largely concerned with Polish
cases and with information available to him from Polish Intelligence
sources, including the fact that Gehlen Organization reports were
reaching them from the Soviets.

According to this theory, the Russians had learned what Goleniewski
was up to, decided to use him for their own purposes, and to that end
re-hired him as a KGB agent. The KGB was using him as a disinformation agent, so much of his most significant information probably
was sent before he became an unwitting instrument of the Soviets. But
the lead to Felfe was so direct and so blatant, and its source—
Gribanov's boast to Goleniewski—so suspect, that there were those
who believed it had been deliberately planted on Goleniewski by the
Soviets, to be forwarded to the Americans. The KGB would sacrifice
Felfe to destroy the reputation and credibility of Gehlen and his BND.

Shortly after Goleniewski sent the Felfe lead, the Soviets made a
move which they knew would catapult him into the arms of the
Americans. First, his travel was restricted. Then he was given a new
task, searching for a Polish Intelligence officer who was providing
secret information to the West—he was assigned to find himself. At
that point Goleniewski knew the game was up, and dialed the emergency number.

From the time Goleniewski came over to the West, Howard Roman
was his constant companion—a combination of baby-sitter and hand-
holder. In the first days of January, 1961, after a brief stay in Frankfurt,

Roman took him and his lady friend on a MATS flight to Paris. From there they headed for Washington, via the Azores. It was an uneventful flight, but Goleniewski livened it up for Roman, saying "If the KGB knew we were on this plane, they would shoot it down." When they got to the Azores, they went to the Officers' Club where Goleniewski dropped everything, including the "poor, pathetic girl" he had brought with him, and fed an endless stream of coins into the insatiable maws of the slot machines. The girl, whom Goleniewski eventually married, knew nothing, not even that her lothario was an intelligence officer.

After the plane landed in Washington the passengers got into a car and headed for a safe house, but Goleniewski was suspicious. "He was a sly fellow," Roman said, "always trying to outwit and see through us. So he immediately decided we were trying to hide our destination from him. He informed us he knew we were driving him around in circles and that it was quite unnecessary; he wouldn't tell anyone. We assured him we weren't doing anything of the kind, and we weren't, but he didn't believe us."

Roman stayed close to Goleniewski for some eighteen months, and during that time Goleniewski developed serious delusions of grandeur. "Early on," Roman said, "Goleniewski told us his father worked in a State brewery in Poland, that he was a State employee and stoked the fires. And he told us his uncle was a streetcar conductor in Warsaw, and that he had an aunt who had married into minor aristocracy—in Poland there was only upper and lower, there was no middle class. But six months later, he informed us he was really the Tsarevich."[13]

During his interrogation Goleniewski added a few scraps to the information he had sent in his letters, which stirred things up in Pullach. He remembered having been told by an officer of the KGB that Stefan Bandera, an active anti-Soviet Ukrainian nationalist living in Munich, had been murdered on the night of October 15 1959 by the man with whom he was having supper. His dinner companion, it happened, had been Heinz Danko Herre, for years Gehlen's friend and closest associate.

This bombshell led the CIA to take a hard look at Herre. "We searched diligently, but found nothing to substantiate the charge. Everything, including Herre's whole history, pointed away from it," says an officer connected with the investigation.[14] The CIA later learned Bandera's real killer was a man named Stashinsky, confirming their conclusion that the Soviets had deliberately planted the Herre story on Goleniewski to make trouble between CIA and the Organization.

But the most indigestible morsel from Goleniewski, one which further poisoned relations between Gehlen and the CIA, concerned information that the secretary to the chief of the German Socialist Party (SPD), was a Soviet agent. It was the usual practice for briefing papers from the Gehlen Organization to be sent to the various political parties in West Germany. Those delivered to the SPD went through the party chief's secretary. Goleniewski said he had information that she had recruited as a Soviet agent the Organization representative in Bonn who dropped off the briefing sheets to her office. The Organization representative in question was a young man with the cover name Justus.

Justus was under consideration for the prime post of Organization representative to the United States, but the real problem was that Justus also was Gehlen's son-in-law. Gehlen had already been told Justus was acceptable to the American government, but after an internal row at the CIA about what to do, a senior officer went to Pullach to tell Gehlen their suspicions about the young man, and to reverse the decision to send him to the United States. Not surprisingly, Gehlen was furious. A subsequent investigation showed there was nothing to the allegations, and once again it had to be assumed that the story had been planted on Goleniewski. "It didn't cost the KGB a thing," one CIA officer said, "and it caused a real breach between Gehlen and the Americans."

Before long, Goleniewski was holding court. "His debriefings were like appointments at a dentist's office, people were shuttling in and out all day," Roman says. "Everyone was questioning him. The FBI, the military, everybody. He sat there behind a big desk with papers spread out in front of him, taking questions, and the interrogator was sitting on the client's side." Roman regrets that so much time was taken up with details. "So much was wasted which could have been used to study him, to probe into his psyche. We could have learned so much of real value." But the clients for his information continued to come.[15]

By 1964 CIA had cut its ties with Goleniewski, who may have revealed more Soviet operations than any other defector in CIA history up to that time. Perhaps his most potent legacies were his direct lead to Felfe, and the seeds of doubt and suspicion which were sown as a result of his revelation that the KGB was so startlingly well informed about the CIA's top secret plan to recruit the Polish Intelligence officer.

Donald Huefner, a big, warmly expansive man, had replaced Thomas Lucid as head of the CIA staff at Pullach in July of 1959. Huefner, who is held in high regard by his colleagues for his sound judgment, chooses his words with care when discussing CIA activities. What lay ahead, he says succinctly, was "a difficult time for us." Sniper's letters had started arriving in March of 1958 and his strong evidence that the Organization was badly penetrated had come that autumn. As a result, the CIA had to exercise extreme caution in its dealings with everyone in the Organization. For security reasons not even Gehlen had been told about Sniper, so the few CIA officers who were fully informed, but at the same time working on a daily basis with Gehlen and his staff, were under considerable pressure. The most Huefner could do was tell Gehlen that the CIA had strong evidence of a serious security problem within the Organization. To have been more specific or to have begun any but the most subtle surveillance could have alerted the quarry.

It was discovered later that Felfe met with a Soviet General twice in the fall of 1958, at the same time Sniper passed on information alerting the Americans to penetrations in the Organization. But even if the KGB knew about Sniper's contact with the Americans at that point, they did not warn Felfe or he would have behaved with greater discretion. That same year, Felfe, who earned roughly 1,700 marks a month, bought a ten room chalet in Oberaudorf, Bavaria, which was estimated to have cost 100,000 marks. When that extravagance was added to his others—his son's private school, his comfortable Munich flat and his above-average wardrobe—it all pointed directly to another source of income. Questions were raised, and Felfe brushed them off by saying that his aunt, who lived in the United States, had recently died and left him a modest inheritance. "What that demonstrated more than anything else," says Clare Petty, who had returned to Washington but was still in touch with events at Pullach, "was the man's contempt for his colleagues, German and American. We checked and his aunt was in good health."

After Goleniewski was safely in the West, the CIA still did not take Gehlen into its confidence about its source. But now Gehlen could be confronted with the evidence implicating Felfe, and the resources of the Organization could be mobilized for what it was hoped would be the final stage of the hunt. The unlikely site for the delivery to Gehlen of this most unwelcome news was the annual Christmas holiday party given in Frankfurt by the CIA Chief of Station in January, 1961. While the other guests were celebrating, Gehlen and the Americans concerned withdrew into a bedroom of the host's house.

An officer who was present described the scene: "It was obvious that something serious was up. We were all tense. One of the liaison staff pulled a piece of paper out of his pocket and handed it to Gehlen. It had a list of names on it. Then he told the Doctor more or less what Sniper had said, that two people who had been on an orientation trip to the United States were Soviet agents, and this was a list of those who had gone. He was asked to pick from that list the names of those he suspected. Then an interesting thing happened. Gehlen didn't say anything and his face didn't change expression, but he turned red. His face flushed so that it turned truly red.

"He studied the list for a couple of minutes and finally he pointed to a name and said: 'For no particular reason, I pick this Felfe.' Nobody said anything, and he went on studying the list. After another couple of minutes he picked several other names, too. But I think we all knew Felfe was our man."

"Felfe was damned good at shaking tails," Huefner says ruefully, but then he picked the terrain most favorable to him. He met his Soviet contact on Sunday mornings in Vienna—when its boulevards were devoid of traffic—and he used a classic maneuver to see if he was being followed, making four right turns in a row. A full-scale, top secret effort, cooperating with units from the Organization, had been directed against Felfe; his telephone was tapped, his mail was opened, and he was put under surveillance. A CIA team had been recruited to follow him so there would be no chance of his recognizing an Organization agent. All the bases had been covered, and according to the novelists it should have been easy to catch him red-handed, but it was not so simple as that. Although his stalkers found out a great deal, the essential hard evidence was elusive. After it was all over, the CIA learned that Felfe had had one meeting with his KGB case officer only thirty mintues after the CIA team had lost him.

Surveillance quickly revealed that his old Dresden comrades Erwin Tiebel and Hans Clemens were working with him. Clemens received the messages from their Soviet masters, while Tiebel acted as courier. Telephone calls between Felfe and Clemens were frequent and repeated references were made to "Alfred" having called. The Organization broke into Felfe's house, did a black bag job, but they came away empty-handed. An American intercept station picked up KGB coded radio messages which could not be read, but were sent on a schedule which meshed closely with Clemens' movements. However, that only provided one more intangible. No one doubted what Felfe and Clemens were up to, but something solid was required.

It was a risky game for those whose secrets were being plundered; to alter Felfe's status, to limit his access or to act in any way which might suggest distrust would alert him to danger and ruin any chance of snaring him. Frustrations grew and provocations of various kinds were discussed, and dismissed. Then one day in November Felfe got careless, and his pursuers were there to spring the trap.

Clemens put in a call to his friend—one CIA officer close to the events remembers it as being on a Friday—and he had a complaint. "Alfred," Clemens said, had sent a "letter" which he could not read. What should he do about it? Clemens was a lazy man and this was not the first time he had failed to make the effort necessary to decipher a complicated message. This would be anathema to the meticulous and energetic Felfe, who in any case hardly had the time to spare to do Clemens' work as well as his own, and would not fancy making an extra trip to the outskirts of Bonn where Clemens lived. So Felfe made a mistake: he told Clemens to send the "letter" to him by registered mail.

"We intercepted the envelope to Felfe," a CIA officer said, "and there it was. A page of instructions, in code, from Felfe's KGB case officer. So we copied it, sealed it up again, sent it on and waited for Monday."

"The compound was sealed off," Huefner says. "Nobody, including the Organization security people, knew why, but no one could get in or out." The final scene had been carefully planned, and it would be played out in the office of General Lankau, one of Gehlen's oldest associates and head of a section that went by the misleadingly neutral name of Strategic Intelligence.

In terms of casting for the part, General Lankau was exactly right for his role in the brief drama that was to unfold. Even more than Gehlen, he relished operating in the shadows. His detractors joked that he considered himself so secret he pretended to himself that he did not even exist. He also had a taste for conspiracy, and it is said that on occasion he would lock the door of his office and refuse to open it except to an agreed signal. Felfe was summoned to this office on November 6, 1961, after his escape routes had been blocked.

There was always a studied casualness in Felfe's manner—Howard Roman says "he slouched through the door" when entering a room—but today Felfe's aplomb lasted only as long as it took him to glance at the document placed on the desk, a copy of the intercepted message from Clemens. In an instant Felfe had grabbed a half-inch square of microfilm from his billfold and thrust it into his mouth, but security guards wrestled him to the ground and prevented him from swallowing it. On that scrap of microfilm was a summary sheet of requirements which he had received from the KGB in Vienna. The fact of his carrying it about inside the confines of Pullach was as all-inclusive a gesture of contempt—for the Organization, its people, its purposes, and the nation it served—as one could find.[16,17]

Sniper: The Trail Leading to Heinz Felfe

Immediately after his arrest—which, ironically, occurred fifteen years to the day after his release from prisoner of war camp by the British—Felfe, in an effort to lighten his guilt before going to trial, tossed a fellow KGB spy to the West. The cynicism of this action was compounded by the fact that some time before Felfe's exposure the Soviets had chosen the unwitting agent for sacrifice. Evidence of the agent's espionage activities had been given to Felfe for just such an emergency; the KGB gave him a life with which to try to buy himself a better deal.

Forty-six year old Peter Fuhrmann, a former District Attorney in West Berlin of apparently independent means, had built a reputation as a result of his many court duels with a prominent lawyer from East Berlin. But the versatile Fuhrmann was also an undercover agent of the Militärische Abschirmdienst (MAD), the West German Army Intelligence service, and a Soviet spy. Having worked his way into the core of MAD's counterintelligence division, a position which allowed him to warn the Soviets about forthcoming operations in time for them to take countermeasures, Fuhrmann was a bargaining chip of some consequence.

The evidence Felfe turned over to the West Germans, which he claimed had come to him accidentally, condemned Fuhrmann out of his own mouth. Felfe reported to his Soviet case officer on large rolls of magnetic tape. When they met they would exchange tapes, Felfe giving his contact a full roll in return for an empty one. Felfe claimed that his case officer had given him, by mistake, a tape which had not been fully erased. To his surprise, Felfe declared, he found his supposedly empty tape contained part of an operational meeting between

Peter Furhmann and *his* case officer. With an eye to the uncertain future, Felfe tucked the evidence away in a safe place.

The KGB does make mistakes, but this wasn't one of them. Tapes are degaussed mechanically by putting a stack of them into a machine which takes everything off at one time, and it is inconceivable that the KGB could have left any part of a conversation on a tape by accident. Fuhrmann had been cold-bloodedly set up by his own people. But the scheme would take one year off Felfe's sentence, a sentence which he knew from the start was irrelevant since the Soviets, sooner or later, would buy his freedom.

After his arrest, Felfe was held in Koblenz, much of which was still in rubble even in 1962. The jail, which is old and solid, with thick walls and pitched roofs, had not been damaged. It is a formidable structure, but not as coldly awe-inspiring as American prisons. Dormers breaking the roof line, and sand castles outside the walls where the prison governor's children played, softened the look of it. That softness, it developed, was not confined to this prison or to prison architecture, a circumstance Felfe would discover and exploit.

In March, 1962, Howard Roman and Clare Petty, with one member of the Gehlen Organization, two secretaries, boxes of files, and a secure communications link, set up a base near the prison and prepared to interrogate Felfe. Roman had been chosen for the task because he had had charge of Goleniewski, and was fluent in German. Petty, the counterintelligence specialist whose analysis pinpointed Felfe in 1957, had known Felfe for several years. Since this was a German case— Felfe was being held on suspicion of treason—it was legally necessary that the CIA officers be accompanied on their visits to Felfe by a Gehlen representative. That proved to be more complicated than it sounds.

Humiliated by the revelation that it had been harboring Soviet agents, and by now thoroughly gun-shy, the BND agreed to do what it had so vigorously resisted; it would subject the agent assigned to accompany Petty and Roman, a man well qualified by training and background, to a polygraph examination. To everyone's dismay the candidate flunked. That was how it happened that the BND represen- tative who finally did sit in on the interviews with Felfe, a pleasant titled gentleman with impeccable credentials but little to qualify him for such a debriefing, did little more than sit.

An old lantern hung over the big double doors to the prison; inside there was a courtyard to cross before entering the building. "The first time we went to see Felfe we had to talk to him in the Visitors' Room,"

Roman recalls. "Those places are all much the same, I think. You sit opposite the prisoner in something like a booth in a restaurant, with wood partitions on either side. It was an awkward arrangement, it didn't work well, so after that we were able to use a nicer room." Up a winding staircase, on the top floor, they were allowed to use one of the relatively large dormer rooms. Because it was used for educational purposes, courses for young offenders and cultural programs, there were blackboards and a piano.

"We weren't actually supposed to tape the interviews," Petty says, "but I had stuck a tape recorder in my briefcase, and when we got into the room I snapped it on and hid it in the piano. It was a great idea except there was something wrong with the machine and a shrill screeching noise, which we pretended didn't exist, came from the general direction of the piano one whole morning." What Petty's recorder otherwise would have caught with greater clarity was a good performance by Felfe. "When he came in," Petty says, "Felfe greeted me like an old friend. In effect he said to us: 'I'm sorry about the whole thing, but I want to be perfectly frank.' " The rest of what he said was no more honest.

Another mechanical failure put the CIA men at a psychological disadvantage. Late one afternoon, as they were getting ready to leave their dormer room, there was a loud "click." They discovered the door had been locked automatically, presumably by a time clock. The three interrogators were imprisoned with the prisoner. After knocking on the door for a time and getting no response, the Gehlen representative went to the window and, while trying to appear casual, started shouting to attract attention. Nothing happened. Then he banged on the bars with a piece of metal. Finally, when the pounding and the shouting had proved useless, he found a fuse box high in the corner of an adjacent room and unscrewed the fuses. With that, alarm bells suddenly started ringing, guards came running, and the men were rescued. To the irritation of his interrogators, Felfe had remained sprawled comfortably in a chair watching the undignified proceedings with wry amusement.

"We met with him ten times," Roman says. "The main thing we wanted to discover was what cases he had betrayed. But it led nowhere, we got nothing. I didn't believe anything he told us. He had been well trained by the Soviets; there are so many levels of deception, you could keep digging and digging and never hit bedrock truth." "He told us what he knew we already knew, nothing more," Petty adds. "His memory for everything else was remarkably poor." When the interrogations were over, Gehlen thanked Roman and Petty, but Roman wonders what for. "The longer I was with Felfe, the less I believed him. We got nothing."

Felfe's imprisonment did not mitigate his contempt for West German security measures. Not long after his interrogation by Petty and Roman, he was transferred to the Riefstahlstrasse prison in Karlsruhe to await trial. There he contrived to breach the citadel's defenses in a way that heaped still more embarrassment on the German authorities. In an unprecedented gesture of generosity to the man whom the press had characterized as a dangerous traitor and Germany's most successful Soviet spy, the prison authorities granted him permission to leave his cell on weekends to play chess, unsupervised, in the prison library. This action was later dubbed "incomprehensible" since those suspected of political crimes, and particularly of treason, were supposed to be held under the strictest control. Comprehensible or not, granting him the freedom of the library allowed Felfe to resume contact with "Alfred," his Soviet case officer, from within the walls of the prison.

Under the guise of letters to his mother, Felfe was writing to Alfred and the letters were smuggled out by fellow inmates—an operation which continued for at least a year. Under his cover text, the actual messages were written in secret ink concocted by Felfe from alum he pinched from the prison laundry. The letters provided the Soviets with various items of interest and also gave them a list of things to do for him. But his smoothly running communications channel was cut in Feburary, 1963, when a former prison mate walked into a police office in Stuttgart and handed the startled officers a letter from Felfe to his "mother." In it Felfe asked if a specific amount of money had been deposited in a certain account; when the Gehlen Organization checked, they found it had been done.[18]

General Gehlen's "Lowest Ebb"

By the time Felfe and his two henchmen, Clemens and Tiebel, came to trial, the German public had been saturated with scandals about its security agencies, most notably the by now notorious Gehlen Organization, the BND. Allegedly riddled with former Nazis and a nest of Soviet spies, the Organization was pictured as a moral slum. The trial came on the heels of the Spiegel Affair, a scandal whose focal point was the influential news magazine Der Spiegel, but which embroiled Gehlen, Adenauer and his powerful Defense Minister, Franz Joseph

Strauss. Relations between the ambitious, hard-driving Strauss and Gehlen were at best strained, the subject of greatest contention between them being the role of Defense's Intelligence agency, MAD. In the course of the Spiegel Affair the two became open combatants.

Flash point was reached in 1962 when Gehlen sent to Adenauer an evaluation of information he had received from Washington suggesting that there could be trouble ahead over Germany's defense policy. The indications were that if Adenauer endorsed Strauss' plan to expand the country's arsenal dramatically, making it part of a European nuclear defense community, there might well be a confrontation with the Kennedy administration which strongly opposed such a move. When Adenauer passed Gehlen's evaluation on to Strauss, the Defense Minister reacted badly: Gehlen had gone too far. Not only had he reserved for his Organization all positive military intelligence, and its evaluation, now he appeared to be trying to make national defense policy. MAD, which in any case had been chafing under the restraints placed on it by the government, thanks to Gehlen, took its cue from Strauss' anger. It began to mobilize for an attempt to wrest some of Gehlen's responsibilities from him and to increase its own.

Timing is all-important, and this state of affairs coincided with the preparation for publication of an article by Der Spiegel—a magazine roughly equivalent in power and influence to the American Time in those years—designed to "expose" Strauss as a dangerous threat to democracy. Gehlen, it has since been charged, saw an opportunity and took it. Adolf Wicht, head of the Gehlen office in Hamburg where Der Spiegel's offices were, allegedly passed information to the magazine which was damaging to Strauss. To make matters worse, some of the material apparently was classified.

As soon as the article appeared on October 8 1962, the Ministry of Defense moved to have the magazine's editors indicted on suspicion of treason. While the Public Prosecutor considered, MAD took action. Surveillance teams followed the editors and, on October 23, arrest and search warrants were issued against two of them. At 9:00 P.M. on October 26, the Federal Criminal Police took over the Spiegel offices in Hamburg and in Bonn and confiscated uncounted numbers of files. Then, on November 2, MAD moved against Gehlen. His Hamburg representative, Wicht, was arrested.

This drama, played out in full view of the public, now brought the shadowy Gehlen himself on stage. On November 12 1962, he was summoned to the Chancellery for a confrontation with the Public Prosecutor. While he was subjected to the indignity of being kept waiting in an anteroom, it is said that Adenauer, who by now was entirely disenchanted with his former protégé, ordered Minister of Justice Stammberger, to arrest Gehlen. Stammberger, citing lack of evidence, refused. Gehlen survived, as he always did, and in the end it was Strauss who was driven from the government. But this time Gehlen was badly crippled. He had irrevocably lost the support, and the friendship, of Chancellor Adenauer.[19]

A pall still hung over the reputation of Gehlen and the Organization when a few months later the Felfe affair was reignited in the public mind. On Monday, July 8 1963, in a courtroom in Karlsruhe with five red-robed judges presiding, Felfe and his co-defendants, Clemens and Tiebel, were brought to trial. Spread out on a table before them were the tools of the spy's trade: tape recorders; miniature cameras; radios; and a suitcase of soft leather with a hidden compartment which could hold as many as twenty miniature spools of tape and fifteen miniature reels of film. Not in evidence were the cans of baby food which had been sent to Gerda Clemens, Hans' wife, when she was expecting a baby fathered by her husband's Russian contact, Max. Those tins, too, had been used to transmit secret messages.

Because of the sensitive nature of the testimony, most of the trial took place *in camera,* but enough happened in open court to feed a sensation-hungry international press. Clemens was the first to face his judges, and he was blatantly unrepentant. He regarded the Gehlen Organization, he said, as the enemy for many reasons, not the least of them its connection with American Intelligence. "I hate the Americans," he roundly declared ". . . I hate them like the plague." After the destruction of Dresden during the war, he told the court, he had made a vow: "I shall repay them doubly and triply." And, the Tiger of Como claimed, his resentment had been further inflamed by his treatment at the hands of the Americans after the war. There is no doubt Clemens worked hard to get his revenge, if indeed that, rather than money, was his motive. Except for a period during 1955, Clemens claimed he had met with the Soviets approximately every eight weeks to hand over information, from 1951 until his arrest ten years later.

Felfe, who described being a double agent like "dancing at two weddings, with the Russians and with Gehlen," told the court of two meetings with a Soviet general. The general, he proudly proclaimed, had come direct from Moscow to see him; once in Vienna, once at the Soviet headquarters at Karlshorst outside Berlin. Felfe also confided that he was far from being the only one in the Organization working for the Russians. His Soviet handlers, in fact, had advised him to get a transfer from the counterespionage section because there were already too many of their agents in that department.[20]

Having an audience, Felfe took a number of other swipes at the Americans and the British. He claimed to have been given information about the conferences at Teheran and Yalta during the war by an (unnamed) associate of Allen Dulles, then OSS representative in Switzerland. And he gave vent to his bitterness over the beating and torture of fellow prisoners of war he claimed to have seen administered by the British. The British, the former SS man Felfe aserted, were guilty of "bestial conduct." Erwin Tiebel was the last to appear, and the former Senior State's Attorney and construction firm manager made poor copy for the press, having acted only as a courier for the others.

The defense attorneys appealed to the court for leniency for the major players Felfe and Clemens on the ground that "their hatred for the United States had clouded their judgment." Sensing that his rotund client might be suspected of acting out of greed rather than anti-Americanism, Clemens' lawyer, Kurt Schon, insisted that money was not his motive, and once again trotted out the destruction of Dresden. Felfe's lawyer was more imaginative. His client, he pleaded, had been embittered by the American Morganthau plan, despite the fact that it never had been acted upon, to dismantle Germany's industry after the war and turn the nation into an agrarian society.

In view of the penalties handed down for treason in other countries, the trio got off lightly. In addition to fines equivalent to what they had been paid by the Soviets, Tiebel was sentenced to three years in prison, Clemens to ten, and Felfe to fourteen. In Felfe's case the judges shaved one year off the fifteen-year maximum allowed by law because he had named Fuhrmann as a fellow Soviet spy.[21]

The final scene in the drama of Heinz Felfe took place in 1969, the year following Gehlen's retirement. It was an ending Gehlen had bitterly opposed, but now he was powerless to stop it. It was a cold, bleak evening in February on the frontier between East and West Germany. Two cars, a Mercedes and a BMW, and a Russian-made bus, moved slowly along the road that wound through the trees toward the Wartha border, 360 kilometers southwest of Berlin. They stopped on the East German side, several miles short of the frontier. An East German security officer got out of the BMW and directed the bus, with its human cargo, to back into a clearing off to one side of the road; then he returned to his car where, like the others, he waited.

In the Mercedes were two lawyers from opposing camps. Their

responsibility was to protect the interests of their clients and to assure that the transaction they had so painstakingly negotiated on their behalf was carried out as agreed. Wolfgang Vogel, a bon vivant who defied the image of the dour East German by driving his brightly painted sportscar at high speed through the streets of East Berlin, represented the East German government. The more restrained Jürgen Stange was acting for West Germany. Both now waited, exchanging few words, as the tension grew. Every precaution had been taken. The minimum number of people had been informed and security was extremely tight, but there was always a possibility that something could go wrong.

At last an empty West German bus approached from the direction of the border and stopped when it reached them. Once again, the East German officer got out of the BMW and this time, after examining the documents given to him by the West German bus driver, he went to the parked East German bus, opened the door in the rear and ordered its passengers out. Without speaking, each carrying a suitcase, the men and women clambered awkwardly out of one bus and into the other. The transfer made, the West German bus turned around and, together with the BMW and the Mercedes, headed for the frontier crossing.

On the West German side of the line, Heinze Felfe, under guard, also was waiting. When the caravan from the East reached the first barrier on the Wartha side of the crossing, the court order which formally released Felfe from prison on parole was read to him. Then he was taken outside. As he watched, the Mercedes and the bus, having passed the first barrier, traversed the 900 yards of no man's land and the second, West German barrier was raised.

Felfe stood with several members of the Organization, and as Stange and Vogel approached them the tension was palpable. The hostility of the Gehlen officials toward their former comrade was barely suppressed, as was Felfe's own anxiety. The formalities were brief: Heinz Felfe, having been released from West German custody, and having chosen East Germany as his place of residence, was officially handed over by Jürgen Stange to the representative of the East German government, Wolfgang Vogel. As Stange watched, Felfe and Vogel walked over to the Mercedes and went back to the place from which they had come: East Germany.[22]

The price the Russians paid for Felfe was twenty-one human beings. Fifteen men and three women who had been held as political prisoners, and three West Germans from the University of Heidelberg who had been convicted of espionage and imprisoned in the Soviet Union: hostages for just such an exchange. The years of political maneuvering, the repeated Soviet overtures, Gehlen's adamant refusal to sell Felfe to the Soviets, all had ended swiftly—in less than an hour—and in near silence.[23]

In the aftermath of the Felfe trial, Gehlen and his Organization, still reeling from the disastrous Spiegel Affair, reached their lowest ebb. Calling it an "unprecedented scandal," editorial writers blamed Gehlen for the sloppy personnel policies which allowed Nazis to be hired, and berated the Organization for peppering its ranks with leftovers from "the Nazi leadership corps." On July 23 1963, Deputy Leader Erler of the opposition party, the SPD, referred to an "abyss of treason."[24]

In an analysis done for the CIA, Tennant Bagley, Jr., in the 1960s a senior member of the Agency's Soviet bloc division, reflected on what the Soviets had achieved in West Germany. There, he said, Soviet agents "provided the KGB not only with secrets but also with control of the intelligence apparatus itself . . . moles [in the BND] were able to manipulate the careers of their fellow officers so as to promote and strategically place other KGB moles."[25] There was no way of knowing, after Felfe, how many remained in the Organization, how deeply they had burrowed, or how high they had climbed.

Reports circulated that the Organization was to be completely overhauled, and that on October 1, 1963, Gehlen was to be replaced. One CIA officer remembers running into a senior Organization member in Bonn. "He was skulking like a shadow, tiptoeing along the halls of power. He used to march through them, as if he owned them. No one in Bonn would see any of the Gehlen people any more. When I asked him what he was doing he said: 'My job is to save what can be saved.' Gehlen survived, if you can call it that, but only because there was no one to put in his place."

The Felfe trial and the storm it provoked took its toll, and once more he had not been swept away. But by now his strength, both personal and political, had been sapped, and his reputation as well as that of his organization had been irreparably damaged. Although he withdrew more and more from active supervision of his staff and their activities, still he clung to the thing he loved above all, *Der Dienst,* the Organization.

A generation had passed since the Americans had decided to bring Gehlen back to Germany and embark on what was essentially an experiment. Some twenty years had elapsed since that small band of former Fremde Heere Ost officers was reunited in the Blue House at Oberursel and formed what Friedl von Glinski called "a family, really." At Pullach the family had grown into a bustling community complete with a nursery school for the children of both the Germans and the few Americans. Now the Organization was an institution, the BND. The site, in the peaceful Munich suburb of Pullach, with its tree-lined streets and neat gardens, remained the same; behind the tall electrified fence that enclosed the entire complex, even some of the old American World War II prefabricated huts were still in use. But as one of the major intelligence services of the Western Alliance, the BND was a powerful contemporary enterprise.

Unable to agree on a successor, the government extended Gehlen's tenure for a year beyond the retirement age of sixty-five. But then, at last, on April 30 1968, Reinhard Gehlen was awarded the Grand Cross of the Federal Republic of Germany's Order of Merit, and ushered into retirement. And Gerhard Wessel succeeded him for the second time in twenty-eight years, just as he had in 1945 when he had taken over as chief of Fremde Herre Ost while Gehlen fled to the mountains to await the Americans.

Gehlen retired to his house on Lake Starnberg, not far from Pullach.[26] There he spent much of his time writing his memoirs, apparently undertaken to answer the endless stream of criticism being directed at him and his Organization. They are bland, uninformative, and occasionally wrong, and if their purpose was to set the record straight, they failed. Nor did they silence his critics. But Gehlen also pursued other, uncontroversial interests, such as sailing in a sleek little craft several of the original CIA team had used and then given him on their departure. He made an effort to stay in touch with former colleagues; startled senior CIA officers received large color photographs of the notoriously camera-shy Doctor, in full evening dress, resplendent with the Grand Cross of the Order of Merit hanging from a broad silk ribbon on his chest.

And Gehlen continued to see his old friends, John Boker, Eric Waldman and James Critchfield, even in his last illness. On June 9, 1979, Gehlen died quietly at his lakeside house.

Conclusion

The late historian Theodore White said, in another connection, that the United States has two traditions in diplomacy: the crusade and the deal.[1] At the end of the war these two incompatible approaches to the conduct of national policy converged, and Gehlen was the beneficiary. Just as unconditional surrender had been the nonnegotiable goal of the war against Hitler, halting the spread of communism became the focus of America's postwar defense of democracy. The Americans had a new crusade, and in an effort to further it they struck a deal with Gehlen.

Crusaders tend to be naive, they see issues in black and white, and adopt unyielding postures. Deal-makers, by contrast, are more likely to be flexible and, if not cynical, certainly pragmatic. At the time Gehlen was taken on, most Army Intelligence officers were inexperienced in the subtleties and ramifications of high-stakes international politics, but they had the crusading spirit. They viewed Gehlen's unit as a useful weapon in achieving their goal. If they stopped to consider what was in it for him, they probably did not go beyond the obvious advantages it gave him over his captured brother German officers.

Gehlen, however, was a seasoned veteran and had learned how to maneuver in the most hostile environments. He knew how to make a deal. He had navigated some slippery terrain as Hitler's least favorite Intelligence officer. He had witnessed Germany's secret rearmament under the noses of the very same governments which had just defeated

173

it again. And above all, he had planned, and executed his daring escape to captivity—including the "liberation" of the all-important secret FHO files—in the dangerous and paranoid atmosphere of Hitler's last days. A master at manipulating situations to his own advantage, he approached his deal with the Americans from a different perspective. While the single-minded Americans were exploiting the knowledge and experience of their captured asset, Gehlen was exploiting the leverage that relationship gave him to further his own agenda.

By the spring of 1946, as the Cold War grew in intensity, the Americans had pulled the bulk of their troops out of Western Europe, while the Soviets had radically increased their armed presence in the East. The threat of war was real, and the Americans realized they were at a critical disadvantage militarily. What they didn't know was how great an advantage the Soviets had, or what their intentions were. The Americans were desperate for information, and Reinhard Gehlen was there to give it to them. Having satisfied themselves that he was not a war criminal nor a supporter of neo-Nazism, they returned him to Germany and put his knowledge, experience and resources to work.

It was a risk politically, but the undertaking was shrouded in secrecy, and the gamble quickly paid off. Reliable information about the military buildup in the East came in. The Americans finally had the operational intelligence they needed, and because secrecy had been maintained there was no political price to pay back home.

While the Americans were focusing on the short-term goal of instant intelligence, Gehlen was taking the long view, and circumstances conspired to help him. Gehlen knew that if Germany was to come back to life it would have to be as a democratic state allied with its former enemies. Moreover, if Europe was to regain its economic strength Germany, with all its resources, natural and human, would have to play a central role. Further, convinced as he was of the growing Soviet threat, he believed that eventually, together with its economic and social rebirth would come some kind of new German army.

Given this view of his country's future Gehlen recognized that leaders would be needed, German leaders with contacts and influence in the country. So he used his unique position with the Americans to gather in and give shelter to former General Staff officers who could form the core of such a cadre of leaders. It is fair to say that in mounting this rescue effort Gehlen knew he stood to reap handsome rewards from the intervention of those he helped if events unfolded as he foresaw. Most of these officers, many bearing distinguished names and reputations widely recognized in Germany, had had no connection with intelligence and hardly qualified as professionals able to help him carry out his mission. But from the start, the Americans' control over Gehlen was loose.

This failure in oversight became critical during the next phase, the heady days of rapid expansion when a grossly understaffed and inexperienced American presence failed to rein in and impose restrictions on Gehlen's recruiters. Lax oversight played a major role in the Organization's recruitment practices which were, at best, slipshod. The partition of Germany left the West German government vulnerable to penetration by agents from the East, and continuing Soviet success in exploiting that weakness was demonstrated as one spy scandal followed another. But after the earliest days, when identity files became readily accessible, there was no excuse for hiring former Nazis, SS men whose backgrounds could be checked with ease, as the CIC's Operation CAMPUS demonstrated.

Most knowledgeable observers agree that Gehlen gave the Americans at least some of what they wanted, although there are widely divergent views about the overall value of the relationship. But some in the Intelligence community remain vehemently critical of both the Army and the CIA for taking him on. Their criticism flows in large measure from the conviction that it was unprincipled to protect Hitler's Gehlen and a group of his senior officers in the first place, let alone to support his single-minded ambition to create and control Germany's Intelligence service. To them Gehlen was an opportunist prepared to trim his sails to whatever political breeze was blowing within Germany, witness his virtually simultaneous overtures to both Adenauer and the SPD. As they see it Gehlen, in his bid for power, manipulated the Americans from the start, exploiting their lack of sophistication in international affairs (they could not even speak the language), and of professionalism in the field of intelligence.

Beyond that, these critics maintain, it was obvious that in order to carry out his mission for the Americans Gehlen would have to recruit former SS men, just as, in fact, the United States Army itself was doing in certain instances. They were the professionals who could get the job done. But Gehlen would do it on a large scale and at a remove from such control as there was over his operation, and that is where the danger lay. This SS element would blend into a German organization corrupting and subverting its stated goals. The Felfe case came as no surprise to those who opposed Gehlen from the outset. They had expected a scandal to erupt sooner or later, and it demonstrated that the whole undertaking had been bankrupt.

A far larger body of those knowledgeable about the subject supports the enterprise, but some with less enthusiasm than others. In considering only the narrow question of his contribution to the American intelligence effort, one former senior CIA officer who was based in Langley says, "At the beginning Gehlen's people filled a gap. They did good work; got lots of observations, numbers of trucks, planes and weapons. But as Soviet security got better even that dried up and pretty soon we were wondering. Gehlen put the emphasis on the wrong place, on clandestine information, and that's a mistake. It's only part of the picture. He was hung up on these clandestine 'reports,' all his analysis was based on them and they were often wrong. Reports were frequently planted on them; they were sitting ducks for Soviet disinformation.

"After they were taken over by the West German government there was a gradual disenchantment there, too. Adenauer wanted to know: What's going on in Pankow? [Soviet headquarters in East Germany]. What's [East German leader] [Walter] Ulbricht going to do next? When Gehlen couldn't tell him because he didn't have anybody in Ulbricht's office, disenchantment set it. As far as we were concerned, by the mid-1950s we didn't have many illusions left about how good they were, but we were in bed with them and wanted to stay there. They were the intelligence service of one of our most powerful allies, we wanted to stay close. But in practice—they faithfully sent us Die Übersicht (The Overview), we got it every week, and nobody ever used it."

Other informed observers see it from a different perspective, considering issues removed from intelligence tradecraft. They defend Gehlen as a valuable political ally, citing his wisdom in providing a haven where the German military leaders that he considered to be most salvageable could be held together. They give him credit for providing an environment where they could be kept abreast of a changing world, and controlled and guided to ensure that they did not get out ahead of the transition of Germany to a member of a Western military alliance against the Soviet Union.

They also point to Gehlen's ability to establish links with other Western intelligence and security organizations, in order to support his own objectives for the emerging democratic West German regime. As one former CIA officer who worked closely with him put it: "Those that judge what Gehlen accomplished solely in terms of their version of good tradecraft do themselves and him an injustice. The broader objectives involved should be weighed. And, finally, it's important to consider where it all came out."

As far as those broader objectives are concerned, the Americans' relationship with the Gehlen Organization ran parallel to that which the United States had with Germany as a whole. As the immediate threat of war with the Soviet Union receded, and as more independence was granted to the German people, there was a shift in emphasis from military to political considerations. This was mirrored in Gehlen's relationship with American Intelligence when control of his organization shifted from the Army to the CIA with its broader range of concerns.

That shift raises two fundamental questions: Should the CIA have taken over Gehlen and the Organization at all? And, once having done so, how effectively was it controlled? Under the Army the Organization functioned as an implement of the occupying force, digging out urgent operational information and, at least in theory, working under direct military orders. CIA, however, looked at it more as a promising political asset, one which had the blessing of those in the highest echelons of the American government, and which was to be handled with diplomacy. The strongest argument in favor of adoption was that the Organization already existed thanks to the Americans, and since it was inevitable that there would be a German intelligence service one day it would be in the American interest to continue to support this known quantity and influence its direction.

Had the CIA decided not to take Gehlen over from the Army it is difficult to see who would have taken on the Organization. Surely not the British, who had their own candidates, nor the French, whose distrust of Gehlen was profound, even assuming either country had been able to pay the bills. It is likely the Organization would have disintegrated, with elements and individuals being picked up by the Americans, French, British and, wherever possible, the East Germans, Soviets and others. However, sooner or later, and probably sooner rather than later, the emerging German government would have developed an organized intelligence capability, a situation which would have left the Americans on the outside trying to look in. As it was, after the CIA takeover the Americans were on the inside, but in terms of control still trying to look in.

Under the Army Gehlen achieved a singular success, he was able to keep the identity of his agents secret from his patrons, the Americans. Without that knowledge there was little practical control. On taking over the Organization, instead of insisting that unless it was given that information all deals were off, the CIA too allowed Gehlen to maintain that vital secrecy. At this critical juncture the CIA should have been much tougher with Gehlen; he needed the Americans more than the Americans needed him. Having failed to force Gehlen's hand CIA liaison officers had to resort to various stratagems to try to discover the true identities of Gehlen's agents, an effort which preoccupied Army CIC as well. The long delay in uncovering Felfe and the nest of Nazis in the Organization is testimony to the seriousness of that mistake, for both the CIA and Gehlen.

Gehlen handled the Americans with great skill. They found him interesting, knowledgeable, a curiosity. His relationship with CIA had its ups and downs, but for many years it was comfortable for both parties. Indeed, the Gehlen operation became a favorite of the CIA. "[Allen] Dulles loved it," said a former senior CIA official who was a long-time observer of the Organization. "It was very secret. It was a kind of club. It was considered a great posting, a plum." And with the transformation of the American-sponsored Gehlen Organization into the German BND control was no longer an issue. Strategic intelligence, political information and influence, the broad and often dangerous concerns of international relations during the Cold War were of paramount importance. Although the Americans moved their liaison office outside the gates of Pullach, in the real sense they remained inside and, regardless of their opinion of Gehlen's tradecraft, were happy to be there.

The democratic development of the Federal Republic defused the question of whether there was a conflict between American interests and Gehlen's own agenda. Binding Germany to the West as a counterweight to the Soviet threat had been an important political goal for the United States. Some of the military leaders Gehlen had "rescued" did move into positions of importance in the new democratic Germany. And Gehlen was recognized by a small circle of men who wielded great influence in both Germany and the United States during the critical mid-1950s. Chancellor Adenauer formed a close relationship with Secretary of State John Foster Dulles. Foster's brother, CIA director Allen Dulles strongly supported Gehlen. And, to complete the circle, Adenauer too had close ties to Gehlen. Yet just how much American ties to Gehlen contributed to the new alliance between old enemies is hard to define.

Within a few years of the end of the shooting war in 1945 the bitter political Cold War engulfed half the world. The United States swiftly grew into its role of Western superpower, gaining in assurance and sophistication. The professionalism and technological capabilities of

American intelligence surged, and while the insatiable need for information about the Soviet Union and its satellites continued, new sources and methods were developed. Accordingly, the relationship between the Americans and the Gehlen Organization changed. However, if the definition of a good deal is one in which both parties are satisfied, then, flawed as it was, on balance the association between Gehlen and American intelligence succeeded.

The Americans got good military operational intelligence when they had few other sources and needed it most. With the shift in priorities to political concerns they used this channel, as well as others, both to wield influence and keep a close eye on political developments in the emerging German state, an avenue the CIA would not have had had it not rescued the Organization when Gehlen's relationship with the Army was at breaking point.

For his part, Gehlen got what he wanted, regardless of the motives ascribed to him. Whether his goal was to help the West stave off Soviet aggression; to help Germany develop a strong democratic form of government with close ties to the United States; to establish and control a German Central Intelligence Agency; to have a role in the formation of a new German army; to have the power to manipulate political events from behind the scenes; or a combination of all those things—his ambitions, in his own eyes, were, for a time, fulfilled.

There were losses to the two parties as well. The Americans opened themselves to the charge of unprincipled hypocrisy by taking on Gehlen and his fellow officers when the civilized world looked at Germany with horror. CIC's secret spying on the Organization and its failure to warn CIA about Felfe arguably allowed him many additional years to loot West Germany's secrets. And the Soviets exploited both American and German intelligence through their failure to assure the security of the Organization. The price paid for this across-the-board laxness was high both in secrets stolen and, for Gehlen, in irreparable damage to his reputation.

Finally, in addressing the question of whether support of the Gehlen Organization was worth the inevitable compromises, it is useful to bear in mind that even when played on a narrow field intelligence is not a game of winners and losers. It is a game of advantages, points gained. Wars are not won by spies.

A Note on Sources

In response to requests made under the Freedom of Information Act, documents were released to me by government agencies including the Department of State, the Department of Justice (Federal Bureau of Investigation), and the United States Army Intelligence and Security Command. Much of this material was classified and had not been released before. I also consulted documents and microfilm held by the National Archives. In addition, I was given access to personal papers and letters which are the property of private individuals.

The U. S. Army Intelligence and Security Command at Fort Meade, Maryland furnished many hundreds of documents in response to my Freedom of Information Act requests on organizations and individuals. In my requests regarding individuals I gave their names and as much biographical information as I had available. Most of the documents I received in return bear the individual's name at the top, indicating he is the subject of the information that follows. Occasionally, however, one individual's name appears in the text of information dealing with another about whom a request had also been filed. Their names also appear on occasion in documents dealing with organizations about which I had submitted FIOA requests.

In many instances relating to individuals there are no indications of where the documents originated, who the authors were, or what their purpose was. Many appear to be photostats of file cards. In citing these documents I have provided as many indicators as possible to facilitate their identification, information such as the agency which supplied them to me (e.g. the U. S. Army Intelligence and Security Command), as well as names, dates and locations that appear on them. (The number and content of these documents indicate CIC surveillance of the individuals named was extremely thorough. These reports frequently recount their activities in detail and describe those with whom they were in contact.)

Many people provided me with information ranging from accounts of personal experiences to professional opinions. I made every effort to find more than one source for what I was told. Since many of the former Army Intelligence and CIA officers I interviewed were associated with Gehlen at the same time, it was very often possible to find a second source. In most instances when it was not, I give the name of the person who provided the information. In cases where a source has requested anonymity, I have honored that request, and refer to him or her only as a former CIC, CIA or Intelligence officer, or as an observer.

Published sources used in this work are cited in the footnotes in the usual way.

Of the books on Gehlen, three are of particular interest.

Reinhard Gehlen, *The Service: The Memoirs of General Reinhard Gehlen*, New York, World Publishing, 1972. (A translation of the original work published in West Germany.)

Heinz Höhne and Hermann Zolling, *The General Was A Spy: The Truth About General Gehlen and His Spy Ring*, New York, Coward, McCann & Geoghegan, 1972. (A translation of the original work published in West Germany.) A later work by Heinz Höhne, *Der Krieg Im Dunkeln*, C. Bertelsmann Verlag, Munich, 1985, (which has not been translated) contains some additional material about the Gehlen Organization.

E. H. Cookridge pseud. (Edward Spiro), *Gehlen: Spy of the Century*, New York, Random House, 1971. Originally published in England. (Not used as a source; see below.)

Other books have appeared in Europe but often are more political broadsides than serious works. One such is Albrecht Charisius and Julius Mader, *Secret No Longer: Development, Organization and Methods of the Imperialistic German Secret Service*. East Berlin, Deutscher Militaerverlag, 1969. Heinz Felfe has also published a memoir, *Im Dienst Des Gegners—10 Jahre Moskaus Mann Im BND*, Hamburg: Rasch und Röhring Verlag, 1986. (These books are not used as sources.)

The only work on Gehlen first published in the United States,

Charles Whiting, *Gehlen: Master Spy of the Century*, New York, Ballantine Books, 1972 (paperback), is sensational in tone and contains many errors. No sources or references are cited. (Not used as a source.)

Gehlen apparently wrote his autobiography to answer the criticism leveled at him and the BND during his last years as its chief, and during his retirement. It must be viewed as a largely self-serving document. Two former CIA officers, one of whom had general oversight of the Organization, and another who made an exhaustive study of it for the Agency, question a number of his assertions. For example, they both state that Gehlen never had a successful high-level penetration in East Germany, or indeed anywhere in the East bloc, and suggest the claims he makes for them in his book result, in the words of one, from "wishful thinking."

Höhne and Zolling's *The General Was A Spy* is based on the series of articles written by them for the magazine Der Spiegel in 1971. Based on interviews with Organization members, personal papers, and drawing on World War II FHO files, the authors are careful to document their sources. However, they appear to have accepted BND claims for espionage coups which are disputed by American Intelligence authorities. The errors regarding the United States' role in the Organization reflect a lack of knowledgeable American sources, a problem which continued to beset Höhne in his later work.

Cookridge's *Spy Of The Century*, regarded by many as the definitive work on the Gehlen Organization, is profoundly flawed. Politically motivated assertions made by polemicists have been accepted as facts. He lists among his sources six works by the East German Julius Mader, co-author of *Secret No Longer* (see above). Openly hostile to the West, Mader has made United States Intelligence a particular target (see his *Who's Who In The CIA*). Cookridge's account of the relationship between Gehlen and American Intelligence is so distorted as to render it useless.

Acknowledgments

It is through the extraordinary interest and generous cooperation of dozens of people that this book was made possible. Many former Army Intelligence and CIA officers who had worked closely with Reinhard Gehlen and the Organization, or with other branches of intelligence, and who had never before revealed their knowledge, shared their insights. I cannot fully express my gratitude to them for their willingness to help, their candor and the time they gave me. Others shared their recollections, helped me in my search for sources, gave me the benefit of their experiences, and showed me great hospitality.

My warmest thanks go to Arnold Andrew Anderson, William Bird, John Boker, John Bross, Anthony Cave Brown, Marjorie Cline, Ray Cline, James Critchfield, General John Russell Deane, Jr., (Ret.), Robert Feldman, Thomas Fox, Harris Greene, the late Frank Harman, Donald Huefner, Ruth Huefner, Ian Hersey, Dr. Robert Gerald Livingston, Peggy Lucid, the late Thomas Lucid, David C. Martin, Dorothy Matlack, Ute Möller, Clare Edward Petty, Melba Petty, the late David Atlee Phillips, the late Howard Roman, Jürgen Stange, Thomas Troy, General Arthur Trudeau, (Ret.), Friedel von Glinski, Rudolf von Glinski, Dr. Eric Waldman, Jo Ann Waldman, and Charles Wheeler.

I am singularly fortunate to have as my editor Mark Carroll, whose enthusiastic support for this undertaking has been tireless, and to have had the invaluable advice and help of Maud Wilcox. The National Archives houses many treasures, as researchers from around the world are aware. Among them are Timothy Mulligan, the distinguished World War II scholar and editor of the microfilmed *Guides to German Records*, and the gracious, courtly, indefatigable and infinitely resourceful John Taylor.

There are former intelligence officers whose help I would like to acknowledge but who have asked that I not use their names, and some who would prefer I not single them out. In some cases they spent many days with me and I am most grateful to them.

Our sons, Mitch and Thornton, have been consistently supportive, showing an active and heartening interest in my work throughout, as well as displaying unfailingly good humor amid the inevitable disruptions in our daily lives. My husband, Mitch, to whom this book is dedicated, encouraged me from the start. His enthusiasm for this project has been unflagging, as is his truly saintly patience and understanding. Living with someone in the throes of writing a book is a test of endurance, yet somehow he has managed to convince me that he cares as much about it as I do. He is my best collaborator, critic and friend.

Glossary

ABWEHR	Literally, "defense." The German Intelligence Service under the High Command of the Armed Forces (OKW). Its chief was Admiral Wilhelm Canaris. In 1944 it was absorbed by the Security arm of the Nazi Party SS.
BfV	Bundesamt für Verfassungsschutz, Office for the Protection of the Constitution. Similar to the American FBI.
BND	Bundesnachrichtendienst. The Federal Intelligence Service. The name given the Gehlen Organization after it was taken over by the German government in 1956.
CIA	United States Central Intelligence Agency.
CIC	United States Army Counter Intelligence Corps.
FHO	Fremde Herre Ost, literally, Foreign Armies East. Unit of the German Army High Command (OKW) charged with eastern front intelligence. Reinhard Gehlen was its chief from 1942 until the last days of the war.
KGB	Komitat Gosudarstvenoy Bezopasnosti, Committee of State Security. The Soviet Intelligence Service.
NKVD	Narodnyi Kommissariat Vniutrennikh Dyet, People's Commissariat for Internal Affairs. Predecessor of the KGB.
OKW	Oberkommando der Wehrmacht. High Command of the German Armed Forces.

OSS   Office of Strategic Services. Predecessor of the CIA.

SD   Sicherheitdienst, Security Service. Nazi Party Intelligence Service, under the SS.

SS   Schutzstaffel, literally, the Protection Detachment. A uniformed arm of the Nazi Party, under Heinrich Himmler.

WEHRMACHT   German armed forces.

NOTES

Introduction

1. Intelligence in Recent Public Literature. 1972 (80) 342 C. A review of four books about Gehlen and the Organization, it appeared in the CIA's internal publication Studies In Intelligence. Made available courtesy of the Carrollton Press.

2. Former CIA officers pointed out that the information I was seeking falls under the "third service rule" by which the CIA will not release to a third intelligence service, or other party, information about or from a friendly service without its formal consent.

Chapter One

1. These episodes are recounted by General Heinz Guderian in his memoir *Panzer Leader*. London: Michael Joseph, 1952, pp. 383, 387, 428.

2. As if to underscore that this was a turning point in their lives, they celebrated Herta Gehlen's forty-first birthday with as much optimism for the future as they could muster. Reinhard Gehlen, *The Service: The Memoirs of General Reinhard Gehlen*. N.Y.: World Publishing Co., 1972, pp. 101–2, 106–7.

3. Reinhard Gehlen, p. xxi.

4. The late Glenn Infield quoted Karl Deeter, with whom he had a conversation in Heidelberg on July 2, 1972.

5. David Irving was the translator of Gehlen's memoirs and as such spent

a considerable amount of time with him. In a conversation with Irving, he told me Gehlen "tended to return again and again to what was of greatest interest to him. It was a bit like dealing with a broken gramophone record. Things would move along smoothly for a time, then he'd hit a groove and we'd be back to the German General Staff again. And again." (Conversation with Irving, June 2, 1983.)

6. Walter Görlitz, *History of the German General Staff.* N.Y.: Praeger, 1957.

7. Some of Germany's enemies, however, held a harsher opinion. In the intemperate words of British Brigadier General J. H. Morgan, a member of the Inter-Allied Military Commission of Control in Germany from 1919 to 1923, ". . . the German Officers' Corps has blighted like a pest every green shoot of modern thought and progress that might otherwise have taken root in Germany . . . The great humanitarian movements of the 19th century, in particular the humanization of the laws of war, the growth of international law, the development of a 'social conscience' . . . left the moral standards of the Officer's Corps as primitive and as ruthless as they were in the days of Frederick the Great and indeed of Attila. From all liberal and progressive movements, such as they were, within Germany itself, it was equally estranged, and to them it was equally hostile." J. H. Morgan, *Assize of Arms:* N.Y., Oxford University Press, 1946.

8. There was some resistance to Hitler in Germany, and repeated attempts were made to assassinate him. His ability to survive them was uncanny. See, among other works: Herbert M. Mason: *To Kill the Devil,* N.Y., Norton, 1978; Peter Hoffmann: *The History of the German Resistance 1933–45,* Cambridge, Mass., MIT Press, 1977.

9. "This elite group," says journalist William Shirer, ". . . built up by Moltke to be the pillar of the nation . . . had been reduced in the summer of 1944 to a pathetic body of fawning, frightened men." The final humiliation came when Rundstedt, Guderian and the other Generals sat as judges on the Court of Honor [after the July 20, 1944 assassination attempt], expelled hundreds of their fellow officers from the Army and turned them over to the Gestapo for execution. William Shirer: *The Rise and Fall of the German Reich,* N.Y., Simon and Schuster, 1960.

10. Another officer of middle class origins was General Erich Ludendorff. In the period 1914–18 Ludendorff, "the man of steel," was the actual leader of the High Command.

11. For an account of this period see Morgan, op cit. See also Sir Halford Mackinder, *Democratic Ideals And Reality,* 1904, cf Anthony Cave Brown, *The Last Hero,* Wild Bill Donovan, N.Y., Times Books, 1982, p. 800.

12. For insight into the communist uprising of the time, see Eric Waldman, *The Spartacist Uprising,* Marquette University, 1958.

13. Both Gehlen and his wife were and would remain proud of her connection with Frederick the Great's famous General: in the post-war years Ameri-

can intelligence officers at Pullach were amused to receive engraved invitations from the Gehlens to which were appended the footnote that Frau Gehlen was "nee von Seydlitz-Kurzbach."

It was in the mid-eighteenth century, at the Battle of Rossbach during the Seven Years War that General von Seydlitz and the Prussian cavalry achieved lasting fame. With only eighteen guns and seven infantry battalions to back him up, he led the charge on the enemy, routing all 64,000 men within forty minutes.

14. Gehlen's connection with von Seydlitz had another, distant but inviting aspect to it. The complicated leader Frederick the Great, whom von Seydlitz so admirably served, has been called the father of contemporary military espionage. He created and oversaw a large intelligence organization, dividing those employed by it into four categories. Common Spies: peasants and common folk who spied for money. Double Spies: those who worked for both sides, and whose primary value was transmitting false information to the enemy. High Ranking Spies: ambassadors and the like who were handsomely rewarded for their services. Coerced Spies: citizens of captured areas reporting under duress. Frederick made broad use of this organization, and it was extremely effective. "Marshal de Soubise is always followed by a hundred cooks," he said, "I am always preceded by a hundred spies."

15. Information about Gehlen's military career, and FHO, comes from captured German war documents, original and on microfilm, held by the National Archives and Records Service (NARS), Washington, D.C. Of particular interest are the records of Fremde Heere Ost reproduced on 77 rolls of microfilm, reference number T78, rolls 548–591, 670, 673–704. See No. 82, Records of Headquarters, Germany Army High Command (Oberkommando des Heeres—OKH/FHO). Edited and described by archivist Timothy Mulligan, this is Part IV of the invaluable *Guides to German Records Microfilmed at Alexandria, Virginia*, NARS, 1982. Among other documents at the Archives: RG 165, Records of the War Department General and Special Staffs, providing biographical information on Gehlen's life and military career (undated), and reports nos. 5724 and 5725 giving background information (dated 29 August 1945). RG 242, Records of the National Archives Collection of Foreign Records Seized 1941–, German Army General Staff Personnel Card Files reproduces German Army cards dealing with Gehlen's Army service, (latest date December 1, 1944).

16. On February 18, 1944, Canaris was relieved of his post and the Abwehr absorbed by the SS, but the real end came for him in the wake of the July 20, 1944, General's Plot to assassinate him. Although not directly involved, he had aided those who were and was arrested. But Field Marshal General Keitel, in an atypically decent gesture, delayed his trial and thereby prevented him from falling victim to the barbaric bloodbath which followed. It was only a delay, however. Canaris ultimately was tried at Flossenbürg concentration camp on April 9, 1945, and hanged on the same day.

17. Gehlen, *The Service,* p. xxi.

18. The RSHA was formed in 1939. It combined the Security Police (Gestapo and Kripo) and the Security Service (SD). It was a central office of the Supreme Command of the SS (Reichsführung-SS) and the Reich Ministry of the Interior. See Helmut Kravsnick, et al: *Anatomy of the SS State,* N.Y., Walker & Co., 1968.

19. Interrogation of Walter Schellenberg, Appendix VI, pp. 1–2. RG 238, Records of the War Department, NARS.

20. Kaltenbrunner, who also spent time hiding in the mountains, after his capture reportedly was considered as a possible candidate for use by American Army Intelligence. It was a short-lived notion, however, and in the end he was tried, convicted and hanged at Nürnberg jail on October 15, 1946.

21. William L. Shirer's apt description, *Rise and Fall of the German Reich,* p. 324.

22. Schellenberg Interrogation, Appendix VI, p. 65; Pierre Galante, *Mlle. Chanel,* Chicago, H. Regenery, Co., 1973, pp. 179–182. The Germans were out-maneuvered again by one of their most prominent prisoners of war, the son of Josef Stalin. "By staging an elaborate setting [for dinner], ingeniously and craftily arranged to display great refinement and meticulous etiquette, the interrogators sought to embarrass young Stalin, so as to render him ill at ease in the course of the ensuing conversation. Their efforts were futile, as the prisoner was found to be extremely adroit socially, and did not become flustered by the plethora of courses with corresponding changes of silver; on the contrary he distinguished himself linguistically in repartee, as well as in the dialectics of economics. He even succeeded in perplexing his German interrogators during a discussion on Socialism by citing three Hitler quotations, which none of them knew, but which they all affirmed in order not to expose their ignorance in the field of 'Hitlerology,' only to be told that but two of the quotations were genuine, whereas the third was spurious." Interrogation of Prisoner of War Uffz. George Johannsohn, p. 4, RG 165, Records of the War Department, NARS.

23. David Kahn, *Hitler's Spies:* N.Y., Macmillian, 1978, p. 437.

24. There are notable discrepancies between Gehlen's and Schellenberg's accounts of the episode. Gehlen makes little of it, asserting that he telephoned Schellenberg to inquire if Himmler would be interested in a study of the Polish resistance, to see if anything could be learned from it. Schellenberg, he says, called back saying Himmler would welcome such a study. By contrast, Schellenberg gives a detailed account in which he says Gehlen called on him and spent several hours discussing the plan, in which Gehlen suggested they both play a role. Gehlen, *The Service,* p. 111; Interrogation of Walter Schellenberg, supra.

25. Gehlen was at least peripherally involved with the Werewolves. On February 6, 1945, the Strategic Group of the General Staff, of which Gehlen was Deputy Chief, ordered all Army Groups to support and supply any

Werewolf units in their area. See: *History of the CIC in the European Theater of Operations,* p. 45. See also Anthony Cave Brown, *The Last Hero:* N.Y., Times Books, 1982, p. 769.

26. Word of a National Redoubt, a huge, heavily armed and manned underground fortress in Bavaria which would be the headquarters of a fierce German resistance had been circulating for months. Plans apparently had been made, and there are reports that engineers had been sent to study the territory, but the Redoubt was largely illusory. An April 4 1945 cable to OSS chief William Donovan from Allen Dulles, his station chief in Switzerland, however, made it clear that Dulles believed there was indeed such a fortress where the remaining strength of the SS would be concentrated, and from which it would launch a long and costly guerilla war. See Cave Brown, *The Last Hero,* p. 738; Bradley F. Smith: *The Shadow Warriors,* N.Y., Basic Books, 1983.

It was probably the slippery Wilhelm Hoettl, an accomplished con artist, who was primarily responsbile for selling Dulles this bill of goods. An enterprising Austrian Intelligence officer who joined the German secret service in 1938, Hoettl served under Schellenberg. Although the United States was not his target, "Willie," as old OSS hands still call him, was not one to pass up an opportunity, especially not as attractive a one as pesented itself in Hungary.

A company there was marketing an office device with a snappy trade name, The Wolf, designed to shred paper, and the American State Department ordered one for its legation in Budapest. Hoettl made it his business to keep abreast of activities on his turf, which included Hungary, and when he heard about the purchase he immediately spotted its potential for profitable mischief. He paid a call on the manufacturer and quickly came to an arrangement with him. In exchange for an unspecified amount of money the firm would build a special model to be delivered to the Americans, and regular maintenance would be a part of the package. The machine duly arrived and was put into service. It was some time before the Americans realized that while spewing out gratifyingly large quantities of shredded paper, deep in its innards The Wolf retained the originals, periodically giving them up to the "maintenance man" who delivered them to Hoettl. With evidence such as this of Hoettl's ingenuity and imagination even Allen Dulles can be excused for being taken in by him. Wilhelm Hoettl, *The Secret Front:* N.Y., Praeger, 1954, p. 284–291.

Defeat and arrest apparently did little to impair Hoettl's natural talents. He was released from Nürnberg prison on October 18 1945 by the commander of the United States security detachment there, Colonel B. C. Andrus, after Hoettl reminded him of services he claimed to have rendered his new friends. He had given intelligence information to Patton's Third Army; had been of service to the OSS in Switzerland and Italy; and had given evidence against his former superior officer, Ernst Kaltenbrunner, at Nürnberg. Besides, he had ulcers. See Hoettl, *The Secret Front,* pp. 284–291. See also Cave Brown, *The Last Hero,* p. 754.

27. Gehlen, *The Service,* pp. 112–113.

Chapter Two

1. There were those in the Office of Strategic Services (OSS), who had no illusions about Soviet ambitions and were frustrated in their isolation. "The chief driving force in the work of the USSR Division [of the OSS] is the certainty that the problem of the capabilities and intentions of the Soviet Union is the most important of all those that face the United States in the field of foreign relations . . . In some quarters the overwhelming importance of the USSR to the USA has been recognized in theory, but nowhere in the government has it been recognized in practice—certainly not in the allocation of personnel within [the OSS], or within the Department of State, or anywhere else in Washington." OSS document, 6 July 1945. "USSR Division: Survey of Current and Future Work Program." NARS. OSS documents, in raw archival form, are located in the Modern Military History division of the National Archives.

2. John Russell Deane, *Strange Alliance.* N.Y.: Macmillan, 1947, p. 89.

3. Gehlen, *The Service,* pp. 4, 9, 10.

4. Ellen Bracelen Flood, a linguist who joined Army censorship shortly after the United States declared war in December, 1941.

5. David Martin, *Wilderness of Mirrors.* N.Y.: Ballantine, 1980, pp. 12, 29.

6. Martin, *Wilderness of Mirrors,* p. 12.

7. Congressional hearings held before the House Committee on Un-American Activities. "Hearings Regarding Shipment of Atomic Material to the Soviet Union During World War II." December 5, 7, 1949; January 23–26; March 2, 3, 7, 1950.

8. These scenes and conversations are recalled by Ambassador Robert Murphy in his *Diplomat Among Warriors.* N.Y.: Doubleday, pp. 227 et seq. and 246 et seq.

9. Murphy, *Diplomat Among Warriors.* In the absence of guidance from Washington, Eisenhower and Chief of Staff General Marshall had considerable latitude to exercise their own judgment, and in their view Berlin may no longer have been an important military objective. Regarding Berlin, General Marshall cabled Eisenhower: "I would be loathe to hazard American lives for purely political purposes," and Eisenhower cabled back: "I shall not attempt any move I deem militarily unwise merely to gain a political prize unless I receive specific orders from the Combined Chiefs of Staff." Those orders never came, and the Soviets marched into Berlin. Ladislas Farago, *Patton.* N.Y.: Dell, 1963, p. 738. Also see Chester Wilmot, *The Struggle For Europe.* London: 1952, cf Farago, *Patton,* p. 816.

10. The extent to which individuals in the government at this time were responsibile for influencing policy toward the Soviet Union has been and will continue to be debated. (See also Chapter Four of this volume). Certainly there were some sympathetic to the Soviets, and some who gave evidence of having Communist ties. Harry Dexter White, Assistant to the Treasury Secre-

tary Henry Morganthau; Julian Wadleigh, of the State Department; and George Shaw Wheeler, head of the denazification branch of the Military Government in 1945, went to Czechoslovakia in 1947. See: Eugene Davidson, *The Death and Life of Germany*. N.Y.: Knopf, 1959.

11. Quoted from testimony before the Senate Armed Services Committee, 29 April, 1947, as cited in Sanche de Gramont, *The Secret War*. N.Y.: Putnam, 1962, p. 50. This view of American intelligence has been challenged by Dr. Rhodri Jeffreys-Jones of the University of Edinburgh, author of *American Espionage: From Secret Service to CIA*. At the annual meeting of the Society of Historians of American Foreign Relations, August 1983, he said that CIA historians have "belittled the U.S. intelligence methods of the decades preceding the formation of OSS and CIA," and that in his opinion the organization and effectiveness of United States intelligence in the years 1898–1947 was impressive. See Foreign Intelligence Literary Scene, Aug. 1983 issue, vol. 2, no. 4.

12. Herbert O. Yardley, *The American Black Chamber*. N.Y.: Ballantine, 1981 [originally published in 1931] with an Introduction by David Kahn. Yardley, in this landmark book describing his work, reveals himself as an early practitioner of the art of the Intelligence Exposé, precursor of a long line. Yardley referred to his unit by the name the French gave their Cryptographic Office: La Chambre Noire (The Black Chamber). Like its counterpart in Britain, the French unit was well-established, highly regarded and fully supported by its government.

13. Sanche de Gramont, *The Secret War*. N.Y.: Putnam, 1962, p. 51.

14. Cave Brown, *The Last Hero*, p. 171.

15. Cave Brown, *The Last Hero*, p. 2.

16. At the end of the First War the Republican Party wanted to nominate Donovan for Governor of New York State, an indication that his circle of friends was wide and influential. He declined the Republicans' invitation then (although he would run, and lose, in 1932), but nevertheless he was to be drawn into political life. In 1919–1920 he joined the American delegation to the White Russian army of General Koltchak in Siberia as a military advisor, and later served as Attorney General in Calvin Coolidge's administration. But it was his relationship with Roosevelt which led to his leadership of the OSS, and it was that which put Donovan in the history books.

Probably the most authoritative book on Donovan is by Thomas Troy: *Donovan and the CIA*, Frederick, Md., University Publications of America, 1981.

17. CIA document. 1972 (80) 341 E. Excerpted from a review of a book by Richard Harris Smith, *OSS: The Secret History of America's First Central Intelligence Agency*. Berkeley & Los Angeles California: University of California Press, 1972.

18. See Joseph Persico, *Piercing The Reich*. N.Y.: Viking, 1979, for labor reference.

19. Memorandum from Donovan to his senior staff dated 18 April 1945: OSS documents, NARS.

20. John Russell Deane, *Strange Alliance*. His book is the source for much of the material in this section, and all the quotations from Deane are to be found in it.

21. Donovan, himself well pleased with how the negotiations had gone, then endured the kind of irrational obstructionism to which his fellow Americans stationed in Russia, including the American Ambassador, Averell Harriman, were repeatedly subjected. Harriman and Deane had brought a four-engine transport plane to Russia for their use, and proposed to send Donovan, who had urgent business in Washington, back to the United States in it. Foreign Minister Molotov flatly refused. When Harriman protested that his was an unfriendly act flying in the face of their agreement and was, in addition, hindering the war effort, Molotov responded by offering him the use of a Russian two-engine plane.

Despite the many drawbacks, among them the slowness and short range of the aircraft, Harriman, in the interests of getting Donovan home, agreed. But nothing happened. Every morning at 6 o'clock, for eleven mornings, the Ambassador, his daughter Kathy, General Spaulding (head of the lend-lease division of the Military Mission), General Deane and General Donovan made their way through the freezing weather to the airport only to be given some excuse and told the plane could not take off. Every day the party would return to Moscow, Harriman would complain to Molotov—and the scene would repeat itself the following day. On the eleventh day Molotov decided to call the game off and allowed Donovan to leave the country in the American four-engine plane—exactly as the Americans had originally proposed.

22. Cave Brown, *The Last Hero*, p. 425.

23. For a later account of this incident, see Cave Brown, *The Last Hero*, p. 422–25.

24. OSS document dated 31 March 1944: OSS files, NARS. A letter from Donovan to Deane in Moscow.

25. The numbers tell the story. Between October 1, 1941, and May 31, 1945, 2,660 ships were sent to Russia bearing 16,529,791 tons of supplies. These included: 427,284 trucks; 13,303 combat vehicles; 35,170 motorcycles; and 2,328 ordnance service vehicles. To fuel these 2,670,371 tons of petroleum products were sent. Then there were the 4,478,116 tons of foodstuffs. Beyond that there was heavy equipment: 1,900 steam and 66 diesel locomotives; 9,920 flat cars; 1,000 dump cars; 120 tank cars; 35 heavy machinery cars—all of which were especially constructed for the Russian railway gauge. On top of that were over one billion dollars (in 1944 dollars) of machinery and industrial equipment and thousands of airplanes. Not to mention uncounted spare parts, vast amounts of bedding and clothing, and millions of dollars worth of medical supplies.

26. Boston Globe, 25 June 1984, quoted by Joseph S. Nye, Jr., Professor of Government, Harvard University.

27. Winston Churchill, *Triumph And Tradegy*. London: Cassel, 1953, vol. 6, pp. 498–499.
28. Eugene Davidson, *The Death And Life Of Germany*. N.Y.: Knopf, 1959.
29. Farago, *Patton,* pp. 765–771.

Chapter Three

1. Gehlen, *The Service,* p. 102.
2. Gehlen, p. 114.
3. This is a surprising mistake to have been made in Nazi Germany where uniforms were so important. As a general officer, Gehlen wore the red stripe (Hochrot), while some SS Generals wore white-grey stripes on their uniform trousers.
4. Interview with Kreidl. Heinz Höhne and Hermann Zolling, *The General Was A Spy,* NY: Coward, McCann and Geoghegan, 1972 (1st edition) p. 52.
5. Gehlen, p. 116.
6. FHO documents T-77/863, 13 May 1945, NARS, see Höhne and Zolling, p. 56. The order was issued by the head of the Allied Mission for control of OKW.
7. FHO documents T-77/863, 19 & 20 May 1945. From a note by Borchers on his interview with the Russian Commission. NARS.
8. "Report on information obtained from PW CS/2141 Obstlt i G Scheibe. Head of OKW/Archiv Abt, taken at FLENSBURG 19 May 45," a British interrogation report dated 5 June 1945: RG 165, Records of the War Department, SR 1665, NARS. FHO documents T-77/863, a note by Scheibe, 17 May 1945. NARS.
9. Sources for this section also include Leonard Mosley, *Dulles.* NY: Dial Press, 1978, pp. 232–236.
10. Gehlen, p. 3.
11. Gehlen, p. 4.
12. Gehlen, p. 5.
13. There was a considerable amount of innovative spelling of German names by the Americans, which may have contributed to the difficulty in tracing individual prisoners. On an entry dated 28 May 1945, Gehlen was listed as Mjr. Gen. Reinhardt GEHLAR. Document headed GEHLEN, Gneralmajor (Brig Gen), RG 165, Records of the War Department General and Special Staffs, NARS.
14. See report of British interrogation of Scheibe cited above.
15. Scheibe's unit may have been entrusted by Gehlen with the task of preserving some of his papers. A box with documents from FHO was dug up in the Flensburg area in June 1945 and apparently was in the hands of the British. A list of the contents of the box can be found in a document headed Subject: Document targets, 1 Jul 45, RG 331, Records of Allied Operational

and Occupation HQ, WWII, Entry 13B, Box 65, Folder—Miscellaneous Cables, NARS.

16. Of middle-class background and trained as an engineer, the rugged six-foot four-inch Austrian, his face bearing the inevitable duelling scars, was endowed with a contagious enthusiasm for danger and a gift for leadership. He became an authentic hero in September, 1944, when he carried out the virtually impossible task of rescuing the Italian dictator Mussolini from a mountain peak in the Abruzzi. It was a feat of exquisite daring which was exploited to the limit by Hitler's clever Propaganda Minister, Joseph Goebbels. In it and in the debonair figure of Skorzeny he immediately recognized he had an incident and a personality with all the ingredients to create an instant, morale-boosting legend to encourage the increasingly demoralized German people. Sources on Skorzeny: History of CIC, Vol XXV1, CIC in the Occupation of Germany, March 1959, p. 3; Shirer, *Rise and Fall of the German Reich,* p. 1003–4; also Murphy, *Diplomat Among Warriors;* Hoettl, *Secret Front:* Kahn, *Hitler's Spies.*

17. Among the notes on Gehlen by American interrogators: April 1945, "Shrewd outstanding officer, not a Party member. Could be useful to Allies," (The source was General Count von Oriola). And March 1945, "Very military, fanatically Anti-Russian, but a realist." Document headed GEHLEN, Gneralmajor (Brig Gen), RG 165, Records of the War Department, General and Special Staffs, NARS.

18. Gehlen, *The Service,* p. 6.

19. Finding himself in the Soviet Zone of Germany at war's end, Boker's uncle made repeated demands to be allowed to move to the West. In the 1950s the authorities finally agreed. He and his family could go, but on one condition: He would have to leave his books behind. They might as well have told him to abandon his heart or the air he breathed. He stayed with his library, protesting, insisting, complaining, until finally, in the early 1970s the astronomer, and his books, were allowed to leave.

20. Among other things, Boker was given detailed information, including locations of concentration camps inside the Soviet Union in which some three million people were being held. Boker says he was unable to interest any American authorities in this information; the Soviet Union was an ally.

21. The interception by the Americans in March 1942, of a message to Tokyo from Ambassador Oshima, the Japanese envoy to Germany, bears out that this was Hitler's view as well. Ambassador Oshima was reporting a conversation he had had with Hitler in the presence of Foreign Minister von Ribbentrop. The report says in part: "Speaking of the war situation at the time when German-Soviet hostilities began, Hitler said: 'Never in my life did I make such a great decision, but I knew that if I left Russia alone and continued my fight against England, she [Russia] would stab us in the back when we were least able to resist. As Führer, I took it upon myself to do my duty and that's why I began the war against the Soviet Union . . . I knew that without fighting

the Soviet, Germany could never accomplish her plans laid for a hundred years.' " Magic Summary, War Department, Office of Assistant Chief of Staff, G-2, March 31, 1942. NSA document, SRS series no. 559, NARS.

A document acquired by the Germans had encouraged Hitler to arrive at his Great Decision. It was the record of a staff conference at the Kremlin at which Stalin gave a "transfer and assembly order for the Red Army to strike against the Dardanelles." With the Red Army committed to the south, and fully preoccupied with its own plans, Hitler determined the time was ripe to attack his ally. As he did so often in the early part of the war, Hitler gambled and won; the string of victories as the German Army cut through the northern and central regions of the Soviet Union bore out the authenticity of the Russian document. See Interrogation of Prisoner of War George Johannson at PW Camp Forrest, Tenn., 31 May 1945, G-2 Division MIS-Y files, POW 201 files, NARS.

23. Gehlen, p. 11.

24. They included Gerhard Wessel, who had briefly succeeded Gehlen as Chief of FHO and would later succeed him once again as head of the BND, and FHO officers Majors Hiemenz, Hinrichs, and Schöller, as well as German Corps officer Captain Fühner, a former Russian interrogator. Joining them at Villa Pagenstaecher, where they established their HQ, were Colonel Stephanus and Major Lütgendorf.

25. Interrogation of Gehlen at the 7th Army Interrogation Center. "NOTES ON THE RED ARMY—LEADERSHIP AND TACTICS: Source: Gehlen, Reinhard." RG 238, Records of the National Archives Collection of World War II War Crimes. SAIC/R/1&2 Gehlen. The interrogation was conducted in April, 1945, the report dated 21 June 1945. It is noted by the interrogator that the report is "substantially in the source's own words." Reports of other interrogations of Gehlen are noted in Report of Interrogation, No. 5725, 28 August 1945, by Captain Halle. See "Memorandum For Lt. Colonel Parker: Subject: Preliminary Interrogation and Assessment of P/W Brig. Gen. Rhienhard Gehlen, 29 August 1945," (which also contains Report of Interrogation, N. 5724). RG 165, Records of the War Department General and Special Staffs, G-Gehlen. NARS. At Wörgel (near Kitzbühl), he was interrogated by a divisional intelligence officer and gave "only minor details." At Augsburg, at Army level, he was interrogated by a Lieutenant Drake and gave "limited information." At the Special Interrogation Center at Wiesbaden, however, he was interrogated by Captain Boker, and "fullest cooperation was given."

26. At that time the main thrust of the American intelligence effort was directed at retrieving German documents, and both Boker and Gehlen speak contemptuously of the Document Hunters out to bag their quota of paper, yet some of the archives they so indiscriminately swept up proved to be invaluable to historians. On May 20, 1945, in the village of Freimann, CIC agent Francesco S. Quaranta found 150,000 pounds of documents in an abandoned paper mill which would have an impact whose reverberations are still felt today. The

information most assiduously sought at the end of the war was that which would identify Nazi Party members. The conquerors had no way of knowing who was who; the most flagrant Nazi could pass through their hands without their knowing it. Verbal denunciations, some valid, many self-serving, malicious or both began to pour into Allied headquarters. As the scramble to curry favor with the occupiers intensified so did the need for reliable information about the political background of individual Germans.

Told by an informant that Nazi Party documents had been left there by the Gestapo, Quaranta went to the mill and, finding nothing on the ground floor, climbed to the second story. There he discovered a sea of incriminating documents. Among the most significant were records of the proceedings of the highest Party courts; detailed accounts of the actions of highly placed Gestapo figures; and, the greatest prize of all, copies of all the Nazi Party membership cards issued, each with an identification photograph on the back. Quaranta's find eventually was sent to Berlin and forms the core of the Berlin Document Center archive, the primary source of information about the Nazis. History of the CIC, vol. XXVI, p. 61. *CIC in the Occupation of Germany,* March 1959.

27. Thanks to the Document Hunters, and to the German passion for thoroughness, vast amounts of information came to light, not only concerning the recent war and the Nazi phenomenon, but reaching back into the previous century.

On April 17, 1945, after the Ninth Infantry Division had taken the town of Pansfelds, word reached the Americans there that Hitler's Foreign Minister, Baron von Ribbentrop, was hiding in a remote and isolated castle deep in the forests of the region. Special Agent George J. Novak, the only CIC agent attached to the 47th Infantry Regiment, immediately organized a task force to raid the castle, which still lay behind the retreating enemy lines, and take von Ribbentrop. His small convoy of jeeps raced along the narrow roads, passing American troops crouched in ditches on either side returning intermittent enemy fire as they slowly continued their advance.

The castle, surrounded and sheltered by towering evergreens which made it invisible from the air and difficult to see from the ground, looked to be deserted. But as Novak and his men, guns drawn, made their slow and cautious approach a figure suddenly appeared in the doorway: Baron Witilo von Griesheim, armed only with a large ring of keys, identified himself and signaled his willingness to cooperate.

The Baron denied von Ribbentrop was in the castle, but indicated there was something there of greater value to the Americans. Asking Novak to follow him, he led the way down a maze of long corridors, unlocking and thrusting open the doors of one room after another, each of which was filled with orderly stacks of documents, stacks which reached from floor to ceiling. Finally, returning as they had come, von Griesheim showed Novak the master catalogue: every document of the hundreds of thousands stored in the castle was numbered and indexed; the Baron could put his hands on any one of them in a matter of minutes.

What von Griesheim had in his care, as Novak recognized at once, was a treasure of immense importance: the files of the German Foreign Ministry dating from 1871 to 1944. Among the papers were the official communications between Hitler's government and the British in the fateful years when Chamberlain was Prime Minister; records of the Russo-German negotiations of 1939; and a letter dated August 1944 from the French collaborator Marshal Petain to Hitler, begging him to rescind his order to burn Paris. Novak immediately placed guards around the castle and issued the order that no one was permitted to enter or leave the area. He was keenly aware of the historic significance of his find and was determined to protect it.

But it was von Griesheim to whom the credit must go for preserving so much of the stuff of history. The Baron handed Novak a telegram he had received from Berlin earlier that month. It contained instructions that he was to destroy every document in the castle, and to do it at once. Even then, in what most rational Germans recognized as the death throes of the Reich, to disobey a direct order was a profoundly risky business: indeed the risk was greater in those days when fanatical hysteria ruled. But von Griesheim took a chance. Gathering together old piles of newspapers, he lit a smoky fire and kept it going hour after hour to convince any observers of his chimney that he was carrying out his orders. It was impossible for him to destroy over seventy years of documented history; it was important, he told Novak, to preserve the record so that future historians could establish the facts and determine, among much else, the true causes of and responsibility for the war.

After a two-man team of experts from the State Department and the British Foreign Office had authenticated the documents, a caravan of some 200 trucks made their way through the mountains to the castle to carry off their priceless cargo. History of the CIC, vol. XX, pp. 65–67.

28. Gehlen, p. 108.

29. Conversations with John Boker. This incident is also recounted in Gehlen, p. 1; Höhne & Zolling, p. 61.

30. Gerhard Wessel remained behind and served as the contact for Gehlen in Germany.

31. Conversations with John Boker. See also Gehlen, p. 2.

32. For information regarding the Interrogation Centers see History of the Military Intelligence Division, 1941–1945, Chapter V, "The Captured Personnel and Material Branch," p. 99. U.S. Government publication.

Waldman's complaints did produce transcripts of the bugged conversations, and they proved to be illuminating for Gehlen. Two of his men, while loyal to him, appeared to be temperamentally unsuited for the task ahead.

33. Conversations with Eric Waldman.

34. A handwritten note on the first page of a document from the Evaluation Section, Post Office Box 1142, Alexandria, Virginia underscores their special status. Dated 29 August 1945 it is headed: Memorandum For Lt. Colonel Parker. Subject: Preliminary Interrogation and Assessment of P/W Brig. Gen.

Rhienhard (sic) Gehlen. NARS. The notation reads: "1 of seven PO/W specially flown in for the sake of their knowledge of Russia. L D—Colonel Sweet has original; copy to Colonel Shimkin (?) and Major Kisevalter only. For special file." In the vocabulary of intelligence, the word "special" was virtually synonymous with "secret."

35. Conversations with Eric Waldman.

36. Conversations with Eric Waldman.

37. Among the presents Boker gave the group were some pen knives. There is a superstition that the gift of a knife will cut a friendship; to avoid that, the knife must be "paid for," usually with a coin of little or no value. The Gehlen group sewed an array of foreign coins to a card which they decorated, and enclosed it with their notes of thanks.

38. Personal letter to John Boker quoted with Boker's permission.

39. David C. Martin, *Wilderness of Mirrors*, NY: Ballantine, 1980, p. 39.

40. There had been indications as early as October, 1945, that this was the real intention of the Soviets, but no action was taken.

41. Personal letter to John Boker quoted with Boker's permission. Both Boker and Waldman became controversial figures to some degree. Critics of the Army's handling of Gehlen charge that they were too close to the Germans. Without questioning their loyalty, they suggest Boker and Waldman lost their objectivity and began identifying with Gehlen's group instead. Those who support America's use of Gehlen credit Boker and Waldman with recognizing Gehlen's ability and potential, and with preserving his unit.

Chapter Four

1. New York Times, editorial, June 3, 1920, p. 10.

2. The raids ended, but not before some 550 aliens were deported, heads had been broken and American law violated by the nation's own chief lawman. There were bitter exchanges about the legality of these actions between Felix Frankfurter, then a professor of law at Harvard, later a Supreme Court Justice, and Attorney General Palmer. New York Times, June 5, 1920, p. 22.

3. An American Mercury correspondent, unidentified to protect him from Soviet reprisals, filed this report:

"There is an inclination abroad to consider the present terroristic outburst as an isolated and mysterious event . . . The assumption that every new orgy is exceptional enables the [Soviet] propaganda machine in due time to shut out the memory of every extreme expression of the regime's fundamental brutality by laying smokescreens of statistics and apologetics. We have seen how the liquidation of the kulaks, the hounding of intellectuals, the famine, the blood purge after the Kirov assassination, have been treated by the outside world as curious aberrations in an otherwise high-minded and benevolent system . . . The fact that needs emphasis at this time . . . is that systematic ruthlessness has marked the entire reign of Stalin. Brutality is normal, and the occasional benevolence is aberrant. The one constant element in this tumultuous Russian decade has been terror—systemized, undeviating, and cold-blooded terror—with only its magnitude and the choice of its victims at a given moment as the variants." The American Mercury, November 1937, p. 298–306.

Actual figures for those who suffered in Stalin's Terror are impossible to come by, but using the available evidence, in 1938 the toll was: of 12 million in the GULAG camps, 1 million executed; 2 million dead of starvation, disease, exposure, maltreatment, etc.; and 9 million remaining in the camps.

4. On the subject of Soviet anti-Semitism Senator Thomas Dodd, in a speech to the Senate in 1960, said this: "There should be no secret about Soviet anti-Semitism. The terrible ordeal of the Jewish people under the Kremlin's rule has been painstakingly set forth and documented . . . Scattered over a period of 2 decades, moreover, there were some dozens of carefully researched articles in newspapers like The New York Times and New York Herald-Tribune and in magazines like Life.

"But for some strange reason, the terrifying story of persecution of the Jews under communism has not penetrated the public consciousness of the free world . . . Perhaps the Jewish communities in the Western countries did not speak up as loudly as they should have for fear of further endangering their coreligionists behind the Iron Curtain. Perhaps our minds are conditioned far more than we ourselves are prepared to admit by the most powerful and most subtle propaganda apparatus the world has ever known.

"Whatever the reason may be, I am convinced . . . that in the public mind anti-Semitism is far more closely identified with Germany than it is with the Soviet Union . . . But I was appalled at the totality of Soviet anti-Semitism, by its utter ruthlessness, by its doctrinal and practical similarity to Nazi anti-Semitism . . . Between the brutality of Soviet anti-Semitism and the brutality of Nazi anti-Semitism, there is little to choose. About all that is lacking so far in the USSR is the gas chambers. For this deficiency the Communists have made up, at least in part, by employing Siberia and the firing squads as substitute instruments of death . . .

"Jews in the occupied territories who succeeded in escaping did so by fleeing individually or in small groups through the swamps and forests . . . Jews attempting to flee from threatened areas en masse or in large groups were turned back by Soviet guard units . . .

"During the period of Soviet occupation, at least 40,000 Jews were deported to Siberia from Hungary alone and many thousands were deported from Rumania . . . In Poland during the course of 1946 there was a whole series of murderous attacks on Jews which cost several hundred Jewish lives. In the pogrom at Kielce alone, 41 Jews were killed by a mob, while the Communist militia stood idly by—or else arrested the Jews . . . In the fall of 1948, with one sweeping administrative decree, Stalin and his cultural commissar, Andrei Zhdanov, completely eliminated what remained of Jewish cultural and communal life in the Soviet Union . . . At one stroke, all Jewish schools were closed, Jewish newspapers were shut down. The Yiddish publishing house, Emes, was also closed . . . More than 450 Jewish writers, artists and intellectuals—the cream of the Jewish intelligentsia in the Soviet Union—were executed . . .''

"The word 'Jew' is stamped on [a Jew's] internal passport—the document which is the key to a man's existence in every Communist country . . . The marked passports of the Soviet Jews serve only one purpose—the same purpose served in its time by the yellow badge which the Nazis compelled the Jews to wear for purposes of self-identification." Congressional Record—Senate, March 15 1960, p. 5561 et seq. Speech of Senator Dodd (Conn.) "On Anti-Semitism, the Swastika Epidemic and Communism."

5. It was not just in Congress, but throughout the government in 1947 there was growing anxiety about Soviet aims. That year a landmark article, "The Sources of Soviet Conduct," was published in the prestigious journal *Foreign Affairs*. Its author, Mr. "X," was George Kennan, who played a major role in shaping United States policy toward the Soviet Union at that critical juncture. His words were not welcomed by those who believed the Russians were finally emerging from their isolation and joining the community of nations. That, Kennan said, was self-delusion.

"Belief is maintained [by the Soviets] in the basic badness of capitalism, in the inevitability of its destruction, in the obligation of the proletariat to assist in that destruction and to take power into its own hands . . . there can never be on Moscow's side any sincere assumption of a community of aims between the Soviet Union and powers which are regarded as capitalist. . . .

"When there is something the Russians want from us, one or the other . . . features of their policy may be thrust temporarily into the background; and when that happens there will always be Americans who will leap forward with gleeful announcements that 'the Russians have changed . . .' But we should not be misled by tactical maneuvers." A realistic appreciation of the Soviet system, as well as of its goals and methods of achieving them, was essential, Kennan said, and then went on to enunciate and define what would become the cornerstone of American policy. "The main element of any United States policy toward the Soviet Union must be that of a long-term, patient but firm and vigilant containment of Russian expansive tendencies."

6. In March, 1947, President Truman declared the adoption of the Doctrine of Containment to limit the spread of communism, and in a speech on June 5, at Harvard, General George Marshall unveiled the Marshall Plan. In the same year a little-known congressman, Joseph McCarthy, made news with his assertion that even though the communist party was legal in the United States, anyone who belonged to it was ipso facto a traitor. The stage was set for a period of dramatic and divisive confrontation in the name of national security.

7. Gordon A. Craig, *The Germans*. NY: Putnam, 1982.

8. "The United States Army had begun to organize Western Germany long

before the United States government had any clear idea of what should be done with it. While the State Department thought vaguely forward about such great problems as a centralized or dismembered Germany, about the borders and confines of Germany's territory, the proconsuls of the United States Army proceeded to govern Germany on their own, shaping a new society as they went . . . While the civilian statesmen, for whom the uniformed proconsuls developed an easy contempt, talked theory and policy, the Army had to act, every single day." Theodore White, *Fire In The Ashes: Europe in Mid-Century*. New York: William Sloane, 1953 p. 42.

9. Foreign Relations of the United States, Diplomatic papers, The Conference of Berlin. (The Potsdam Conference), 1045, vol. I, Washington, 1960, p. 7.

10. The politicians in Washington were slow to recognize the extent and implications of the deterioration in East-West relations, but it was not for lack of warnings. While Gehlen savored the serenity of the Elendsalm, the final scenes of the German tragedy were being played, and in the immediate aftermath came little incidents, small omens that the foundation of peace was not secure. Within a week of Hitler's death the first faint tremors could be felt in the quickly shifting ground of politically expedient alliances. On May 1 the world heard that Hitler was dead. Six days later, on the seventh, documents of surrender were signed, and the disturbance surrounding these documents foreshadowed the larger shocks to come.

General Jodl, Admiral von Friedeburg, and General Eberhard Kinzel signed the instruments of surrender for the Germans in a little schoolhouse at Rheims where the Supreme Allied Commander, General Eisenhower, had his headquarters. Eisenhower, because of his strong personal distaste for any ceremony of surrender, made the decision not to participate in it and delegated his Chief of Staff, General Bedell Smith, to represent the Americans. The papers were signed on May 7 1945, by all the parties, including the Russians, but there was a hitch; the Americans had made a mistake and submitted the wrong set of documents. The Soviets caught the error and immediately put the worst interpretation on it.

After much discussion and many drafts the European Advisory Commission had prepared instruments of surrender which had been approved by all the Allies. Exhausted and preoccupied, General Bedell Smith had picked up and brought to the ceremonies the wrong set of documents. What he presented were earlier papers which had been drawn up at Supreme Allied Headquarters, not by the European Advisory Commission. There was no substantive difference in the content of the documents, but when the Soviets realized what had happened they insisted on another signing ceremony, this time using the European Advisory Commission instruments.

With a face-saving announcement that the Rheims documents had simply "formalized the surrender," and the "official surrender" of Germany would take place in Berlin shortly, a second ceremony was hastily arranged. Eisenhower sent his deputy commander, Air Chief Marshal Sir Arthur W. Tedder; Field Marshal Keitel signed for the Germans, and the episode was over. It was an embarrassing blunder and the Soviet reaction to it, suspicious and distrustful, was instructive. Murphy, *Diplomat Among Warriors,* p. 242.

11. Anthony Cave Brown, *Dropshot.* NY: Dial Press, 1977, p. 17.

12. In a conversation with the late historian Theodore White, he said the United States at the time was "scared to death." The Russians had dozens of divisions in combat position in Central Europe and many more in reserve. See also his *Fire in The Ashes,* p. 33.

13. American military intelligence had been dealing in information all along, of course, often paying for it with some form of security, and buying it from informants whose backgrounds they had neither the resources nor, in many cases, the desire to check. Even when efforts at verification were made, in the unimaginable confusion of the time, identities were lost, stolen, bought, and sold. It was difficult to know with any certainty with whom one was dealing. The problem of verification was made vastly greater on June 25 1948 when Congress passed and President Truman signed into law "an act to authorize for a limited period of time the admission into the United States of certain European displaced persons for permanent residence and for other purposes." Those admitted were to include "persons who had been of considerable value to Army Intelligence and 'whose removal from the Theater was indicated because of compromise or extreme danger to the individual.' " (June 25 1948, Public Law 774, Displaced Persons Act of 1948. 62 Stat. 80th Congress, 2nd Session, Ch. 647.)

The American occupation authorities were caught in a dilemma here, and a price would be exacted for the course they chose. United States Intelligence had made deals with these individual intelligence entrepreneurs, "persons who had been of considerable value" to them, and in most cases the Americans intended to carry out their end of the bargain; they were going to "do the decent thing" by sometimes less than decent men.

14. Gehlen was a known quantity with a record which could be documented. He was a General Staff officer, not only not a Nazi Party member or one of Hitler's crowd, but one who could claim a connection with men involved in the failed July 20 1944 attempt on Hitler's life. Gehlen's superior, General Halder and his colleague, General Heusinger, were imprisoned for months on suspicion of complicity in the assassination plot, and a former member of his own unit, Colonel von Roenne, had been hanged for his part in it.

Gehlen always maintained that he knew about the plot but, although he protected the conspirators, he claimed he refused to become directly involved because he believed the operation was shoddily planned and doomed to failure. The Americans would have preferred it if Gehlen had been a participant who had somehow survived, but they were willing to accept, and stress, this degree of association with the plotters.

Chapter Five

1. Höhne and Zolling, *The General Was A Spy*, p. 12.
2. Basket referred to the place, while the earliest cover name for Gehlen's unit itself was ZIPPER. It then became known as Operation Rusty. Unlike the usual practice of assigning random words as cover names, Rusty had meaning. It referred to Colonel Deane's newborn son, John Russell Deane, III.
3. General Schow was Deputy G-2, U.S. Forces European Theater. He later joined the CIA.
4. See the section infra dealing with this period. Deane, Sr. was the author of *Strange Alliance*.
5. General Deane's observations are drawn from my conversations with him.
6. Gehlen, *The Service*, p. 17.
7. British and French Intelligence were very sophisticated in their targeting, and acquisition, of POWs who might be helpful to them.
8. Conversations with Eric Waldman.
9. Conversations with Friedel von Glinski.
10. Originally the group was quartered in three houses: the Schloss Kransberg; a hunting lodge which had belonged to George von Opel; and the Blue House. It was the Blue House which was the hub. In addition to apartments, that is where the offices were.
11. Wolfgang Wehner, *Geheim,* Süddeutscher Verlag, Munich, 1960, cited in Höhne and Zolling, p. 63.
12. Höhne and Zolling, p. 66. Baun had not lasted long as chief of Acquisitions; by April, 1947 the job had gone to someone else. But he was still with the Organization in 1949 when it was taken over by CIA. Two members of the early CIA staff were involved in a long investigation of Baun's activities which ultimately resulted in his release from the Organization.
13. History of the CIC, vol. XX.
14. Toast given by Reinhard Gehlen October 4, 1946. Von Glinski, for whom the making of silk purses from sow's ears was child's play, somehow found a small, comfortable hunting lodge, which he dubbed "Himmel," [Heaven], and won permission to take his bride there for a honeymoon. In April, 1948, the von Glinskis left the Organization and Germany for Brazil, where he had worked from 1936–38. Deane had offered, and Waldman got them exit permits. A job and entry permits were arranged by friends in Brazil. From Brazil they emigrated to the United States and the mountains of Colorado where they built a house, "Berghimmel," have raised a family, prospered and give every sign of living happily ever after.
15. Sources for this section include conversations with Eric Waldman, General Deane, and the von Glinskis.
16. Höhne and Zolling, p. 71.
17. General Arthur Trudeau, about whom more later, was Commanding

General of the First Constabulary Brigade, European Command, Germany, 1948–1950.

18. As Gehlen's group built up its networks of informants it also mounted one of the most productive and least dangerous of intelligence operations, code named "Hermes." German soldiers who had been imprisoned by the Soviets slowly were being returned to West Germany, and at each reception area Gehlen's agents were there to greet them. Representing themselves as officials gathering routine information, they amassed quantities of material about conditions in the areas where the prisoners had been held, details of the industries in which they had worked, specifics about the state of the railways, the location and numbers of troops and so on. They also compiled for future reference a "possible enemies" directory of Germans identified by the returning prisoners of war as having collaborated with the Russians.

Gehlen agents frequently followed up their initial interrogations with visits during which they would trade a few cigarettes for coins, ticket stubs, newspapers—anything the former prisoner of war had brought back from the Soviet Union which would provide authentic "pocket trash" for agents who would be infiltrated into Russia. At the same time, the Gehlen men tried to squeeze the last recollection from them, and occasionally the extra effort paid off handsomely, as in the case of the Red Stone.

After his capture, a corporal and former prisoner told his interrogator, he was sent to work on the site of a chemical plant in the Soviet Union, in Djerzhinsk. The plant had one heavily guarded area from which the Germans were barred—all of them except him. An exception was made in his case because it was his job to collect the waste products of whatever it was they were doing and haul them to a dump inside the restricted zone. Much of this waste consisted of chunks of red-colored stone, and at some point it occurred to him that he might be able to use this flinty stuff to make himself a lighter. Which he did. Everyone who passed in and out of this sensitive area was subjected to a thorough search and it tickled him that the guards had never spotted the little chunk of red stone in his home-made lighter. The corporal had even brought the thing home with him as a souvenir.

After the Gehlen agent expressed interest in seeing it, he was so taken with the lighter he offered the former corporal a pack of American cigarettes for it. The agent put the stone in an envelope, together with a full report of the interrogation, and turned it over to the Americans who immediately forwarded it to Washington for analysis. A message of congratulation came back, along with a strong warning that any such material should be handled with great caution, and deposited in a metal container. That sample of the stone the Russians in Djerzhinsk were working with in such secrecy constituted a highly significant piece of intelligence. It was radioactive, and what it told the Americans was the Russians had their own source of radioactive material and were not dependent, as they had been, on mines in Czechoslovakia.

This kind of intelligence work, which involved the establishment of rapport between two individuals, could not have been carried out by the victorious foreigners and it quickly established the value of Gehlen's group. They had had years of experience interrogating Russian soldiers who had come over to the Germans in the thousands during the war, and in analyzing the information they gleaned. Now hundreds of thousands more poured into Germany from the East, a vast reservoir of information which the Germans could exploit. They were professionals in this area, and the Americans recognized it. (Höhne and Zolling, p. 81. See also Mosely, *Dulles,* pp. 274–5.)

The negative side to this was the danger that some of the returning POWs were in fact the bearers of disinformation, but at that time the advantage far outweighed the risks.

19. The relationship between Waldman and Gehlen was close and easy in those early, informal days. After Waldman's wife arrived in Oberursel in September 1946, Gehlen was a frequent guest at dinner, and Mrs. Waldman often travelled with them.

20. "Memorandum for the President. 25 June 1945:"

"The following information, transmitted by the OSS representative in Caserta on 21 June, was obtained from a French agent of the Sicherheitsdienst (SD, the SS Security Service):

"Source declares that he attended a conference at Deisenhofen [sic] near Munich in mid-April 1945, which was presided over by an SS Obergruppenführer whom he did not know. The latter indicated that AMT III B (Internal SD) and AMT IV (Gestapo) of the Reichssicherheitshauptamt (RSHA, the Reich's chief security office under the Hitler regime) had been merged to promote post-war unrest. Trustworthy men, the SS Obergruppenführer said, already had been sent to live in Spain and Switzerland to handle distribution of money. The program would involve the organization of nationalistic movements under the guise of an anti-Bolshevist front, and should culminate in civil warfare. This program would be designed to complicate the Allied post-war task and to permit the Nazis to reappear eventually in a suitable disguise in order to create the Fourth Reich.

"[signed:] G. Edward Buxton, Acting Director." OSS report to President Truman; Papers of Harry S. Truman, White House Central Files, Office of Strategic Services, Harry S. Truman Library.

21. Conversations with Eric Waldman. See also, for an exhaustive study of the Admiral, Heinz Höhne, *Canaris,* NY: Doubleday, 1979.

22. Light from another angle was shed on German activities in Spain by the Soviet spy Harold "Kim" Philby who was working for the British Secret Service. By 1943 discipline at the Abwehr's foreign stations, especially those in Turkey, Portugal and Spain had utterly broken down. British Intelligence by then had infiltrated the Lisbon office of the Abwehr, and Philby reels off a long list of Abwehr outposts in Spain—Madrid, Barcelona, Bilbao, Algeciras, Vigo, and more—whose agents were known to him. He adds, "I knew about the Gehlen unit from the summer of 1943 onwards. It was the anti-Soviet section

of the poor old Abwehr, and the British were reading a great majority of its signals. It seemed to me no better than the other sections of the Abwehr (on which I had been continuously engaged since 1941), which means that it was very bad indeed. No exaggeration, no joke. So I was undismayed when CIA took it over.'' This letter from Philby, dated April 6, 1977, is part of an interesting exchange of letters between Leonard Mosely and Philby which appears in the Appendix of Mosely's *Dulles,* cited above.

23. Cave Brown, *Last Hero,* p. 684.

24. Martin, *Wilderness of Mirrors,* p. 23.

25. Vatican intelligence was indeed catholic in its scope, keeping the Pontiff so well informed that he was able to mention to Mrs. Waldman, who also attended the Audience, that he understood her father was a Methodist minister.

26. According to German journalist Jürgen Thorwald's account of this exploit a third officer defected with them, a Major Tuerr of the Czech General Staff. (Jürgen Thorwald, ''The Man in the Dark; Factual report on General Gehlen and His Organization,'' *Die Welt,* 4 December 1955.) It should be noted that Thorwald was used by Gehlen as a conduit for favorable accounts of his activities, few failures are recorded by him.

27. Klecka's sentence was reduced to five years by General Lucius Clay on March 23 in an effort to head off the ''vengeance'' trial in Prague on trumped-up espionage charges of two American soldiers. Bringing such charges against innocent foreign nationals is a technique that has been used by the Soviets since the early 1920s. In this case, Clarendon Hill and George Jones, arrested in December 1948, were not allowed to see the American envoy, and reportedly were severely beaten. The trial did take place, on March 29 1949. They were sentenced to ten and twelve years in prison respectively. But Clay's effort did pay off: on May 23 they were pardoned and released.

28. Eric Waldman confirms that the account by David Dallin, *Soviet Espionage.* New Haven: Yale University Press, 1955, pp. 376–88, of the breaking of the Czech network is accurate. Other sources for this section include conversations with General Deane, Eric Waldman.

29. Knowledgeable American Intelligence officers rate Gehlen's positive intelligence capability as poor to dismal. But he did have one effective penetration agent, Elli Barczatis, secretary to the East German Prime Minister Otto Grotewohl. She turned over a great deal of valuable material, but ultimately was arrested, tried for treason and executed. In his memoirs Gehlen claims to have had other sources inside the East German government, but this is disputed by several former American Intelligence officers. One former CIA officer who did an extensive investigation of Organization activities flatly denies the claims, citing wishful thinking or faulty memory on Gehlen's part.

30. The handling of Eastern Bloc defectors was in its infancy. But Army Intelligence had a flourishing, well-established clandestine transportation system, the Ratline, through which it made travel arrangements for Nazis who had been ''helpful'' to reach South America. A detailed description of the

Ratline can be found in the Exhibits, which form the appendices to *Klaus Barbie And The United States Government, Exhibits to the Report to the Attorney General of the United States,* August, 1983, Washington, D.C., U.S. Printing Office.

31. Ilya Ehrenburg, in *Pravda.* Cited from Andrew Tully, *CIA: The Inside Story.* NY: William Morrow, 1962.

32. Sir Kenneth Strong, *Men Of Intelligence.* London: Cassell, 1970, pp. 124–25; 135. But having called Dulles one of the last great Romantics of espionage, and having praised his gregarious nature, Sir Kenneth goes on to say, with a touch of asperity that, in his experience, it was impossible to get beyond Dulles' "gusty laugh."

This big man, handsome, charming and sophisticated, with an infectious laugh that seemed to enter the room with him, could hardly have presented a greater contrast to the slight, earnest, former German general, so uncomfortable in social situations. But a special relationship developed between them. Dulles has been quoted as saying that for all he knew Gehlen was a scoundrel, but he was on "our side" and that was all that mattered. "Besides," Dulles is reported to have said, "one needn't ask a Gehlen to one's club." The weight of the evidence, however, suggests Dulles' remarks are apocryphal. Invite Gehlen to his club—such bastions of the Washington establishment as the F Street and Chevy Chase Clubs—is precisely what Dulles did, and frequently, over the years. See the New Republic, 22 April 1972, p. 26.

33. Sources for this section include conversations with General Deane, Eric Waldman, the von Glinskis, members of the early CIA staff and their wives.

34. According to Eric Waldman, Pullach was found by accident. At the Munich PX he overheard two British women who worked for American Civil Censorship discussing their forthcoming move and comparing their future, cramped quarters with their present spacious ones at Pullach. Waldman followed up on it, visited Pullach, and sold the idea to Liebel.

35. As the sensational Felfe case would reveal, Nazis recruited other Nazis, some at Soviet behest.

36. Documents which were to be kept from the Americans were given identifying marks. Evidently the indicators were not always effective, since one former CIA officer recalls that the papers they were not supposed to see had a red line drawn diagonally across them.

37. See Konrad Adenauer, *Memoirs,* Chicago: H. Regnery Co., 1966. Among works on Adenauer are Terrence Prittie, *Konrad Adenauer.* Chicago: Cowles Book Co., 1971; Richard Hiscocks, *The Adenauer Era.* Philadelphia: Lippincott, 1966.

38. Gehlen's own first meeting with Adenauer, however, did not occur until 20 September 1950.

39. Liebel would not be replaced until December of that year. In the interim Lieutenant Colonel Berry, the U.S. Air Force representative at Pullach, served as acting commander of the base.

Chapter Six

1. Critchfield had only a smattering of German and although Gehlen's English by that time was good, Hans Richter, a member of the Organization and a poet, painter and former diplomat, was included in this first meeting to act as interpreter.

2. Gehlen was universally referred to as the Doctor by the officers of the CIA liaison team. Even today in discussing the Organization, former CIA officers automatically and naturally talk about the Doctor. Occasionally he is also wryly called Old Blue Eyes.

3. An account of Eleanor Dulles' experiences in Austria can be found in Leonard Mosley, *Dulles*, pp. 204–213.

4. It was then that the great tragedy of Critchfield's life struck. His wife Connie was travelling from North Dakota to meet him in New York for the journey to Munich. Near Mechanicville, Iowa, a farm tractor with a load of hay suddenly pulled out of a side road, directly in the path of her car, and Connie Critchfield was killed. An Iowa State Police officer telephoned him with the news in Washington. In 1986 his brother published a memoir of the Critchfield family: *Those Days: An American Album*. Garden City, NY: Anchor Press/Doubleday, 1986.

5. Colonel Philp is dead and cannot answer the view voiced by a number of former CIA officers that he was eager to retain his posting at Pullach, and resisted Critchfield's study and a possible CIA takeover of the Organization.

6. Peer de Silva, a 32 year old Californian and West Point graduate, was among the first. A member of the CIA's precursor organizations—the Strategic Services Unit of the War Department (in X-2, the counterespionage section) and of the Central Intelligence Group—de Silva joined Critchfield in December, 1949, remaining until 1951 as his deputy and Administrator of the Pullach base. Peer de Silva, *Sub-Rosa: The CIA and the Uses of Intelligence*. NY: New York Times Books, 1978. (See infra for de Silva's account of his meeting with George Kennan, Ambassador to the Soviet Union.)

7. Among others who came to Pullach in the early days were Fred Stalder, who had been on Allen Dulles' staff in Bern; Robert Feldman, a reports expert; Thomas Lucid, former chief of Army counterintelligence in Austria; and counterintelligence specialist Clare Edward Petty.

Friendly and soft-spoken, his prodigious memory and well-organized mind have led Petty to be dubbed The Computer, while his ability to isolate each thread and trace it through the most tangled web to its source earned him another title, Master of Triple Think. "At one time or another Ed Petty probably suspected everybody at Pullach, but when he came up with something, you paid attention," a former colleague says. "If he said it was so, like it or not I believed him." As will be seen, more attention should have been paid when, after an exhaustive analysis, Petty came up with the name of a possible Soviet agent in the heart of Gehlen's organization.

Thomas Lucid, whose cover name was Herr Lucas, a tall, handsome extrovert whose wit and charm beguiled even the generally aloof Gehlen, became Critchfield's successor as chief of the Pullach base or, in the preferred terminology, Liaison to the Gehlen Organization. He had a streak of the devil-may-care which particularly appealed to Gehlen, who adopted an avuncular attitude toward him and clearly enjoyed his company. Lucid quickly formed an easy relationship with Eberhard Blum, a close, younger advisor to Gehlen who in 1983 would follow in Gehlen's footsteps as head of the BND. Blum not only was particularly well-qualified and capable, he had a light touch not universal among the Germans. Under the spell of this double-dose of charm Gehlen revealed a side that was rarely glimpsed.

Serious business was going on, but the disasters ahead were still out of sight and the atmosphere at Pullach during the Lucids' tenure was lighter and gayer than at any other time. "Peggy Lucid is bright and vivacious," the wife of one CIA officer said, "and she and Tom loved to party. We had a lot of good times." Lucid and Blum became not only colleagues, but friends who shared a certain zany sense of fun which led Gehlen to call them Peck's Bad Boys. It was at dinner at the Lucids' that Allen Dulles accidentally acquired the code name Brussels Sprouts. "We had some people over and I was serving this vegetable, Rosenkohl," Peggy Lucid remembers. "Tom and Eberhard, Eberhard's wife and I were standing together by the buffet table, all talking at once, and we got our wires crossed. At the same moment that his wife was asking me: 'What is the English name for this Rosenkohl?' Eberhard was asking Tom: 'What is Allen Dulles' cover name?' I got my answer in before Tom: 'Brussels Sprouts,' I said. Eberhard looked terribly surprised, then everybody whooped, but the name stuck. Allen Dulles was 'Brussels Sprouts.' "

For the celebration after the christening of his daughter, Lucid invited a number of senior members of the Organization as well as a few other German acquaintances not connected with it, including the owner of the house he leased. "When he arrived," Lucid said, "our landlord looked approvingly around the room and said: 'What charming friends you have. It looks like a gathering of the General Staff.' "

Gehlen took pleasure in heavy-handed teasing of his Bad Boys. On a trip the three made to Paris, Blum and Lucid escorted Gehlen to his hotel room after dinner, the evening apparently at an end. The next morning at breakfast Gehlen peered at each one in turn and observed with mock severity: "I am not sure you gentlemen got enough sleep last night." And in the same vein, when they told him Lucid was being transferred to Washington at the same time Blum was being considered for the post of Organization representative at the German embassy there, Gehlen glared at them and said: "You two together in the same city at the same time without my being there? Never!"

There were not many occasions when Gehlen's lighter side, such as it was, could be seen, but Lucid seemed to bring it out. Lucid and Critchfield remember an incident which took place in 1955 on one of Gehlen's many trips to the United States. They were visiting the New York Port Police, getting ready for a sight-seeing swing around the Statue of Liberty by helicopter. As usual, Gehlen was travelling incognito and was introduced by Lucid as "Mr. Graeber, a senior officer of German Intelligence." Their guide was a tough old veteran of the force, with a manner as blunt as his New York accent. He had recently read about the greeting given another German Intelligence official, Otto John, when he returned to West Germany after his earlier defection to the East. John had been arrested and put into prison. With this apparently in mind, as he shook hands with Gehlen, the old cop gave him a direct look and asked: "Are you a good German or a bad German?" Gehlen, nonplussed, didn't have a chance to think of an answer before the old cop clapped him on the back and cheerfully went on: "Well, anyhow, don't let them put *you* in the slammer when you get back there." To his escorts' relief, Gehlen burst out laughing.

8. Waldman became Chairman of the Department of Political Science and has published numerous books and articles in English and German. Among them: *The Goose Step is Verboten—The German Army Today*, Free Press, 1964; and *Die Sozialistische Einheitspartei Westberlin und die sowjetische Berlinpolitik*, Harald Boldt Verlag, 1972. Waldman and Gehlen maintained their friendship until Gehlen's death.

9. Gehlen, *The Service*, p. 143.

10. In describing the evolution of the CIA's connection with the Organization Thomas Lucid, who succeeded Critchfield as head of the CIA liaison team at Pullach, said: "There were three stages in our relationship with Gehlen. Critchfield had the stormy courtship, I had the happy marriage and Don Huefner [Lucid's successor] had the divorce." That relatively tranquil period had something to do with the smooth meshing of the three personalities, Lucid, Blum and Gehlen. Blum had Gehlen's full confidence, he knew he could rely on the younger man's intellect and judgement. For their part, Blum and Lucid, by using Blum as the middleman, developed a method of "handling the Doctor" which kept friction between him and the Americans to a minimum.

Heinz Danko Herre was the man closest to Gehlen, and his virtual shadow. It was a rare event to meet with Gehlen without Herre being present. He and Gehlen's secretary, Annelore, who had been with him "since time began," were always there; his oldest, most devoted and most trusted associates.

11. Gehlen, p. 146, quoting a 1949 letter.

12. Once the CIA staff in Pullach knew the identity of an agent they would have it checked against existing records. These included documents held by the Army, which had the Nazi Party roster; the OSS "Bughouse" files; the British Primer, and more. The "Bughouse" files were German Foreign Ministry documents captured in Bucharest, Romania, in August 1944 by an OSS team. The files, which were of great value in the Nürnberg Trials, contained SD records, among much else, and ultimately led to the identification of thousands of intelligence officers and agents.

The British Primer was a homely rust-red volume five or six inches thick which contained thousands of names compiled from file cards by British Intelligence. It also contained a touch peculiarly British, a particularly apt quotation from Shakespeare on the front page: "When sorrows come, they come not single spies, but in battalions." [Hamlet, Act IV, sc. V] The British, who had been in the business of German intelligence for a long time, had shared their offices with OSS during the war, and a copy of the Primer remained with the Americans. (The Agency did not have a computer until the early 1950s when Walter Jessel introduced it.)

13. It was virtually impossible to verify the backgrounds of the many thousands of refugees who had poured out of the East.

14. Sources for this section include conversations with Eric Waldman and with members of the early Pullach CIA staff: James Critchfield, Thomas Lucid, Robert Feldman, Clare Edward Petty, and others.

15. The Finns recovered the remains of the codebook from the site of a battle and in November, 1944, OSS chief William Donovan bought the code material from them. Secretary of State Edward Stettinius insisted the code book be returned to the Russians. That was done, but not before Donovan had it copied. See Robert J. Lamphere and Tom Schachtman, *The FBI-KGB War.* NY: Random House, 1986, p. 84.

16. In 1954 von Bolschwing emigrated to the United States, with the help of American Intelligence, and started a highly successful career in the course of which he won the support of political figures and such industrialists as Alfred Driscoll, President, and Elmer Bobst, Chief Executive Officer of Warner-Lambert Pharmaceutical Co. in whose International Operations Division he worked. By the 1960s he had moved to the large multinational Cabot Corporation where he was managing director of German operations. He capped his career when he became President of Trans-International Computer Investment Corporation, an electronics firm in Sacramento, California, which did classified research work for the Pentagon. In 1979, however, the United States Justice Department Office of Special Investigations began to straighten out his tangled past. Information on von Bolschwing drawn from Christopher Simpson, "Not Just Another Nazi," Penthouse Magazine, August, 1983. Other sources for this section: conversations with former CIA officers involved in the Coloredo-Wels operation; Ray Cline; Peer de Silva, *Sub-Rosa.* NY: N. Y. Times Books, 1978; David Martin, *Wilderness Of Mirrors.* NY: Harper and Row, 1980.

17. Information about the hunting lodge meeting was provided by a former CIA officer. State Secretary Carstens is quoted in Höhne and Zolling, *The General Was A Spy,* p. 175.

18. Another misfit organization, Yardley's Black Chamber, also had control divvied up between State and what was then the War Department.

19. Quoted from Glenn Infield's account of conversations with Harry Rositzke.

20. Mosley, p. 289.

21. Mosley, p. 374.
22. Thomas Powers, *The Man Who Kept The Secrets*. NY: Knopf, 1979, p. 48–9.
23. It has been further alleged, in John Loftus' *The Belarus Secret*, NY: Knopf, 1982, that Waldman himself was recruited by Wisner to do "secret research," which Waldman flatly denies. Since the setting for these charges and denials is the baroque world of espionage it may be of interest to those with a taste for anomalies to point out that in Loftus' book Eric Waldman's name is given a German spelling, Erich Waldmann. Waldman did not use that form in the Army, nor at any time after leaving Austria and becoming an American citizen during World War II. This suggests the source of the allegations could be German. As has been noted before, over the years there have been competing interests in Germany, each with a stake in how Gehlen and his Organization are viewed.
24. The root of the allegation that the Organization was taken over by OPC, which has been repeatedly and emphatically denied by the most senior CIA officials, may lie farther to the West than Moscow.
The hypothesis goes like this. Sometime between August and December of 1948 Gehlen did in fact have secret contact with a senior representative of OPC. It was during that period that Gehlen's fortunes were at their lowest ebb, and he was in real danger of losing what he had fought so hard to achieve. The Organization was strapped for money; it was supporting itself on the black market; agents in the field were without adequate supplies; long lists of urgent requests to Washington were ignored; and relations with Colonel Liebel had reached breaking point. In August Liebel was finally recalled, but he was not immediately replaced, and Gehlen remained in limbo. Eric Waldman soon would have his fortuitous encounter with Colonel Philp, who would arrive at Pullach in December 1948, but in the meantime the Air Force liaison officer, Colonel Berry, served as commanding officer for three trying, and nerve-wracking months.
Wisner had been put in charge of OPC in September, and Gehlen's organization, highly vulnerable at that point, must have been a tempting target for his expanding group. For his part, Gehlen might well have viewed OPC as a savior, and he was in desperate need of one. In any event, if such a secret contact was made and discussions were held, they were done without Waldman's knowledge, were inconclusive and were overtaken by events when the CIA's James Critchfield arrived in Pullach in December. If discussions occurred at all, they would have been closely held within Gehlen's German inner circle and never revealed.
25. The name Ludwig Albert (who also used the alias Hermann) together with his Dossier number, D-331202, appear repeatedly in CIC files released by U. S. Army Intelligence and Security Command (U.S.A.I.S.C.). A document headed only ALBERT, Ludwig, and dated 23 Apr 52 identifies Albert as a former Gestapo member and currently Gehlen representative for Land Hessen.

Another, headed HEADQUARTERS REGION III 66TH COUNTER INTEL-
LIGENCE CORPS GROUP UNITED STATES ARMY, EUROPE APO 757
US ARMY, and addressed to Mr. Parkinson at 66th CIC Group, APO 154, is
dated 2 November 1954. The subject is SCHUETZ, Carl. In the body of the
text is the following: "Information contained in the report was gained by
Source from Ludwig Albert, an investigator for the Gehlen Organization." An
undated priority communication from HQ 66th CIC GROUP BAD CANNS-
TATT to CO CIC REGION III (OFFENBACH) alerts the recipients to the
arrest by West German authorities of individuals of interest to them, including
Ludwig Albert, described as being "very well known tech spec and CS team
your rgn." Former Intelligence officials familiar with the case tell the end of
the story: Albert was arrested as a suspected Soviet agent, and killed himself
while in detention at Bruchsal in 1955. (Reference to his suicide is also made
in Höhne and Zolling, p. 286.)

26. A truce of sorts between OPC and OSO began to take shape with the
appointment of General Walter Bedell Smith as Director of Central Intelligence
in 1950. By 1952, Smith had combined the two units, and the level of friction
between them was reduced. Sources for this section include Army Intelligence
documents and conversations with James Critchfield, Ray Cline, and other
former senior Intelligence officers.

Chapter Seven

1. George F. Kennan, *Memoirs, 1950–1963.* Boston: Little, Brown, 1972.

2. Peer de Silva, *Sub-Rosa,* pp. 71–74.

3. Document furnished by U.S. Army Intelligence and Security Command.
It is headed 'Walter Holters," dated "Essen 31 March 1952," and bears the
number 0254 at bottom.

4. Otto John was widely believed to be in the service of the British. Gehlen
never forgave him for testifying against his hero, Field Marshal Erich von
Manstein, at the War Crimes Trials. Von Manstein was tried by a British court
in occupied Hamburg and sentenced on December 19 1949 to eighteen years
imprisonment, a sentence which was commuted to twelve years. Two and one-
half years later, in August 1952, he was allowed medical parole. In 1953, he
was released from custody. (See Gerald Reitlinger, *The Final Solution.* N.Y.:
Beechhurst, 1953, p. 561.)

On July 20, 1954 the question of just which master John was serving became
one of international speculation. On that day John was in Berlin for a celebration in honor of the tenth anniversary of the (failed) July 20, 1944 Generals'
Plot to assassinate Hitler. While there, John disapeared, and when he surfaced
in East Germany shortly afterwards it was to denounce the West German
government as having been taken over by former Nazis. Not surprisingly,
John's defection was assumed.

Eighteen months later, reportedly with the help of the journalist Sefton Delmer, John returned to West Germany claiming to have been drugged, kidnapped, forced to make his anti-West German statements, and taken to Moscow for interrogation. The West Germans arrested and imprisoned him. He was released in 1959.

The timing of his disappearance is of interest, because John had recently returned from a visit to Washington in the course of which he had had an interview with CIA chief Allen Dulles. It is said that Dulles told him then that Gehlen was their man and they would not support any attempt on John's part to supplant him.

A sidelight on this incident comes from Thomas Fox, who later would be Chief of Counterespionage for the Defense Intelligence Agency. While he was with CIC in Germany Fox made it his business to get to know Otto John—indeed, Fox had spent the evening before John's disappearance out on the town with him. Although he did not have responsibility for John's security, because John knew the identities of many Military Intelligence agents, Fox assigned an agent, Ed Hofer, to keep an eye on him.

There was great confusion after John vanished, and it was immediately assumed that because of the sensitive nature of his work and all that he knew about West German affairs he had been kidnapped to the East. Believing that Hofer, because of his connection with John, might also be a kidnap target, Fox gave him a pistol and six rounds of ammunition to protect himself. To Fox's horror Hofer used the gun to kill himself.

It was widely rumored at the time that Fox had discovered Hofer was in some way responsible for John's diappearance—perhaps that he had been involved in the plot—and Fox had given him the gun and the classic option: either you do it or I will. Fox flatly denies that there is any truth to the allegation. (Sources include conversations with Thomas Fox.)

One former CIA officer described the enigmatic John as "part idealist, part Nazi opponent, part Soviet agent, part crazy." A number of accounts of the John incident have been written, and there is also his own memoir: Otto John, *Through Both Lines*. N.Y.: Harper and Row, 1972.

5. Sources include *The Times* (London), 10 November 1953; *Die Welt*, 10 November 1953; *The New Republic*, 4 October 1954, p. 13.

6. For accounts of a complex communications operation, the Berlin Telephone Tunnel, see Martin, op cit, and Chapman Pincher, *Their Trade Was Treachery*. London: Sidgwick and Jackson, 1981.

7. The word *Femme* derives from "punishment" in old German. Originally, in the Middle Ages, applied to secret courts using the star chamber process, the term was later used for radical right wing gangs which committed political murders during the tumultuous years of the Weimar Republic (1919–23).

8. Thomas Dale made such a mark in Germany that on the principle of "If You Can't Fight Them, Enlist Them," the CIA, in the person of James Jesus Angleton, the controversial chief of counterintelligence for the Agency, even-

tually hired him away from the Army. But that came after the Agency, embarrassingly late in the game, discovered CAMPUS.

9. As an example of the inexperience of officers in critical Intelligence positions, a Colonel whose concern had been chemical warfare in Utah was suddenly put in charge of counterintelligence for Europe.

10. Conversation with a confidential source.

11. Many government agencies besides the CIA and the armed services had agents operating in Germany, including the State Department and the FBI.

12. Document dated 19 February 1949. Subject: Kurt Merk, Klaus Barbie. Addressed to Commanding Officer, 797th CIC Group, Reg. IV, APO 407-A, US Army, Attn: Technical Specialist. Signed by Major George B. Riggin, CAC. It contains this passage: "The new plan of action has been instigated to obtain all new sources, seeking out as many old Gestapo and SS informants as possible, and especially those whose mission was KPD [Communist Party Germany] penetration under the Nazi regime." See *Klaus Barbie And The United States Government, Exhibits to the Report to the Attorney General of the United States.* August, 1983, Washington, D.C., U.S. Government Printing Office (not paginated).

For those sufficiently interested in this subject to take on the poor reproduction quality of the documents contained in it, the *Exhibits,* which form appendices to the Barbie Report, contained in a large separate volume, are recommended.

13. Headquarters 66th Counter Intelligence Corps Group, Incoming message. From: LO OCA Mehlem. For Action: CO 66 CIC Group. Dated Dec 54. REF NR: 0-398. "Subject is Amt Blank Intel Sec Ref Friedrich Wilhelm Heinz case and attempted Sov penetration of Amt Blank setup." The rest of the message is blacked out until the final paragraph which is quoted in the text. There are numerous other examples of selective distribution of information indicating the lack of cooperation among American Intelligence agencies. For example, another report from Headquarters 66th Counter Intelligence Corps Group To: Assistant Chief of Staff, G2, Intelligence, APO 403, ATTN: Chief Counter Intelligence Branch, dated 11 December 1954. Subject: Heinz, Friedrich Wilhelm. "It is requested that further dissemination of the attached report be restricted to military channels." And a report from Headquarters U.S. Army, Europe, Office of the Assistant Chief of Staff, G-2, to Commanding Officer, 66th CIC Group, APO 154, dated 15 February 1956, Subject: Gehlen Organization (C). "It is requested that no distribution of this information be made outside of US military channels." This is of particular interest since it reveals Army Intelligence interest in the Gehlen Organization. Documents furnished by U.S.A.I.S.C.

14. One of Gehlen's most serious rivals was the aristocrat Count Gerhard von Schwerin. A panzer division leader during the war, he was the selected British instrument to oust Gehlen and replace him as head of the German secret service. The British, however, overplayed their hand when their Ambassador began pushing their man with Chancellor Adenauer.

Adenauer had not forgotten that the British had removed him as Bürgermeister of Cologne. Nonetheless, when Britain's Ambassador Steel called on him and regretfully informed him that his country could not support Gehlen, offering Count von Schwerin instead, Adenauer listened. Despite the fact that he was close to Gehlen, the Chancellor said he would be willing to talk to the Count sometime in the future. It was then that the Ambassador made his mistake. Instead of judiciously playing out his hand, Steel produced von Schwerin there and then out of his waiting car, like a handkerchief out of his sleeve, and Adenauer reacted badly. The beneficiary of the failed British ploy was Reinhard Gehlen. (See also Höhne and Zolling, *The General Was A Spy*, p. 184.)

15. Among the U.S.A.I.S.C. documents relating to Busch is the Final Report of Interrogation dated 15 September 1945 from the 307th Counter Intelligence Corps Detachment, Headquarters Seventh Army. The earliest is an Arrest Report dated 26 July 1945, the latest a Memorandum from Headquarters, 66th Military Intelligence Group, United States Army, Europe dated 7 July 1961. The Addressee is illegible, but the Subject is Fritz [sic] Busch, and the substance of the Memorandum is a request for any interrogation reports on Busch.

16. Among the U.S.A.I.S.C. documents relating to Hans Sommer is one dated 4 May 1951, headed CONSOLIDATION OF CPI CARDS, File D-95421. Other documents, some undated, are copies of cards on which Sommer's name appears. The information dates from July 1945 to 6 May 1955.

17. U.S. Army Military History Research Collection, Senior Officers Debriefing Program. Vol. II, 13 Jan. 1971 to 13 July 1971. Also, conversations with General Trudeau.

18. Conversations with General Trudeau.

19. Globke, one of Adenauer's closest and most powerful associates, came under heavy fire when it was revealed he was co-author, with State Secretary Dr. Wilhelm Stuckart, a convicted war criminal, of the 1936 Legal Commentary to the three Nürnberg Race Laws of 1935. Many unimpeachable witnesses came to his defense, however, and he was able to make a convincing argument that his contribution to the laws had been designed to mitigate the plight of the Jews and that he himself had acted to help them. (Detailed information about this incident can be found in the doctoral thesis of Donald D. Dalgleish, "The Nazi 'Past' In The Communist Cause," University of Colorado, 1963.)

20. As to what exactly was on the infamous cards, neither General Trudeau nor James Critchfield seems able to remember in any detail. "This was information about penetrations of the Gehlen Organization," Trudeau offered, while Critchfield said "It is my impression that they had nothing to do with Felfe. If they had it would have been brought to my attention."

The real end of the Trudeau affair came much later when Felfe flatly stated that he was far from being the only Soviet agent in the Gehlen Organization. That there were many more, each unknown to the other.

Other sources for this section include conversations with James Critchfield and other former CIC and CIA officers.

Chapter Eight

1. Clemens was captured by the Canadians at Como 28 April 1945, and was interrogated. A document provided by the U.S. Army Intelligence Security Command, dated 27 May 1945, from "C. C. No. 1 SCI Unit" reads: "First Detailed Interrogation Report on SS Hauptsturmführer [sic] CLEMENS, Hans." The report was not provided and may not be in the Army Intelligence and Security Command files. Another, undated, document headed "Surname: CLEMENS" notes under Brief Case History: "Has been interrogated CSDIC/ CMF/SD7, but no copy of report available." Several efforts were made by the 66th Counter Intellegience Corps Group to obtain information about Clemens. Among other documents supplied to the author are an undated request to the Berlin Document Center, signed by Mr. A. B. Boenau, that NSDAP records be checked for Hans Clemens, and an undated one page report headed "(Clemens, Hans (also: Johannes), Max)," signed by Manfred Guggenheim, Executive Officer, Berlin Document Center. Another request from Mr. A. B. Boenau, this time to the French, is dated 23 April 1954. It is directed to: L'Administrateur J. M. Arnold, Chef des Services et Conservateur des Archives WAST. A single, undated, page, apparently the last of two or more, does not name Clemens but contains biographical information clearly indicating he is the subject. The document is signed by A. Sadowsky for J. M. Arnold from the Services d'Exploitation des Archives WAST of the Gouvernement Militaire Français de Berlin. The date of the request, 1954, demonstrates CIC's early interest in Clemens.

2. Tiebel also worked with Felfe on the Swiss Desk at SS headquarters in Berlin during 1943 and 1944.

3. TACTICAL INTERROGATION REPORT, A.S.O., South Holland. Report No: R040/2. Date of Interrogation: 17 Jul 45. NAME: FELFE, Heinz. The interrogation report is signed R. T. Robinson, Capt. 1 Cdn Army Interrogation Pool. Det, C/o. A.S.C., South Holland, and dated 4 Aug 45. U.S.A.I.S.C. document.

4. Report from Headquarters, 970th Counter Intelligence Corps Detachment, European Command, Region VI (Bamberg), Sub-Region (Bayreuth) U.S. Army, dated 2 April 1948. File number VI-B-99.4. Subject: Felfe, Heinz. Re: British Intelligence Agent. The report includes Felfe's NSDAP Party number and notes he worked in AMT VI, RSHA, as did Erwin Tiebel. U.S.A.I.S.C. document.

5. Information for the material concerning Felfe's activities is drawn from conversations with former CIA officers.

6. In the opinion of at least one CIA officer it is not surprising that Gehlen

was duped by Felfe. "Gehlen," he observed, "had no grasp of the psychology of treachery, he was a ready victim for a treasonous employee."

7. Some CIA officers who were close to the investigation of Felfe say this assessment of the situation gives the Soviets too much credit, endowing them with, among other things, "clairvoyance and a superhuman ability to manipulate men and circumstances."

8. Information about the material Felfe transmitted to the Soviets comes from conversations with former CIA officers, and press reports at the time of his trial, especally *The Times* (London): July 9, 10, 24, 1963.

9. Conversations with Charles Wheeler.

10. Information from Howard Roman and other former CIA officers who examined the letter. The quotation is from Martin, *Wilderness Of Mirrors*, p. 97.

11. It was George Blake who disclosed to the Soviets the existence of the elaborate clandestine Allied listening post, the Berlin Telephone Tunnel.

12. Sniper provided the leads to, but never actually named Felfe.

13. Sources include conversations with Howard Roman, Clare Edward Petty, and other former CIA officers; also Edward Jay Epstein, *New York Times Magazine*, 28 September 1980, p. 34.

14. This was not the only time suspicion dogged Herre. Several years later, while Herre was the official representative of the West German Intelligence service in Washington, it was discovered that there was an uncanny similarity between Herre's intinerary on a trip through South America, and that of a Soviet "agricultural attaché," Bagramov, widely believed to be an intelligence officer. This coincidence was followed by another, when Herre and his wife travelled to Denver, Colorado, and Jackson Hole, Wyoming, at the same time as two Soviet officers, one of whom, it was known, had contacts with Bagramov. The CIA also assigned a man and woman to follow Herre on a trip to Bermuda. Each time Herre was put under scrutiny he was cleared. Information about the suspicion of Herre was provided in conversations with former CIA officers.

15. Howard Roman's interest in the psychology of the defector Goleniewski and the question of what happened to him when he was "cut off," raises the matter of American handling of such people. In conversation with the Soviet defector Vladimir Sakharov he discussed his own unhappy experience of being virtually "dumped on a street corner" after having been "squeezed dry" by the CIA. He expanded on our discussion in an article, "The Defectors: Why They Do It, Where They Go And What Happens To Them," in *Foreign Intelligence and Risk Management,* a newsletter of which he is Editor. In 1986 the American government undertook to study the question of how defectors are treated.

16. The only tangible evidence of Felfe's guilt was the instruction sheet sent by his KGB case officer, and radio messages retrieved from Clemens. The messages were on one-time pads which Clemens was supposed to decipher

and pass on to Felfe. Clemens found it difficult to deal with cipher and against all the rules of espionage he kept the messages around. Some fifteen one-time pads, and Clemens work sheets, were recovered from his house.

17. Heinz Felfe published a memoir, *Im Dienst Des Gegners—10 Jahre Moskaus Mann Im BND,* Rasch und Röhring Verlag, Hamburg, in 1986.

18. Sources for this section include conversations with Howard Roman and Clare Edward Petty. The story of Felfe's arrest was widely covered by the press in Germany, and by *The Times* of London. *The Times:* December 11, 14, and 16, 1961.

19. The Strauss scandal/Spiegel affair constituted one of the most important episodes of the Adenauer period. Its impact was profound and had far-reaching consequences which go beyond the reach of this work. Numerous accounts have been written about this event. Among those in English is David Schoenbaum's *The Spiegel Affair,* N.Y.: Doubleday, 1968.

20. Sources close to the case say that Felfe in fact did apply for a transfer into the communications section, which would have been a rich hunting ground for him.

21. Clemens, Felfe, and Tiebel also recieved money from the Soviets. Reports from the trial put the amounts at 178,000 marks ($44,500), 135,000 marks ($33,750) and 5,000 marks ($1,500) respectively. The actual amounts undoubtedly were far larger.

22. I am indebted to Jürgen Stange, who acted for the West German government in the Felfe prisoner exchange, for his generous help. While adhering scrupulously to his obligation not to reveal any information of a sensitive nature concerning the transaction, he was kind enough to verify for me the accuracy of other reports of the incident which I presented to him.

23. Two of the students from Heidelberg, Peter Sonntag and Walter Naumann, were arrested by the Russians two months before Felfe was taken into custody by the West German police, but they were not tried and sentenced until some two weeks after Felfe had been charged. Intelligence officers tend to be wary of coincidences, and the timing is of interest.

On September 3 1961, the CIA sent the students on an "amateur" mission to the Soviet Union as tourists. They were to photograph power plants, radar stations, and military movements. On September 17 the Russians arrested them and, on November 22 1961, they were tried in Moscow and sentenced to twelve years in prison.

Felfe was arrested on November 6 1961. Eighteen months later, almost immediately after Felfe's trial and sentencing, on July 22 1963, the students were first offered by the Soviets as barter for Felfe. It was not until six years later, with the addition of nineteen more men and women, that the deal in human beings was completed.

24. Department of State telegram number 325, July 24 1963 from Bonn to the Secretary of State reviewing media coverage of the decision in the Felfe case. In a television broadcast 23 July, Erler reminded viewers that Adenauer

had used the phrase "abyss of treason" in regard to the Spiegel affair and questioned why the Chancellor did not speak out in this case. The trial was heavily covered by the German press. The New York Times ran stories on it on July 9, 10, 12, 14, 17, 19, 20, and 24, 1963.

25. Edward Jay Epstein, New York Times Magazine, 28 September 1980.

26. Over the years much has been made of this house. Critics, claiming it was bought for Gehlen with CIA money, point to the house as evidence of the extent to which he was a creature of the Americans. The CIA did provide the funds, but in the form of a loan. Even former officers who are otherwise unenthusiastic about Gehlen say such loans are not uncommon, and that he repaid it in full.

Conclusion

1. White, *Fire In the Ashes,* p. 394.

Index

225

228   *Index*